FIVE IN A ROW
VOLUME 2

BY
JANE CLAIRE LAMBERT

FIVE IN A ROW PUBLISHING · GRANDVIEW, MISSOURI

Five in a Row, Volume 2
Revised Second Edition

ISBN 1-888659-01-7

Published by:
Five in a Row Publishing
14901 Pineview Dr.
Grandview, MO, 64030-4509
(816) 331-5769

Send all requests for information to the above address.

Original cover oil painting created for *Five in a Row* by:
Deborah Deonigi
P.O. Box 1140
Maple Valley, WA 98038
(206) 413-9118

For

Hannah, Allison, Mallory, Lewie and Tess

and

Melissa, Kristin, Tim, Sam and Sharon

...and to the boys who were so excited to see the real
little red lighthouse and gave me the idea to use that book.

Table of Contents

Introduction

Good books have always been the doorway to learning. That doorway leads to growth and an appreciation for the wonders around us. Come along on a learning adventure using picture books to open the door to art, history, vocabulary, geography, science, human relationships, math and writing!

No matter how young, children get a substantial educational head-start from books, *Five in a Row* has been created to bring excitement and fun to learning and to enrich children's lives. These lesson plans are simple in concept, but rich in results. Read the chosen book in its entirety *each day for at least a week*. After each reading, choose an exercise to share with your student. Then watch his world expand as you begin to show him facets of the story he would never have recognized without your purposeful guidance. As a teacher of this material, you will find that you become excited and interested in a variety of subjects, too. You'll rediscover the joy of learning and you'll build a special bond between you and your student as the two of you go on a learning adventure together.

This curriculum is intended to be extremely flexible. It allows you the option to do any or all of the exercises for each story. You may elect to skip over certain exercises which do not fit the needs of your student. You may place additional emphasis on certain exercises which seem appropriate. You will find more exercises than you can use in a week, so enjoy choosing just the right lesson elements for your student.

You can adjust classroom time to fit your needs as well. By using only one lesson element each day, you can work through *Five in a Row* in as little as thirty minutes daily, including the time to read the book. If you choose to use all of the lesson elements, field trips and follow-up exercises, you could easily spend several hours daily. Use *Five in a Row* however it best suits your needs and the needs of your student.

The technique of reading the same story for at least five days in a row is one that I have tested in teaching for more than eight years. I continue to be amazed at the effectiveness of this technique! Each book will become very special to your student. He will remember more and more about the story. More importantly, even a four-year-old will begin to think more critically as he begins wondering how certain portions of the story came to be, or how the characters solved a certain problem. These results could never be achieved in just one reading.

Your student will see how the illustrator accomplished certain effects and he'll be encouraged to begin exploring those techniques in his own art. You'll see your student learning about science, math and history by the things you bring to the discussion every day. Your student will have the opportunity to try new activities and learn more about a variety of people, places and animals. You'll also discover him asking more questions than ever before. By the end of the week, the new book will have become his friend for life.

Perhaps the most valuable benefit of using *Five in a Row* is that the young student will learn to completely critique (with your guidance). That skill will serve him well as he learns to read for himself. Your student will begin looking to see whether a book is a

Caldecott or a Newberry Medal winner. He will quickly classify a new book as either fact or fiction. He'll be able to articulate the point of view from which the story has been written. A wide variety of literary techniques and the ability to recognize them will soon be at his disposal. You'll be delighted when your student begins to evaluate the illustrator's medium and technique.

All of this is imparted in an enjoyable learning environment. Your student will think you're just reading him a book, but he's learning so much every day! The more lessons you do together, the more skills your student will acquire; skills which will benefit him through high school, college and throughout life!

Welcome to the wonderful world of *Five in a Row*. You are the leader for this adventure, so gather the children around you and have a great time!

Jane Claire Lambert
December, 1994

The goal of FIAR instruction is to lead children to fall in love with good books and and to embrace the joy of learning.

About the Books Themselves

Sutherland and Arbuthnot write in <u>Children and Books</u>, "*Aesthetic satisfaction comes to small children as well as to adults, and the development of their taste depends not only on their initial capacities but also on <u>the material they encounter and the way in which it is presented.</u>*"* (emphasis added)

Most of us can directly attribute a lifelong interest in at least one topic to the quality and creativity with which some particular teacher or a parent introduced the subject. You may also have nurtured a lifelong distaste for certain subjects because a parent or teacher made it seem difficult or boring.

Sutherland and Arbuthnot go on to suggest that by selecting excellent children's literature and reading it together each day, children have the opportunity to "*catch a new theme, savor the beauty, the subtle humor or a special meaning that eluded them at first.*"

"*Sometimes,*" the authors suggest, "*an adult has the privilege of seeing this discovery take place. The children's faces come suddenly alive; their eyes shine. They may be anticipating an amusing conclusion or a heroic triumph. There is a sudden chuckle or breath is exhaled like a sigh. The book has moved them, perhaps even to laughter or tears, in any case there is a deep inner satisfaction and they will turn to books again with anticipation.*"

Sutherland and Arbuthnot conclude, "*Once they have experienced the joy of reading they have acquired a habit that will serve them all their lives. It is important, therefore, that those who guide their reading select wisely.*"

It is within this context that the titles for *Five in a Row* have been chosen. In each case content was of supreme importance. Books were chosen that showcase close family relationships, personal triumphs, and perseverance in times of trial. There are books with people characters and stories with animal characters. In each story the characters touch the reader's heart and demonstrate life's truths. Please remember, however, that our selection of a particular title by an author does *not* mean that we endorse *everything* from that author. We're aware of several cases where authors have written marvelous books and very questionable books as well. Please take the time to review any book you bring home from the library *before* reading it to your children!

In addition to content, the books cover a wide range of artistic expression from the beautiful portraiture of Allen Say to the hilarious pictures of Marjorie Priceman; from the warm homey drawings of Robert McCloskey to the action-packed illustrations of Virginia Lee Burton. Each illustrator's work was selected for the utter appreciation and enjoyment of children. We have chosen titles with art to appreciate, art to learn from and art to be remembered for a lifetime!

It has been said that some stories must be talked over or listened to while *someone who knows and loves them* reads aloud. (emphasis added)* If *you* come to love the stories, your student will, too.

With these standards in mind we hope you and your student find a special place in your heart for these stories and for the concept of *Five in a Row*.

*Sutherland and Arbuthnot, *Children and Books*, Harper Collins Publishers, 8th ed., 1991.

How to Use *Five In a Row*

Select a book to study with your student. There is no right or wrong order for covering the material. However in the Appendix, you'll find a suggested semester reading calendar for the spring term which links some stories to the appropriate seasons of the year.

Some teachers will choose to purchase each book as a valuable addition to their permanent library. Of course, any public library should have (or be able to request via Inter-Library Loan or ILL) each of the titles in this book. (For extra help and ideas see "Finding the Books" in the Appendix.)

Important Note: *Please* take the time to read the book aloud to your student each day **before** covering the lesson material. *Five in a Row* was designed for each book to be read daily! The repetition is essential to your student's learning process, and the time you spend reading together is just as important as the lesson material itself.

In the Appendix, you will find a weekly sample Lesson Planning Work Sheet for *The Tale of Peter Rabbit* You'll also find a Blank Work Sheet which you can reproduce and use. Or, feel free to design your own worksheet. The sample sheet shows how to correlate the suggestions in the teacher's guide to the five days of the week. Some teachers don't use planning sheets at all and work directly from *Five in a Row*. Do whatever works for you!

Notice the lesson plans are outlined briefly and give you a quick reference for the week. Not every lesson suggested under *The Tale of Peter Rabbit* is listed. There are too many lessons for one week. Choose the ones that are especially suited to your student. The subjects Math, Science, Art, etc., do not have to be used in the same order every week. The plan is completely yours. Use only the subjects and topics you wish. Remember when planning that this curriculum builds on itself. Whatever you study on Monday will be recognized by the student when you read the story again on Tuesday. When you read the story a third time on Wednesday, the lessons you introduced on Monday and Tuesday will not escape the student's notice as he hears or sees the examples again. So each lesson, except the one for Friday, gets at least one review and some lessons get four reviews. The topics you think are most important, therefore, should be scheduled toward the beginning of the week. Some teachers put off Art until Friday. Try to use this topic earlier in the week, perhaps Wednesday, so the student can study the pictures for several days as he hears the story read and reread.

Also in the Appendix, you will find a sheet of story disks. These are quick, symbolic representations of the twenty-two titles included in *Five in a Row*. They may be used to make a **literary map**. First, color each disk and put the name of the book on the back of the disk. For greater durability, laminate the disks before you cut them apart. Now take a large map of the world (a laminated map is more durable). By placing a velcro dot on the disk and the other velcro dot on the map where it goes, you can quickly take it off and put it back on each day. Teacher's tacky putty (available in office supply stores) will also work, and you or the student can locate the disk and attach it daily. Eventually, you will be able to track each of the stories you have read from all over the world. Even young students will learn some map basics. Any stories with fictitious settings can be placed in the margins of the map as the "Land of Make Believe."

There is also a page of mostly blank disks in the appendix so you can make your own pictures for these stories or replace a lost disk. You might also like to make disks for other stories you read outside of *Five in a Row*.

Social Studies

Because there are only five subject categories (to correspond to the five days of the week), many different topics are included under Social Studies. Each story presented has been identified according to the geographic area. Often the culture of that area is discussed. Making a flag is recommended as an interesting and informative activity. Geography also includes the mention of oceans, continents and geographic regions. (An excellent illustrated children's geography book is Rand McNally's *Picture Atlas of the World*, illustrated by Brian Delf. You'll find it informative and fun!) Under the topic Social Studies, you will also find lessons about cities, small town life, minority ethnic groups, occupations and discovering our own unique gifts. In addition, the Social Studies unit includes history. Under this heading, you will see lessons which create opportunities to discuss slavery, civil rights, Civil War, Hanukkah, Appalachian lifestyles, patriotism, United States Wars, and explorers like Columbus. Social Studies also includes several lessons about people and their relationships to one another. In this category, you'll find subjects such as fathering, self-image, stewardship, friendship, taking responsibility, envy, jealousy, forgiveness, manners and generational ties, just to name a few. As you can see, many subjects are included under Social Studies.

Choose the topics you'd like to discuss and either mark them your in *Five in a Row* book or write them on the Planning Sheet (see Appendix) under whichever day it seems best to cover them. If you use the Planning Sheets, be sure when presenting the material *to tie it in to the story.*

Finally, in the Geography section of Social Studies, you'll find the directions for placing the geography disk for each book you read.

Language Arts

There are many techniques for teaching Language Arts using children's literature. Increasing vocabulary, learning literary devices, learning list-making skills, composing short stories, acting out dramas, are just a few of the ways. Teaching Language Arts is a natural extension of the enjoyment of children's literature.

Vocabulary is enriched by hearing new words like **bubee** (*Mrs. Katz and Tush*), **vagabond** (*Mirette on the High Wire*) or **etiquette** (*To Duet or Not to Duet*). A child's vocabulary is much greater that just the words he can read or spell, and reading a story which contains new words five times in a row will help increase his recognition and understanding of those words.

Two methods for organizing vocabulary words are the file box and the notebook. The file box method uses four by six inch, unlined index cards with alphabet dividers. Either the teacher or the student can print the word at the top left of the card. Write in a short definition at the left and add an illustration, either drawn or cut from a magazine to show the word visually. Keep the words alphabetized and encourage your student to go through the cards frequently. (To help in remembering which story the vocabulary word came from, write the name of the book on the back of the card.)

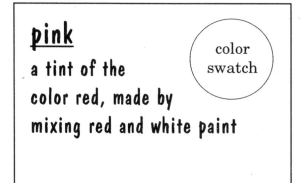

| **windmill** |
| a machine that uses wind power to grind grain, pump water, and make electricity |

| **pink** |
| a tint of the color red, made by mixing red and white paint |
| color swatch |

A second method of keeping track of vocabulary words is to list them on a page in the Language or Vocabulary section of a notebook. Print the word (large if necessary) on notebook paper. Then illustrate the word with a drawing or magazine picture. Your older student could alphabetize each separate list on another sheet of paper. Review these words from time to time while remembering your favorite incidents in the corresponding stories.

A notebook is good for more than just vocabulary words. In fact, it's a great way for your student to keep his work organized and ready for quick review and easy reference. For the grade level student, this isn't unusual. But for your pre-schooler to have *his own* notebook is special. Let him use colored dividers so he can find the subjects, even if he cannot yet read. In this way, he can proudly find his Science or Social Studies section and show someone his drawings or projects. With color dividers he'll be able to look up his Art or Vocabulary section by himself. He can then share the new words he has learned and his illustrations of these words, as well as his art projects.

List-making is another Language Arts skill that develops vocabulary, memory, associations and creativity. It is also a skill that has lifetime value in many different areas: grocery lists, lists of people to invite to a party, "to do" lists, lists of ways to solve a problem, descriptive lists to inform and many others. There have been great eloquent lists made by famous people of the things they liked, disliked, or the things they wished for. Once, while travelling together in a car, a friend's family began an oral list of methods of transportation. Many miles down the road, the list had grown to gigantic proportions with the hilarious inclusions of walking on stilts and walking on your hands added to the regular methods of riding in a car, bus, taxi, etc. What began as a list-making exercise became entertainment. The art or skill of good list-making is included in this curriculum to provide both a learning experience and a *good time.*

There are many Literary Devices explained in this book and tied in to the lessons from children's literature. Certainly not all of them will be used, but they are included to remind the teacher of them and give opportunities for casual inclusion in the reading lessons.

As you come to each new Literary Device, a list can be made with examples and pictures. Keep your list in the Language section of the student's notebook. For instance, Personification (giving human qualities to non-human things) might be defined and then illustrated with a magazine picture of the Pillsbury Doughboy® in showing how a lump of dough has been made into a person. There are many examples of Personification in magazine pictures. The other devices can be illustrated as well. Keeping a chart or list of these words makes review easy and interesting. The student can use his list for inspiration when he is creating his own works.

Ideas for leading your student into writing include letting him tape record his stories for you to transcribe. Often your student will enjoy listening to his own story tape. Writing rebus stories, where a picture takes the place of a certain word throughout the story, is an interesting way to begin writing skills. As you follow the curriculum, you will find lessons explaining what makes a good story, different story elements and ways to achieve variety. Your student will begin to appreciate the choices an author makes to create a story and the careful thought that goes into writing.

Many times this curriculum asks questions such as: "How did the author make the story exciting? What words did he use? How did he ...?" Eventually, as your student sees these techniques modeled before him, he will begin to include such elements in his own writing. The suggestions after every lesson to imitate an aspect of the author's work is optional, and depends on the interest and abilities of the student. Try it, and if the response is not favorable, then concentrate on the appreciation aspect of the lesson. In time the rest will follow.

If, however, your student enjoys writing "after the manner of" imitating aspects of the author's story, then he will like the suggestions to try a fable, an instructional story or a poem. He'll also begin to include in his own stories: a good setting, interesting characters, an exciting climax, or an important denouement (final outcome of story), personification or repetition. Each of these is a separate lesson in the curriculum. Again, keeping a chart with definitions and examples or a good list in a notebook, will give your student ready reference when he is writing his own stories and makes review easy. Just add to the list or chart on an on-going basis as you come to different lessons. You might title the chart or list: *Choices A Writer Can Make.*

Remember, there are too many language topics to be covered in a single day. Choose the ones appropriate for your student and jot them briefly on your weekly Planning Sheet under the day you think best. Remember, if you are going to teach vocabulary it is a good idea to do this at the beginning of the week, perhaps on Tuesday. As the book is read and re-read throughout the week your student will spot the words providing a built-in review. And remember, choose only a *few* words from each story.

Art

When you choose good children's literature, you will frequently discover exceptional illustrations as well. Water color, pastels, charcoal, beautiful colors, active lines, funny characters and balanced compositions are all part of fine illustrations for children.

Furthermore, they can be used to introduce children, even young children, to the fundamentals and techniques of art.

Art appreciation is learning to recognize the many techniques and concepts which combine to produce effective art while learning what you like and why. Some pictures have a rhythm, balance and choice of color that combine to make them pleasing. Some illustrations are meant to evoke strong emotions or to provide information. Even a young child can begin to identify great art, not only enjoying it wherever it's encountered, but beginning to know *why* he likes it. By teaching about the artists and their methods, your student's taste in art will expand to include a rich and wonderful variety of work.

As you look at illustrations with your student, ask "What do you think the illustrator used for his medium?" Sometimes it's hard to tell. There are combinations of pen and ink with water color washes, etchings with strokes from oil or acrylic and the wet, transparent blends of water colors. Look for the shading in a charcoal or pencil sketch, or the build up of color by successive layers of colored pencils. Learn to identify the deep texture of pastels.

After you've discussed the medium, ask **why** and **how** questions. "Why do you think the illustrator chose this color, style, view point, etc.? How did the artist make it look like night time, etc.?" These kinds of questions will open a doorway to art appreciation for your student.

Let him study the illustrations as he tries to answer your questions. You may want to suggest some answers as you discuss the methods the artist used and how the illustrations help tell the book's story. Does the artist's work provide additional story information not included in the text? Does the choice of color palette convey the tone of the story?

Asking lots of questions will cause your student to look with a more critical eye, poring over the pages to find answers. He will gain a love of art based on newly discovered information and an emerging appreciation for great illustrations. Don't ask all the questions at the same time, but bring them up conversationally from time to time as you study each book.

One of the best techniques for teaching art fundamentals is to imitate a particular technique from the painting or drawing of a known artist. In *Five in a Row*, the lessons attempt to identify and single out a specific artistic element and to encourage imitation. Your student will be invited to mimic specific styles, colors, designs, etc. Remember that appreciation usually precedes imitation. Therefore, look for examples of the element you are studying in other books, magazines, etc. Let him examine and enjoy these additional examples before he begins experimenting with the technique himself.

In order for you to be ready to meet your student's needs, you may want to have certain supplies on hand:

Kneadable eraser
Drawing pencil or #2 lead pencil
Charcoal (**Teacher's Note**: Supervise the use of charcoal, since it can get messy!)

Oil pastels	The favorite medium of many young students. It doesn't smear as much as chalky pastels. **(Adult supervision required.)**
Markers and	
Colored pencils	
Crayons	
Water colors	Prang® brand is good. Tube water colors are also extremely easy to use for mixing exercises.
Acrylics	Acrylics aren't required, but give your student a chance to paint layer upon layer using lighter colors on top.
Brushes	You'll need brushes with several different bristle lengths and widths. If you want to paint fine-lined tree branches, you need the right brush!

Water color paper
Canvas paper for acrylics
Drawing tablet or paper
Tracing paper
Ruler
Cardboard templates of geometric shapes

(**Teacher's Note:** Realize that you do *not* have to be personally accomplished in all these media and techniques before introducing them to your student. *You* are invited to learn and experiment *together*. Above all, remember that creative art is an intensely personal subject. If you wish to demonstrate a technique, do it on a separate piece of paper; never on your student's work! Be wise with critique of his work and grant him the respect you would grant any artist. Go slow, letting him *catch* the enthusiasm for the ideas you present.)

Math

In many of the books chosen for this curriculum, young children ages four to eight will enjoy finding practical ways to use the new concepts they are learning in math.

For the youngest learners, there are many opportunities for counting practice. It may be counting the stars in one special illustration or the pickets of a fence in another. Finding and counting all the corks in *Ferdinand* can be fun while providing an opportunity for the teacher to observe his/her student's counting skills.

Money and shopkeeping are covered in the lessons for *Down Down the Mountain*. You may also introduce grouping by twelves and the concept of dozens by discussing the number of riders in *Mr. Gumpy's Motor Car*.

Concepts of relative size, measuring, time and money may be found in the stories of children's picture books. A book about quilts offers a chance to talk about geometric shapes. Because the concepts are linked to an enjoyable story, your student will remember them with pleasure.

If time is available, especially in the summer before school starts, make math manipulatives using ideas from the story illustrations. For instance, if you are going to read a book for a week that is about trains, make flash cards with the facts printed inside train cars. Use bright cheerful colors and write the answers on the back. Laminating the cards will help them last. The cards can also contain any term or new concept on one side with the definition on the other.

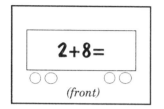
(front)

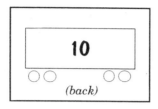
(back)

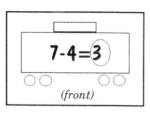
(front)

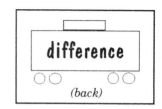
(back)

Reading the lesson story all the way through, enjoying the closeness of the teacher, and the entertainment of the book establishes a good environment for presenting a math lesson derived from the story. Even the lesson will be a shared experience. If there are more math ideas than are appropriate for one day, choose the ones you wish to cover and write them on your weekly Planning Sheet (see Appendix for Planning Sheet) for the day you wish to cover Math.

Science

Open wide the door to children's literature and find within the stories a vast array of scientific educational opportunities: gazing at the stars, wondering about our sun and how shadows are made, insect growth, how a lever works, volcanoes, pollution, seasons, nutrition, animal behavior and much more.

After reading the book for the day, bring up conversationally the science topics suggested in the lessons and other ideas that you may have. Don't try to use all the topics. Just choose the ones you think are appropriate and mark them on your weekly Planning Sheet for whichever day seems best.

When presenting your science lesson, *be sure to tie it into to the place in the story.* For instance, in *Gramma's Walk,* you might say, "Remember when Donnie was at *the beach?* What kind of things might you find at the beach?"

A Science section in your student's notebook with a page for Ocean Life and a page for Simple Machines, etc., will help in reviewing and in referencing. If he likes, let your student illustrate the topics with his own diagrams, magazine cut-outs or drawings of the story, and how the topic applies. This could be part of a beloved notebook by year's end.

(**Teacher's Note** - Throughout *Five in a Row* you'll find students referred to as "he." Obviously, this is strictly a literary convention to avoid cluttering the book with hundreds of "he and or she" clauses! *Five in a Row* was created to be gender-neutral and you'll find hundreds of fascinating lessons to appeal to both boys and girls. Also, please note that we've referred to **student** in the singular, even though many of you undoubtedly have more than one student. **Also, see the interesting ideas for Review Week, p. 166.)**

THE GIRAFFE THAT WALKED TO PARIS

Title: *The Giraffe That Walked to Paris*
Author: Nancy Milton
Illustrator: Roger Roth
Copyright: 1992
Summary: Relationships are reconciled through the gift of a giraffe, in a
                story which will delight and intrigue both children and adults.

Social Studies: Geography-
Egypt, France and the Mediterranean Sea

The story of the giraffe that walked to Paris begins in Egypt, a country on the continent of Africa. The giraffe is transported to France on the European continent. The shortest route of travel crossed the Mediterranean Sea. For younger students, the mention of these names is a good introduction. For older students, you may wish to make continent and sea disks to label these points of interest and have your student place them on the map.

Egypt: Examine the pictures on the first through the third pages and discuss the details you see regarding the culture of Egypt. Notice the clothes of the pasha and his stablemen Hussan, Youseff and Atir (not to mention their names!!) Look at the architecture of the buildings and the pyramids. The pasha is seated on a pillow beneath a tent. Ask why and see if your student understands the tent offers protection from the hot sun. Note also the palm trees, plants, eating utensils, colors and patterns of pottery and rugs and the camels in the distance.

France: When La Girafe, as she is called in France, arrives in Marseilles (Marsay), everyone wants to see her. Find the picture of Hussan walking her past the sidewalk cafe. Notice the cobblestone street, the white buildings with red roofs and palm trees (because it is warmer in the south of France). Notice the nineteenth century French clothing styles. Continue to turn pages looking at the coaches and soldiers on horses, the buildings, and finally, as the procession nears Paris, looking down on the city itself. In the illustration where King Charles X finally sees La Girafe, can your student locate the professors wearing purple and green robes with white fur collars in the crowd? There is also a reference to the river in Paris, the Seine (sane or sen).

Social Studies: Citizenship

Due to the international atmosphere of this story, as well as the diplomatic relations portrayed, it might be a good time to discuss **citizenship**. What does it mean to be a French citizen, an Egyptian citizen or a citizen of the United States? What are the various benefits and responsibilities of citizenship such as voting, obeying the laws, etc.?) Use this opportunity to introduce the beginning concepts of government, diplomacy (the same kind you use within your family) and citizenship.

Social Studies: Relationships-
The Right Word At the Right Time

King Charles X's counselor is able to persuade the King to wait for spring through polite, respectful speech. Knowing that the King has authority to do whatever he wants, the counselor acts wisely with good explanations and well-thought-out reasoning. In a most respectful manner, the counselor suggests that it is warmer in Marseilles. This allows the King to see the wisdom of not bringing La Girafe to Paris in the winter. The good reasoning and polite respectful manner makes it easier for the impatient King to make the right decision. The counselor knows how hard it is for the King to wait, but he is kind in finding a scientist to draw a picture so the King will have something to look at. (Even though the illustration turns out to be inaccurate, the kind intention is still there.) Talk with your student about making wise (well-thought-out), timely suggestions, and the advantages of making them in a respectful way.

Social Studies: Relationships- Reconcillation,
Deep Affection for a Public Symbol and Giving Honor

La Giraffe is given to France by the Pasha of Egypt as a symbol of **reconcillation** and **friendship**. You may wish to discuss these terms. The people of France adore La Girafe. This love and adoration toward La Girafe lasts till her death. Even after she dies she is preserved by a taxidermist, and is still displayed today in a museum on the west coast of France. (Read about this on the last page of the history notes at the end of the story.) Isn't it amazing that you couldactually go and see La Girafe? (**Teacher's Note**: Years later in 1884, France gives the Statue of Liberty to the people of the United States, as a gesture of friendship, much like the Pashah gave La Giraffe to the King of France.)

With your student, go through the text and pictures and make a list of all the things the people of France do to honor La Girafe: Her picture appears on signs. The people talk about her and write letters to their relatives. There are newspaper stories about her. Soldiers dress in their finest uniforms; professors wear long robes of purple and red and green with white fur collars. Horses dance and prance with generals on their backs. They give her a garland of flowers and a special blanket with the symbol of Egypt and France together. There are also thousands of visitors who come to see La Girafe at the zoo. Her picture appears on dresses, shirts, purses, plates, cups, and coffee pots. There are hairstyles to honor her, and gingerbread giraffes are made. People go out everyday to see her walk and drive their wagons out to meet her!!! Think together of things you could do to "honor" someone for something special, like a birthday or an accomplishment.

Social Studies: History

"This is a true story,"...these are words you don't often hear in a children's picture story, especially one in which there is so much fairy tale appearance. With the pasha of Egypt's bright colors and exotic belongings, and kings and pageantry, not to mention a giraffe in a raincoat, it is hard to believe there was a real La Girafe that actually walked to Paris! The author has taken a real event and real people and added illustrations and detail to help us *see* in story fashion how things might have actually happened. By adding illustrations, the author helps us imagine how things appeared at that time. Because the events in this story happened such a long time ago, no one is alive today who remembers *exactly* what happened to La Girafe, but Nancy Milton has helped us imagine what it must have been like to be there through the medium of a child's picture book.

Language Arts: Setting of the Story

Every story has a setting. The setting establishes the *where* and *when* of a story. Stories can be set in the past, present or future and they can be set in real or imaginary places. The setting for this story includes Egypt and France and two main French cities: Marseilles and Paris. It is set in a time of political tension between Egypt and France, and spans the years 1826 to 1845. Consider joining two story disks together with a piece of string or yarn between Egypt and France. (For another great children's book set in France, try *Bon Appetit, Bertie* by Joan Knight which contains a wonderful map of Paris and its landmarks, ISBN 1-56458-095-0. You may also want to look again at the lesson for *Madeline, FIAR* Vol. 1, p.23)

Now help your older student make a list of ten other "settings" for a story he might like to write. Vary the settings to include both real and fictional locations and be sure to include both past, present and future time settings.

Language Arts: Italics

Let your student observe the difference in the regular print of the story and the slanted, *italic* print of the ship named *The Two Brothers* (on the page which begins, "In the year 1826..."). Italics are used in the printing process, but when a story is hand-written <u>underlining</u> is used instead of italics. We always italicize the name of ships. Italic print is used for other purposes, also, such as the names of books, etc.

Language Arts: Vocabulary

pasha   a high civil or military official

ambassador someone who represents (goes on behalf of) a country to make good, friendly relations with another country, and to know and report what is going on in foreign countries

port   an area safe from wind and waves for ships and boats to stop; usually a city or town where the goods are taken from the ship and sold or loaded onto the ship for transporting

counselor someone who helps by giving advice. (In this story the counselor gave the King advice.)

difficult hard or complicated

impatient unwilling to go slowly and wait; wanting everything immediately

popular liked by people
excellent very good; outstanding.

silent without any noise

journey trip or travel

professor a highly educated teacher

impossible not capable of being accomplished

procession a long line of people (In this story the people were following La Girafe.)

Art: Appreciating Expressions and Body Movement

Roger Roth shows an overall fine artistic ability including perspective, architecture and the use of color. One of his most notable skills in *The Girafe That Walked to Paris* is his ability to show intriguing expressions and a seemingly infinite variety of body posture and movement. This is true whether the picture showcases one person or an entire crowd!

Have your student look for interesting facial expressions on the main characters in the story. The cover picture shows Atir looking up at La Girafe with a proud and happy expression. The face of King Charles X displays a variety of emotional expressions. Look for different expressions on the King's face. Which of the King's expressions is the most intriguing to your student?

Now, look at the faces of the people in some of the different crowd scenes. Have your student look carefully at them. Even though many of the figures are small, their hand and feet gestures show action, and their faces reveal much feeling. The longer you look, the more you see the excitement among the people. Even the face of La Girafe herself and the other animals in the story are well done with personality and detail. Bravo, Mr. Roth!

Art: Knowing Your Subject

The scientist that draws King Charles the picture of the giraffe had never actually seen one. It is easy to understand why (from looking at his picture) an artist needs to know his subject! What mistakes did the scientist make? Just for fun, try drawing a composite, imaginary animal, combining different features from various animals and thinking up a good name, the type of climate or area it could be from, what it might eat, etc.

Now try drawing a real starfish, goldfish, or other animal from a photograph or other drawing. Pay as much attention as possible to the correct form and details. Most artists work from live models or pictures. They pay a great deal of attention to the details of their subject.

Art: Humor

Have your student look for illustrations that are humorous to him. One example might be the picture where King Charles X of France finally gets to see La Girafe. She is so tall that her head disappears! The King is surprised. Some of the people are surprised. Even the dog is surprised!

Math: Counting

There are lots of counting opportunities in *The Giraffe That Walked to Paris*, especially counting the crowds of people and the people in the parades. You can even count, women, then men, and then children, and end with a count of the animals pictured on the fourteenth and fifteenth pages. Remember to include the pictures of La Girafe on the signs and billboards!

Math: Measuring

There are lots of measuring opportunities for your student after reading *The Giraffe That Walked to Paris*. Remind your student that La Girafe was eleven feet tall. How tall is your student? How tall are you? How many inches are in a foot? How many feet are in a yard? Using a tape measure or yard stick, spend some time measuring. Be sure to measure eleven feet (on the floor if necessary) and let your student see how tall La Girafe was.

Science: Wind Power

With your student, look at the ship on which the giraffe sails to France. Ask him how the ship moves. What makes it go? See if he knows about sails and wind power. Does the wind always blow? Mention how a sail boat or ship is "becalmed" when there is no wind. If your student shows an interest, explore other wind-related subjects; windmills, kites, etc. Perhaps you'd like to try flying a kite together and feel the power of the wind as it pulls on the string. It's this same power that propels sailing ships around the world.

Science: Animal Care

Notice how carefully the preparations are made to ship the giraffe. See if your student can name them. (three cows to give milk and a person to milk them along with two helpers; a hole cut in the deck; straw bumper padding, and a canvas over her head like a canopy to protect her from sun and rain) The preparations are well thought out. They take the very best care of the animals, which is a wise and kind thing to do. Ask your student if he has pets. Are there special preparations made when traveling with pets or in having them cared for while the owners are traveling?

Science: Animal Behavior

King Charles X notices that the giraffe does not walk like a horse–that's observant! It is fun to spend time watching animals and insects and learning things that people who don't take time to be patient and observe will never know. Ask your student if he remembers how La Girafe walks and why. (La Girafe swings both of her right legs and then she swings both of her left legs because she has a short body and long legs. If she didn't walk that way, her back feet would step on her front feet.)

King Charles X of France said he never imagined such a creature as a giraffe. It is amazing how many animals there are to observe, and animals you've never even seen before. It is a wonder to realize there are animals, insects, birds, and plants still waiting to be discovered! (If possible, find a picture of a duck-billed platypus and let your student examine it. Ask him how he would describe this animal to someone who had never heard of one and if he thinks the person would believe him.)

Science: Zoos

There is an excellent explanation of the beginning of the "public zoo" or *menagerie*, as it is called in France, in the historic section at the end of the story. If you can, visit a zoo with your student and spend some time watching the giraffes and observing their behavior, how they eat, walk, etc.

Science: Seasons

Autumn or Fall: The ship *The Two Brothers* sets sail and reaches Marseilles (Marsay), France in October. In what season of the year does October occur? What are the other months of fall in the Northern Hemisphere? (September and November)

Winter: The King is hoping to see the giraffe by Christmas. When is Christmas? What season is December in? What are the other winter months? (January and February)

Spring: The King agrees to wait until spring to see his giraffe gift. What months are generally considered spring in the Northern Hemisphere? (March, April and May)

Summer: But the giraffe doesn't reach Paris till summer, on June 30, and King Charles X doesn't see her until July 9. What is the other month usually considered summer in the Northern Hemisphere? (August)

For your younger student, just the mention of the seasons and some of the months contained therein is sufficient. For older students, the names of the seasons are probably familiar and learning exactly how the twelve months are divided into each season is a timely lesson. You might enjoy naming months of the year in which your student's family's birthdays occur. Let him tell you whether each birtday is celebrated in the spring, summer, winter or fall.

THREE NAMES

Title: *Three Names*
Author: Patricia MacLachlan
Illustrator: Alexander Pertzoff
Copyright: 1991
Summary: Text and illustrations give a generous taste of prairie life along with a great-grandfather's colorful memories.

Social Studies: Relationships - Pets

In *Five In A Row* you have explored many relationships among people. *Three Names* provides an opportunity to explore the relationship of a boy and his pet dog. For centuries man has enjoyed the companionship of certain animals: dogs, cats, horses and certain birds, etc. Does your student have a pet? Does it sometimes seem as if a pet can understand our thoughts? Why do pets seem to enjoy human companionship? Scientific studies have proven that people benefit from having pets around. The loving relationship and faithful friendship of a dog, for instance, can be a special encouragement to some children, older adults and the handicapped. The friendship between man and animal is a mystery that both parties enjoy.

Social Studies: Prairie Life

Many children are well acquainted with the word *prairie*, from the *The Little House on the Prairie* books and television show. If they have heard or read these books they know life on the prairie was quite different for the Ingalls family than their life had been in "the little house in the big woods."

(*Teacher's Note:* A prairie is a region that is flat or hilly and has a covering of tall grasses with few trees. It is the area once roamed by the bison (or buffalo). The North American prairie includes the prairie provinces of Alberta, Saskatchewan, and Manitoba in Canada. In the United States prairie extends from central Texas northward and includes most of Oklahoma, Kansas, Nebraska, Iowa, North and South Dakota, and parts of Montana and Minnesota. Ask your student if he lives on prairie land, or if he has a friend or relative in the prairie region of this country or Canada. (There are other prairie lands in South America, South Africa and in parts of Russia.)

Man has altered most of the prairie land and the native grasses have been replaced by fields of corn and wheat or by grazing herds. Some small areas of prairie land are protected by the government. If you can view a natural prairie area you can see the kind of land that Three Names knew, and wonder if *you* would ever get lost on the vast prairie.

Your older student might enjoy drawing a prairie scene for his notebook. He might want to include tumbleweeds, a slough, prairie dogs, prairie grasses, Indian paintbrush, wheat, a ruffled grouse, wide open spaces, not many trees, etc.

If your younger student is interested, you could find magazine photographs or make simple drawings of prairie items. Then let your student glue them on a page he has decorated with a horizon line, blue sky and with brown and green grasses underneath. No matter how "primitively drawn" the items are, it is fun to make a composite picture that shows how different things live and grow in different geographic regions and zones.

Social Studies: History - One-Room School House

Explore the wonders of the American one-room school house. There are all grades in one room, where the older students can help the younger. There is a wood stove; too hot close up, never hot enough in the corners of the room. And what about the outhouse? But, there are still those things that never change: geography, writing and arithmetic. There is still a teacher and students, lunches, friends, siblings, games to play, and still twenty six letters in the alphabet! And maybe, if you are very fortunate, a dog like Three Names.

Roast some potatoes for lunch and have a crock of butter handy! It helps bring the story to life. Your student loves these kinds of "hands on" surprises!

Language Arts: Interesting Title

(**Teacher's Note:** *You might discuss the story title before reading the story for the first time.*)

What does your student think of the title? Does it make him want to read the book to find out what it means? A good title draws you into the story. After you've finished *Three Names,* make a list of other titles that could have been used for this story.

Language Arts: Vocabulary

slough	a depression filled with mud or mire; also, as in this story, a pond that is partly overgrown and marshy
aggie	a round, playing marble made of a rock called agate
graduation	a ceremony celebrating a moving on from one form to another, as from high school to college or college to career.
tethered	in this story, tying the horse to a stake, in a manner, allowing him to graze in a circular path

Language Arts: Literary Device - Simile

For your older student, try reminding him of simile which is a comparison of two unlike things using the connective words such as *like, as, seems*, etc. See if he can hear and identify similes in this story. For example:

(prairie dogs) with eyes black **as** berries

the nights were crisp **like** apples

children looking small **like** tumbleweeds

watching the prairie stretch out **like** a quilt

Three Names would turn around and sigh, settling **like** a sack of grain

Your young student may enjoy the images that these similes create. By appreciating them now, he may make use of this type of literary device later in his own writing.

Language Arts: Literary Device - Hyperbole

Hyperbole (hi purr bow lee), is exaggeration, usually made for emphasis. *Three Names* contains two examples of the same hyperbole. "When my Great-grandfather was young–a hundred years ago, he likes to say," and "high topped shoes that took a long time to lace–a hundred years." The text quickly admits that neither of these statements is true, but Great-grandfather is fond of making this exaggeration.

Language Arts: Writing Description

On p.17 there is a splendid description of a barn. Reread the paragraph. Can your student see it? Can he smell it? (Of course, this is not easy if he's never been in a barn, but if he's ever been inside a barn this description will surely be reminiscent of his visit) If there is an opportunity, visit a stable or barn and let your student feel the coolness, see the darkness, and smell the sweet smell of hay, the tangy odor of harness leather, and the comfortable aroma of horses whether that are pinto, gray or blaze.

If your student would like, have him dictate, tape record, or write a description of something he knows well. Have him remember that his readers need to be able to "see, hear, feel, taste, or smell" whatever he is describing. Remind him that he can choose to use simile and metaphor to help his readers understand his description more clearly.

If you have a young horse lover, find some good picture books of horses that show the beauty of a Palomino, the stoutness of a draft horse, the lines of an Arabian, etc. Libraries usually have large picture books full of excellent photographs of horses. Check the adult section as well as the juvenile section of your library.

Art: Games to Play

Great-grandfather plays games at school, including:

Marbles: Does your student have an old sock full of marbles? Does he know how to play? Marbles are still available from toy stores, but wonderful older ones can be passed down from family members or found in flea markets, junk or antique stores. Surprise your student with an old woolen sock full of marbles, find a dusty spot, draw a circle and enjoy! If you need to brush up on the rules try your library card catalog, or request *The Complete Book of Games* by Clement Wood and Gloria Goddard, Garden City Books, and see p. 866!

Fox and Geese and Hide and Seek: These games have been played and enjoyed for many generations. You may have some stories to tell your student about times when you played Fox and Geese or Hide and Seek. (For some, Fox and Geese was a winter game played in the snow, while for others tales of events, adventures, and mishaps abound on the subject of Hide and Seek. Other old fashioned games included Statue, where one had to hold a certain position, and Mother May I, etc.) If you are unsure of the rules, some of the games of yesterday can be found in game books at the library, or variations in the memories of parents and grandparents.

Take time after lessons or for recess and gather some players for a great old fashioned time. Pretend you are drinking cool water from the well, in tin cups, or have some lemonade and cookies.

Art: Shadows and Light Source

Alert your student "shadow chasers!" Look for examples of shadows in Alexander Pertzoff's paintings. By now, your student will probably understand some things about shadows. He may already know that shadows are cast when a solid object interrupts a bright stream of light. He may also be able to find the light source of a picture in this story and thus show you the direction from which the light is coming.

Look at the painting of Three Names running on the back of p. 31. Take your finger and trace it from the right side of the picture, across the lighted part of the dog's face and through the middle of the shadow. That is the path of the light and it comes from the right upper corner of the picture. Compare this picture with the one of Three Names running into the picture on p. 9. Where is the light coming from? (Ahead of him and slightly to the left of the picture.)

Next, have your student look at the picture of George giving his graduation speech. Notice the shadows, especially behind George, and the light on the backs of the other students. Can your student trace the path of light? (It looks like it is from the horizon line at the left of the picture edge to a little above the lower right-hand corner.)

Now, notice the shadow on Great-grandfather's face on p. 6. Where is the sun? (overhead and a little to the left of the picture) Finally, look at the shadow Great-grandfather's mother made behind the sheet! What was she doing? (crying because her children were going off to school and she would miss them) Where is the light coming from? (clues:

brightest sky on left side of picture, behind the house; also, shadows of chickens and wagon and house) Trace the path from the middle of the house to the lower right corner of the picture. Ask your student if all the shadows in this picture follow this path. (yes) Getting back to Great-grandfather's mother, look at the series of shapes the artist used to give the effect of her figure behind the sheet. (For fun, find an old sheet and hang it so that someone standing behind it with bright light behind them will cast a "people" shadow. Have them act out crying, dancing, singing with hand gestures, jumping, etc. Let someone else guess each action.)

Only for the most avid shadow chaser: Check the shadows cast by the wheels against the wagon on p. 13. Find the light source. (The light source, from the right side of the picture about horizon level, can be seen on the faces of the dog and children.) If they are starting off to school in the *morning,* what direction, north, south, east or west, is the light coming from? (east!)

Art: Vanishing Point

Have your student look at the road on p. 16. How does the artist give the effect of a road that seems to stretch back into the picture until it disappears? Notice that this road is wider at the bottom or foreground of the picture. The two sides of the road grow closer together as the lines rise on the paper. If you could see past the figures in the road, you could see these lines actually touch each other (the point at which the road vanishes!) The fence posts are also taller in the foreground and smaller the farther up the lines go. This gives the effect of the road moving back into the picture. Try this simple road on a piece of paper. See if your student can begin to understand and possibly draw this effect. Then, someday, when he has a picture "in his mind" that needs a road, he will know there is a way to make that road seem to "disappear into the distance." He'll have the beginning understanding of how to use vanishing point to help create perspective.

Art: Interpreting a Painting

Look at the picture of the title page. Ask your student why he thinks the artist painted the boy looking away.

There is no right answer unless the artist himself could tell us what he was thinking when he painted the picture, but we can interpret what the picture "says" to us. Maybe the boy looking back is inviting the reader into the story. Maybe the picture was painted that way to symbolize Great grandfather's reminiscing (looking back at his childhood), or maybe it was to focus the reader's attention on Three Names, the title character who is always at Great-grandfather's side.

Art: Surface Lines-Element of Perspective

Did your student ever wonder how an artist takes a flat piece of paper or canvas, and creates something that looks round or rounded? One way an artist can accomplish this is the use of surface lines to give depth and roundness to figures. We show the roundness of an object by drawing or painting small curved lines. Look at the boy on p. 20, the one on the right with his back to the reader. See the darker brown lines on his tan shirt that show how his arm and side are curved? There are very dark lines along the left side of his pants, also, which make his leg look rounded. Can you find any other examples in this story? Look for surface line in the works of other artists and try some on your own figures until you can do it easily yourself.

Art: Music

Great-grandfather mentions that Martha played her fiddle. This was a popular instrument for the people of the prairie. It certainly was easier to obtain than something heavy like a piano. By the time a piano traveled from the east, jostled by wagon, it might not be in the best condition. A piano was also much more expensive than a fiddle. (Remember Pa had a fiddle in the book *The Little House on the Prairie*?)

This might be a good time to sing a few choruses of *Home on the Range*. (Not an original cowboy song, but one that became popular in the twentieth century. Still it accurately captures the feeling of the range and the prairie, the place where the buffalo roamed.) You might also want to check out *"Westward Ho,"* a Hear and Learn tape with accompanying book that includes fourteen songs such as *Home on the Range* and *Little Sod Shanty*. ISBN 1-879459-05-1 This tape is available from many curriculum suppliers.

Math: Perspective in Measurement

How long is a foot? Have your student look at a twelve inch ruler. How many feet in a yard–see how many ruler lengths you can lay on a yardstick.

For an older student, teach the number of feet in a mile. (5,280 feet per mile) That would be 5,280 rulers laid end to end. Great-grandfather usually rode to school in a wagon, but once he says he walked how many miles to school? (3 miles) Three miles is how many feet? Your student could remember that changing miles to feet would be going from the larger unit (miles) to the smaller unit (feet). This means that the problem requires multiplication to solve. Have him multiply 5,280 feet by 3 (for the miles) and see how many feet that would be. Remember to use the comma to divide the hundreds' from the thousands' place.

Math: Ordinal Numbers

Ordinal numbers name the order or position in a series. *"On the first day of school Three Names pranced and danced around the wagon."* and *"Great-grandfather's mother always cried the first day of school for her own reasons."* Both of these quotes from the story *Three Names* demonstrate the use of the ordinal number *"first."* When standing in a line, ask your student to name the position of the person wearing the red sweater, or the baseball cap, etc. Allow him to practice his ability to say ordinal numbers even into the teens and twenties if possible. Also, you may wish to ask a younger student what position is the letter "g" in the alphabet (seventh), etc. You can ask what month of the year is August (the eighth month), etc.

Science: Weather - Wind

There are strong winds and even tornadoes on the prairie. Wind can be a slight movement of air across the surface of the land or water, or a stiff breeze or a destructive force as a hurricane or tornado. There are many vocabulary words associated with wind: *gale, breeze, drafts, puffs, gusts*, and a new word seen often in the media today "*wind shears*." Wind shears are strong, sudden down-drafts that can cause airline crashes. There are many good library books available on the subject of weather and wind. These range from extremely simple texts to those with more advanced information. Search with your student for age appropriate books that include the topic of wind.

Science: Fraternal Twins

"The Twilling twins, who did not look alike, walked because they lived close by." Is your student a twin? Does he have any twins in his family? Does he know any twins? Are they identical or not? Some twins are identical in appearance, of the same sex, etc. Others, called *fraternal twins* are not identical. They may be of the same sex or they may be a boy and a girl. Of course, there are also triplets, quadruplets, quintuplets, etc.

If it seems appropriate, you may want to discuss the genetic origins of identical and fraternal twins. Identical twins occur when one sperm fertilizes one egg which subsequently splits, producing identical twins with the same genetic makeup. Fraternal twins occur when two separate eggs are fertilized by two separate sperm resulting in two simultaneous, but dissimilar children.

Science: Wells and Well Water

Great-grandfather gets his water from a well. Where does your water come from? City residents usually receive water via underground pipes from area purification plants which pump the water from rivers or reservoirs. Many small towns have water towers, which contain water purchased from cities, etc. Some rural families either collect their water in cisterns, purchase their water by the truckload, or pump their water from underground wells.

Why is well water cool? (Because the water comes from deeper underground). As you go further underground, away from the sun's warmth, it becomes cooler for the first several hundred feet. It was once quite popular to keep vegetables and some fruits in root cellars (underground rooms that stay cooler than the buildings above-ground when the temperature is hot). These cellars would keep the vegetables and fruits fresh for a longer period of time. Also, the temperature does not fluctuate as quickly when it is cold, in underground storage cellars, so the fruits and vegetables do not freeze when the above-ground temperature is freezing. A typical underground well or root cellar is approximately 50 degrees Fahrenheit year round. This is warm enough to prevent freezing and cool enough to preserve freshness. Ask your student if his home makes use of a root cellar. Has he ever visited anyone's home and seen their cellar? Perhaps he could write or ask his grandparents if they had root cellars. Maybe they would tell him about them.

WEE GILLIS

Title:	*WeeGillis*
Author:	Munro Leaf
Illustrator:	Robert Lawson
Copyright:	1938
Award:	Caldecott Honor Book
Summary:	A young lad with a big decision to make finds a way to be himself.

Social Studies: Geography - Scotland

Scotland comprises the northern third of the island of Great Britain. Scotland's rugged highlands cover the northern two-thirds of Scotland, with the lowlands the southern third. It is one of the countries of the United Kingdom of Great Britain, which includes England, Northern Ireland, and Wales. Edinburgh is the capital of Scotland, while Glasgow is its largest city. Many of the people live in the central industrial area. They work in shipyards, mills and other industrial businesses that frame the economy of this country.

The Highlanders came from an area much like the United States' Appalachian Mountains. (Remember the mountain coal region in *The Rag Coat*, by Lauren Mills, FIAR Vol. 1, p. 31) In fact, many of the the Scottish Highlanders who immigrated to the United States settled in Appalachia because the mountains reminded them of home.

Though the reader isn't told exactly, it appears the story of *Wee Gillis* took place many years ago in Scotland before there was much industrialization, in a more rural time. In this story, there are cottages, kilts (knee-length skirts, made of wool with pleats, worn by the men of the Scottish Highlands), tam-o'shanters (soft wool hats with flat round crown, perhaps worn more by Lowlanders), rugged highlands, misty lowlands, stags, long hair cattle, oatmeal, and words like "wee" (which means small or young). In addition, "Wee Gillis" is basically a nickname because the young man's Scottish name is too long: Alastair Roderic Craigellachie Dalhousie Gowan Donnybristle MacMac. Many of the Scottish family names were long and just reading this list gives your student an idea of the "sound of Scotland." The long list of names could also be Mr. Leaf's touch of humor!

If you can, look up Scotland in *The World Book Encyclopedia* and share the pictures with your student. If there is special interest, find good books at the library to increase his knowledge of the country and the culture. Don't forget to fix a bowl of oatmeal and maybe get some shortbread for a treat! Now, place the story disk on Scotland.

Social Studies: Relationships - Making Decisions and Controlling Emotions

Within families there are sometimes struggles for affection or power. The manner in which such times of stress are handled can make a difference for a long time to come.

In the story of *Wee Gillis*, it would seem that the young man is old enough to settle down for himself. His problem is to decide whether to associate himself with the Highlanders or the people of the Lowlands. What does your student think of the way he tries to decide (before the man with the bagpipes appears)? Does the fact that he is cheerful and amiable (happy, friendly, sociable) help him in this family dilemma? Does Wee Gillis seem overly upset when the two men fight over him? As they appear to get more and more angry, what is the look on Wee Gillis' face? Does this calm demeanor seem a good thing to your student? Remember the poem about keeping your head when all about you are losing theirs? The poem is entitled *If* by Rudyard Kipling. It begins:

> *"If you can keep your head when all about you*
> *Are losing theirs and blaming it on you...*

and ends,

> *"And—what is more—you'll be a Man, my son!"*

Language Arts: Family Names

In the story of *Wee Gillis*, the boy's real name was extremely long. It obviously included many family names. Just for fun, have your student research some of his family names on both sides and let him see what his name would look like if he added these between his first and last name.

Language Arts: Foreshadowing

(**Teacher's Note**: Use this lesson after you have read the story several times.)

Foreshadowing is a literary device that suggests what is to come later in a work by giving hints and clues. In this case, it is not the text but the illustration that gives a clue to the ending of the story. On about p. 4 where it explains the dilemma of Wee Gillis, the picture opposite shows him standing not in the Lowlands, nor in the Highlands, but rather on middle ground. By the end of the story we can look back and recognize that picture as a foreshadowing clue. It foreshadows the outcome of the story because the middle is exactly where he stays.

Language Arts: Poetry

If you or your student has a love of poetry, this story presents a good introduction to the poems of Robert Burns, especially one called *My Heart's In the Highlands*, of which the following is a part:

"My heart's in the highlands, my heart is not here,
My heart's in the highlands a-chasing the deer,
A-chasing the wild deer, and following the roe,
My heart's in the Highlands wherever I go." .

(**Teacher's Note:** Burns uses the word "roe" as a synonym for deer. Other words associated with deer include: hart, stag, doe, fawn, buck, etc.)

Language Arts: Descriptions and Balance

Using both text and especially illustrations of this story, ask your student to write or dictate to you a list of descriptive words about the relatives of Wee Gillis. Make two columns; one for the Highland relatives, and one for the Lowlanders. Describe each with as many different words as possible. For instance:

Lowlanders   valley dwellers
long-haired cattle raisers
wear woolen pants and jackets and tam-o'shanters
think the Highlanders are foolish for chasing deer
volatile tempers

Highlanders   mountain dwellers
stag stalkers
wear kilts and other garb of highlands
think the Lowlanders are foolish for milking cows
volatile tempers

These descriptions, as well as the basic flow of the story, give a sense of balance. The Highlanders are on one side and the Lowlanders are on the other. Who seems to be in the center? This type of writing with balanced segments is a common technique used by authors. A well-known story, *Blueberries for Sal* by Robert McCloskey, uses the same type of balanced segments when he writes about the little bear and little Sal, and what little bear did and what little Sal did, and what little bear's mother did and what little Sal's mother did, etc. Your student might try such a story, but he needs to choose a subject which has two clearly opposite components, such as something that happens every summer and something that happens every winter, or something's happening in space at the same time other things are happening on earth, or the left hand wanting to do everything that the right hand does, back and forth till a solution is reached. The story can be humorous or serious.

Art: Medium - Monochrome

From reading about the artist/illustrator, it appears the medium used for this book was brush and black tempera paint. The look is similar to pen and ink. Even though the pictures are in black and white, there is much expression, action and description. In fact, we see these more clearly because we are not preoccupied with color. Black and white drawings can be a powerful means of artistic expression. Look in magazines for exceptional black and white photographs. Have your student watch for black and white art that is interesting and creative. Encourage your student to try drawing an object or subject using colors. Then let him try drawing the identical subject again, using only black on white. When an artist uses only **one color** to draw or paint his pictures he is said to be working in **monochrome**. His picture is then monochromatic.

Art: Compare and Contrast

There are two pictures of Wee Gillis eating his oatmeal that seem to be the same. On closer examination there are a number of differences. Let your student look carefully at both pictures and see if he can spot the differences. (One mug has a long haired cow on it, the other mug has a stag deer. One hat rack is made of cow horns while the other is made of stag's antlers. The knife blades are the same but one handle is made of cow horn and the other of deer horn. The spoon handles are different, too.) There are some things in these two pictures that are the same. Can your student name them? (There is the same chip in the bowl; the spoon is full of oatmeal. Wee Gillis has the same clothes and hat, etc.) Have your student try two simple pictures of something that can be almost the same but in small ways is different. If he shows his pictures to a relative, will they notice that the pictures are not supposed to be exactly alike?

Art: Cross-Hatching

With your student, look at the picture showing Wee Gillis holding his breath. His mouth is on the bagpipe, just before he starts to blow. How can you tell (with a black and white picture) that Gillis is red in the face? For one thing, you have to know that when a person holds their breath in that manner their face turns red. Using that knowledge, look again at how the artist has darkened Gillis' puffed up cheeks. Even though this picture is black medium on white paper, we realize his cheeks are supposed to be red. The technique that Robert Lawson used to make the cheeks darker than the rest of the face is called **cross-hatching**. In drawings, it is a way to make shadowed or darkened areas by making a series of marks going one way, and then crossing them once or twice at different angles. Try cross-hatching by making a row of one inch squares. Show your student how to make free hand pencil lines parallel but close to one another in the first box. Repeat this same pattern in the second box and then make another series of parallel lines crossing the first ones. Repeat both of these steps in the third box, but make yet another set of parallel lines crossing at a different angle than either the first or second box. Now look. Each succeeding box should look darker than the one before it. Have your student look for other examples of cross-hatching whenever he sees drawn illustrations.

 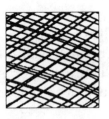 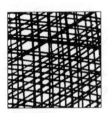

Art: Shadows

Opposite the text where the relatives find just the right deciding place, is a good example of shadows. Have your student place a ruler or long pencil along and parallel to the shadows, extending the ruler off the book page to the right. Explain that the source of light that is making the shadow (in this case the sun) is coming from the direction of the upper part of the ruler. Since it cannot shine through the men, wherever the light is stopped it casts a shadow. Remind your student that he can first decide where the source of light is coming from in his pictures. Then he'll know where to draw his shadows. Draw several identical drawings of a simple tree, stick figure, lamp post or stop sign. Now, have your student try placing the shadow at various angles as you "show" him where the sun is located in each picture. When you tell him the sun is high and to the right, for instance, he would draw a short shadow to the left. If you told him the sun was located low and behind he would draw a long shadow straight forward or down on the page, etc.

If your student is a shadow chaser, let him hunt for other shadows in these illustrations. (A favorite is the shadow under the long haired cows as Gillis drives them home. The light source is coming almost directly from behind the tall, skinny tree, directly toward the reader!)

Math: Half

When Gillis is being encouraged to choose which set of his relatives to live with, he must have felt nearly pulled in half. Explore the meaning of the word **half** for whatever age is appropriate: Half a century or a year (what is that?), half a dollar (how much is that?), half an hour (how long is that?), half time (the middle of a football game), half sister or brother (when only one parent is in common), half a pie (the part I'd like!). The definition of half: a part that is approximately equal to another part which put together make a whole. How many different ways can you write one half or its equivalent? (one half, 1/2, .5, 50/100, etc.)

Math: Calendar

"On the first day of the new year Wee Gillis went up into the Highlands." Ask your student if he knows what month on the calendar begins a new year. You may hint that it is in the month following December (on a Western Calendar). Show your student or ask him to write the date of the first day of the year. (January 1) Often, the beginning of the new year is marked by a re-evaluation of achievements and a new evaluation of goals. In keeping with this custom of "January new beginnings,"Wee Gillis changes direction on the first of the new year and goes to try the Highlands. What is January like in the area of the country where your student lives? Are there any January birthdays in his family?

How many months are there in a year? In a half year? Set up the division problem on paper or work the problem by grouping 12 items into two equal groups. (6) In a quarter year? Set up the division problem on paper, or work the problem by grouping 12 items into four equal groups (3).

Can your younger student recite the months of the year? Can your older student read them on the calendar? Can he write them in a list? Can he divide them into seasons? How many of the 12 months are in each "season"? (This is another way to approach the "quarter year" division problem in the paragraph above.)

Science: Weather - Fog

The valleys of Scotland often have fog and mist. This is, in part, due to its island location. Also, while the fog seems to dissipate faster in the windy highlands, it settles in the valleys, where there is less wind. Discuss with your student the conditions which cause fog. Fog occurs when the temperature falls below the dewpoint. First dew drops occur, and eventually the moisture in the air forms visible droplets of water, or fog. Fog occurs when humidity is high, temperatures are low and the wind is calm. In some areas of the United States, fog occurs more often in the fall and early winter months as temperatures decline and winds are calm. Yet, other areas might experience routine fog near bodies of of water, i.e., bays, rivers, marshes, lakes, etc. Begin to notice with your student the times of the year and the conditions that create fog where you live.

Science: Sheep

In Scotland, sheep are grown for their wool which is turned into clothing. Notice in the drawings the rough, almost thistle-like texture of the stockings, jackets and pants of the people. Show your student an article of wool clothing, perhaps a scarf, skirt or jacket. Have him feel the texture and compare it with cotton and synthetic fabric. There may be opportunities in your community to learn more about wool. You may know someone who has sheep on a farm, or perhaps you know someone who cards, spins and weaves wool as a hobby. If you have the opportunity, a field trip to see the actual process of carding, spinning, dying and weaving wool would be fascinating. Sheep are also raised for food. While lamb is not as popular in the United States as it is in other foreign countries, many people enjoy leg of lamb, rack of lamb, shish kabobs, or lamb chops. Consider cooking some lamb with your student for lunch or dinner or researching the components of Scotch broth.

Special Note: Video Available of *Wee Gillis*

There is also a video available of *Wee Gillis*. This is an actual nineteen minute film and not just an animation of the book. While the film doesn't perfectly follow the book, it will give your student a wonderful opportunity to actually see the highlands, kilts, long-haired cows and bagpipes, as well as hear the actual accents. The video, in VHS format, is from Churchill Films and edited by Pieter Van Deusen and George McQuilkin. I ran across it at my local library, so check yours first. Perhaps they have a video search/request service. You might also check with local video rental stores as well.

Title:	*Owl Moon*
Author:	Jane Yolen
Illustrator:	John Schoenherr
Copyright:	1987
Award:	Caldecott Medal (Remember to show your student the medal usually displayed on the book cover. Remind him it is given for the most distinguished *picture book* for children published during the pervious year in the United States. He will then know about the Caldecott Award, to whom it is given and for what accomplishment (illustration). You may want to discuss with your student that awards do not necessarily guarantee that a book is truly great. He still must learn to use his own discernment to evaluate a book's contents and pictures.

Summary:	A young child experiences a look at nature–a look that turns out to be too special for words.

Social Studies: Relationship - Father and Child

Owl Moon shows us a relationship between a father and his child. This relationship may be traced in the illustrations as well as the text. The picture opposite the first page of text shows father and child walking together away from their house. The following pictures show the shared experience of searching for an owl. The last picture shows the intimacy that comes from a shared experience–a closeness that does not even need words to express the wonders they have seen.

Ask your student if he can describe a special time he has spent with an adult, perhaps a father, aunt, uncle, teacher or friend. Ask him what made the time special, and how he felt about an adult spending that time with him. He may want to draw a picture of what they did together.

Social Studies: Relationships - Rules

Discuss the *"rules of the house"* with your student. Ask him what he thinks the reason is for each rule. Do some of the rules provide protection from danger? Do some of the rules provide a disciplined atmosphere in which to live, such as "clean your room" or "help with the yard" or "empty the trash"? Living in a chaotic atmosphere makes everything more difficult. Sometimes this type of atmosphere causes people to be constantly irritated. Rules can provide a measure of safety and a calm, neat enviornment in which to live.

Are there other kinds of rules? Ask him if he knows what the word *"flexibility"* means. In *Owl Moon,* the father exercises flexibility (momentarily changing the rule for a reason) when he takes his child out late at night. The wise parent can choose times to suspend a rule for a special occasion. The young person in this story is especially happy to be allowed this adventure with Pa. Flexibility is a good quality, and in *Owl Moon* Pa uses it to add "spice" and fun to his child's life. Can your student think of occasions in his family when a rule was set aside for a special event? Ask him to describe the event or maybe write a paragraph about it.

Social Studies: Maturity
Self Control, Bravery, Realistic Expectations

The text of *Owl Moon* reveals, through conversation, information to let the reader know that the child has experienced growth and maturity. Sentences like, *"But, I never called out. If you go owling you have to be quiet...",* and *"I had been waiting ... for a long, long time.",* and *"I could feel the cold. But I never said a word."* Also, *"If you go owling you have to be quiet.",* and *"I didn't ask what kinds of things hide behind black trees...When you go owling you have to be brave.",* and *"I was not disappointed. My brothers said sometimes there's an owl and sometimes there isn't."* Each of these sentences show either a gaining of self-control, the growth into bravery, or the ability to wait for something in a mature manner. Also, we see the child growing in the ability to have realistic expectations and enjoy the trip, even if the goal cannot be met (in this case actually seeing an owl). Choose one of these ideas and explore it with your student.

For instance, in discussing self-control it is good to talk about the fact that while many people feel "self-control" limits their actions, actually it allows one to do far more things and to be more productive than when self control is *not* exercised. Sometimes children are not invited to certain activities because they have not yet learned self-control. They may be unable to control their voices, language or actions. Sometimes, adults are passed over for a promotion in the work-place because their lack of self-control hampers their work productivity. Lack of self-control, loosing one's temper, putting off work that needs to be done, etc., has many negative effects on our family relationships, neighborhoods, and society. On the other hand, maturing and growing in this area can open many doors of opportunity and fulfillment, enriching our relationships with others. Encourage your student by explaining these rewards of self-control.

Social Studies: Setting - Woods

The setting for *Owl Moon* is a wooded area near the farm house in a northern area of the country (snow and cold). The text itself does not define a particular town or state but the book jacket tells us that the farm featured in *Own Moon* is the Schoenherr farm of illustrator John Schoenherr. We can tell from the illustrations that the story is set in a northern climate and has woods enough for owls. (**Teacher's Note:** See additional information on owls and the forest habitat in the Science section of this story's lessons.)

Social Studies: First-Time Experiences

If you have not taught about first-time experiences before *(The Very Last First Time, FIAR* Vol. 1, p. 83), you may want to use this story as a discussion springboard. Or use this lesson as a review by asking your student why the young person in this story has to wait so long before they are allowed to go owling? (This is a late night activity, and involves walking long distances in the snow. Also, the self control to remain quiet is needed so that they can actually have the chance to see an owl. Bravery is also necessary in order not to be afraid of the dark woods, etc.) Some first-time experiences are dictated by law, such as being able to drive a car, vote, etc. Sometimes a parent's rules or finances cause a wait for something special. Younger children might be anticipating their school or mucic lessons to begin like their brother's and sister's, or waiting for permission to answer the phone, etc. Ask your student if there is something he is waiting to do for the first time? (Perhaps to ride a horse, play baseball on a team, sew on a machine, etc.) Ask your student the reason he is waiting for that particular event. Share with him, too, any special first-time experiences you remember.

Language Arts: Poetic Language - Metaphor and Simile

The story *Owl Moon* is a gentle, quiet, yet exhilarating story of people enjoying the wonder and awe of pure nature as it was created. The text is filled with phrases that help bring the sights, sounds and feelings to the reader by comparing them to other things that he has known and experienced. Metaphor and simile are comparisons of one thing to another reminiscent of the first thing but not actually like it. For instance, on the first page the author writes, *"The trees stood still as giant statues."* Has your student ever seen a statue? If he has, he knows they some statues are quite large and they do not move at all. This is a good word picture of huge trees that are still because there is no wind. (There is no reason for young elementary students to memorize terms like metaphor and simile. The idea is to introduce them to the concept of comparison and help them begin to enjoy the technique of comparing things so that their future writing can be more descriptive.)

(**Teacher's Note:** The word *"as"* comparing trees to statues is what makes this phrase a simile. Simile compares two unlike things using the connecting word **as**, **like**, or **seems**, etc. On the first page "...a train whistle blew... like a sad, sad, song." This is also a simile. An older student may enjoy going on a hunt for similes. There are others in this text: quiet **as** a dream, snow whiter ***than*** the milk in a cereal bowl, owl lifted off the branch ***like*** a shadow, etc. There is another poetic form of comparison called metaphor. Metaphor is like simile, but it **does not use** connecting words such as *like, as, seem, than,* etc. It suggests that one object is actually another, yet they are dissimilar things. For example, on the next to the last page, *"I was a shadow as we walked home,"* is a metaphor. Had the author said, *"I was like a shadow"* it would have been a simile. Another metaphor appears earlier in the text, *"The moon made his face into a silver mask."*–not it was *like* a silver mask, but it *was* a silver mask.)

Here are some examples of the difference between simile and metaphor.

Simile	**Metaphor**
The clouds looked *like* marshmallows.	The marshmallow clouds flew by.
Last night the harbor lights shone *like* jewels across the black water.	Last night the harbor lights were jewels in the black water.

Your older student might like to write some phrases that use similes and metaphors while your younger student might have fun just saying phrases that you begin for him: Simile starters: "The grass was green *like*..." (frogs in spring, etc.), or "The sand felt sharp *like*..." (stepping on Legos®, etc.). Metaphor starters: "My swollen fingers *were*..." (fat sausages, etc.) or "The giant lake *was* a..." (dark mirror, etc.)

Language Arts: Literary Device - Hyperbole

Hyperbole (pron. high purr bow lee or high purr buh lee) is x exaggeration or overstatement made for the purpose of emphasis. In this story by Jane Yolen, when Pa turns the flashlight on the owl, the text says, *"For one minute, three minutes, maybe even a hundred minutes, we stared at each other."* The hyperbole is the "*hundred minutes.*" It is improbable that they actually stood in the cold and watched the owl for an hour and forty minutes. The author uses this figure of speech to help the reader understand the child's reaction to that special moment.

Discuss with your student that people use hyperbole in speech as well as in writing. Some common conversational examples might be: "My teacher gave me *tons* of homework." "We were gone *forever*." "That idea was *pure gold*!" If your student grasps the idea of hyperbole, have him look for examples in speech, books or magazines. If not, point out now and then an example that *you* find. Your student will eventually begin to understand the concept of hyperbole. This is one form of literary device that you would not want to overuse. A little hyperbole goes a long way.

Language Arts: Imagery

Imagery is painting a quick specific picture with words which are so carefully chosen they create an instant mental picture when reading them. You can *see* what is being described. In *Owl Moon* the line, *"We reached the line of pine trees, black and pointy against the sky..."*, is an example of imagery. Rather than trying to teach the word to younger students, it might be good to point out the concept of imagery by saying, "When you read the line about the pine trees, can you *see* them in your mind?" If your student has ever noticed how pointy pine trees can be and how they outline themselves on the skyline, he will respond. If he has not and you have the chance to point such a scene out to him, you will have broadened his awareness of his world. Good pictures (illustrations, photographs, watercolor or oil paintings) can be used to show such scenes if your student lives where pine trees are scarce. These will help him understand Yolen's word imagery.

Imagery often comes from contrast: the pearl white egg on the cool green grass. (Can you imagine this?) At other times imagery may be the result of a carefully described subject which brings an image to your mind. Try creating some phrases that paints a specific picture and leave an image, such as, "Slowly, one by one, the purple petals fell on the polished wood floor."

Language Arts: First Person Point of View

Ask your student who is telling this story. (The young owling person is speaking about the adventure. Words like *"I"*, *"us"*, *"my"*, *"we,"* (all of which are *first person* pronouns) let us know that this story is told from the *first person* point of view. For your young student, just an introduction to the idea of telling a story from the "I" point of view is sufficient. Have him try to write a story in that manner or dictate one to you. For your older student, a more focused lesson on first person pronouns* may be practical. He also could try writing a story from the first-person point of view. It can be simple. Have him recount an adventure or event of his own. If he is a practiced writer, let him try a fiction story from the first person point of view.

*First Person Personal Pronouns

	Nominative Case	Possessive Case	Objective Case
Singular:	I	my, mine	me
Plural:	we	our, ours	us

Art: Details

Some artistic styles rely on broad, impressionistic renderings while others use a more detailed, realistic style. John Schoenherr has included lots of wonderful detail for us in *Owl Moon*. On the title page, the young person is looking out the door. Ask your student to tell you or write a caption for this picture, e.g., *The Adventure is About to Begin*, or *What Will it Be Like?*, *Will We See An Owl?*, *My First Owling*, *It Looks Dark Out There!*,etc.

The text talks about a train. Can your student find it in the picture on the first page of the story? What kind of animal is on the second page of text? And opposite the sec ond page of writing? What about the third page of text? What kind of animal is pictured? On the fourth page, fifth page (opposite), (I couldn't find one in the sixth??), the seventh and eighth (both opposite text) and opposite the eleventh page, there is a hidden animal. Ask your student to hunt for them and identify them. Isn't this an enjoyable and subtle way to let children know what animals they could expect to find in the woodland habitat?

It is a certain that John Schoenherr loves the woods and the animals. His "love" is evident in his work. Remind your student that artists often paint what they love and the subjects with which they are familiar. Some artists take time to study the real subjects and make many sketches before they paint or draw the illustrations for a story.

Art: Aerial View

Notice with your student the illustrations on the first page of text. This view of the farm is almost as if we are seeing it from the owl's point of view, as he would see it if he flew over the farm. It gives the reader a beginning sense of the drama to unfold, that the people are not the primary figures in the up-coming events but they are a part of the grand scope of the scene. Has your student ever flown in an airplane and noticed how things look from up high? Even looking down at buildings, cars, and people from a tall building will help him understand an aerial view. He may want to try a picture of his home or neighborhood as he thinks it would look from an owl's point of view. As a beginning exercise, have him look down on smaller objects such as toy cars, Lego® houses, etc., and try drawing them. Now, have him try to visualize his own home or neighborhood, imagining how it would look from an airplane or hot air balloon above.

Art: Trees and Shadows

(**Teacher's Note:** Most people tend to draw what they *think* a tree looks like. They already have an idea in their minds: draw a stick and put a ball at the top, etc. It is sometimes difficult for them to stop and take the time or have the patience to draw what they actually see. Therefore, you might preface this lesson by saying to your student: "You know how to draw tees, but here is another way you might like to try." Then, proceed gently with this lesson of drawing exactly what you see. It is an important lesson to begin to introduce. Always be positive in your criticism and speak encouragingly to your student. These suggestions are introductory art lessons only. It may take several years to bring about successful results. The goal for your student is happily to try these art ideas and enjoy experimenting with them. Please read this entire lesson before you begin.)

On the first page of *Owl Moon* there is a large tree with its shadow just to the left corner of the farmhouse and another at the extreme right of the opposite page of text. Have your student pick one of the trees (the one on the right is much more simple) and try to draw that tree as exactly as possible with pencil. He will have to concentrate on each line and where the line turns and bends. It is helpful to have him begin at the bottom of the trunk and work his way upward. Then, he can try to add the shadow.

For your older student, look at a real tree (pick out one that is simple). Ask him to look specifically at the tree. How many branches does the tree have? Which branches are straight? Which ones are curved to the left or the right? Does one branch pass in front of another, etc.? Ask questions to help your student really *see* the tree. If there is interest, go on other outings and be sure to take a sketch book. Remind your student to sketch exactly what he sees, taking his time with each branch, drawing the curves and bends of that particular branch, etc. He then may want to progress with a more advanced lesson by using a fine line paintbrush and trying to copy the trees with watercolors. At this point, we're only concerned with the tree itself, but other figures could be added to make a scene later.

For your young student, you may want to take a very simple object like a large paper clip and see if he can follow the line and imitate the shape exactly. Then perhaps a ball point pen or a hair clip can be drawn. In other words, trees may not be the place to begin, when teaching the technique of drawing what you actually see.

Math: Units of Time

When the owl watchers finally saw the owl, they stared at each other *"for one minute, three minutes, maybe even a hundred minutes."* This is a good way to introduce (or review) the number of minutes in an hour. (60) In two hours (120), etc. From there you can discuss the number of hours in a day. (24) In two days (48), etc. For your older student make multiplication problems out of these kinds of facts.

Also, for your older student, try the problem of finding out how many hours and minutes there are in a hundred minutes. Remind him that going from minutes to hours is going from a smaller unit to a larger one and that requires division. There are sixty of the smaller units to one of the larger unit so use sixty for your divisor and the hundred minutes for the dividend. The answer or quotient will be expressed in hours. The sixty minutes will only go fully into one hundred once. We end up with forty "left over" minutes The answer then, is one hour and forty minutes. You can make more drill problems in this manner.

You may wish to introduce the concept of the length of a minute. Ask your student to raise his hand for what he considers to be one minute. Time him with a stop watch or the second hand of a watch. Tell him how close he was in his estimate. Then tell him to raise his hand, as you begin to time exactly one minute. Tell him to lower it when a minute is up. Did he think it was a long or short amount of time? (There are 1,440 minutes in each 24 hour day for his use!)

Math: When Time is Altered

Try introducing this concept to your older student. Jane Yolen writes, *"Nothing in the meadow moved...we watched silently...."* Then the owl watchers stared at the owl *"for one minute, two minutes, maybe a hundred minutes..."*, and the reader understands that the young owl watcher has had an exciting moment. The exaggeration of time (a hundred minutes) is a result of the moment being so special that the *"real"* counting of time has been suspended. In this case, it seemed as if the owl stared at them for a long, long time. Sometimes, when a person writes about a special moment he might say that," it was as if time stood still." Another person might write, "We were in awe, it seemed as if time lasted forever." When a person is concentrating on something they may be unaware of the passing of time. This perception of altered time is one that your older student might want to incorporate in his stories as a way to express the very special moment of an adventure or event.

Math: Hours of Daylight and Dark

You can also keep track for a day the hours of daylight and of dark. Discuss the fact that this amount of light and dark hours changes with the seasons. In the winter you might discover only ten hours of daylight and fourteen hours of darkness while in July you may discover just the opposite. Since *Owl Moon* takes place in the winter of the northern hemishpere, the hours of darkness are longer than the hours of daylight.

Science: Owls

Owls are fascinating birds. They have large heads and eyes, very sharp hooked beaks, and strong feet with sharp claws. Their eyes, which see extremely well in low-light situations, are surrounded by rounds of feathers called the facial disk. The eyes of an owl point forward (unlike many birds whose eyes are located on the sides of their heads). These forward pointing eyes focus together on an object, much as do human eyes. The difference is that owls cannot move their eyes in their sockets. To compensate they have a greater range of head movement. They have the ability to almost "look behind themselves," and they must move their heads to keep an object in view.

Their feathers differ from other birds. They are fluffier, which silences the sound of the wind, going through them as the owl flies. Therefore, the owl is able to come on silent wings and snare his prey. This consists of mammals: mice, rats, and shrews (larger owls will eat rabbits and squirrels). There are many interesting characteristics and habits of owls. If your student shows an interest in owls, he should be encouraged to seek additional books from the library and report on facts and discoveries he makes in his research. Be on the lookout for owls. Even on the edges of cities, an owl can occasionally be seen at dusk on a telephone pole or in an old tree.

The owl pictured in *Owl Moon* seems to be the great horned owl. These large owls have a tuft of feathers at the sides of their heads that look like ears or horns. Their silhouettes against the night sky and theirlarge size make them unmistakable. (Your conservation department may have a color poster and information pamphlet about the owls of your area. Often, the information is free.)

If possible, find a copy of *Owl Lake* by Tejima, 1987 Philomel Books, New York, ISBN 039921426-7. The beautiful woodcut illustrations create a quiet, yet powerful view of woods and lake. You will feel that you've visited there. A nature lover's special find! Another book, *Moths and Mothers, Feathers and Fathers* by Larry Shles, has good pen and ink close-ups of owls. While not a pure nature genre book, the illustrations are worth examining. The author uses the subject of owls in his attempt to define "love."

The Great White Owl of Sissinghurst by Dawn Langley Simmons is also a beautifully illustrated story of children who stay at the famous white gardens of Sissinghurst Castle in Kent, England. This story based on fact, features a great white owl and its brush with danger. If your student has an interest in owls, this book continues the learning experience. (White gardens were created by cultivating only white forms of flowers and foliage such as white roses, white delphiniums, lambs ears, etc. The famous white gardens were a special section of the gardens at Sissinghurst.)

Science: Bird Calls

The father in *Owl Moon* is able to make a sound like the call of an owl with his voice. It is realistic enough that the owl calls back. Discuss with your student the fact that creating a convincing bird call takes careful listening to know what the sound is like. A person must practice to make his voice imitate the sound. Some people use wooden devices (duck calls) to call ducks and turkeys.

Ask your student how many different birds he has seen. See if he knows the names of them. If not, encyclopedias have good pictures by which to identify birds. The conservation departments of many states have posters and pamphlets of the birds in their state which make identification even easier. After the student has become aware of the different birds around him, help him to differentiate the sounds and calls these birds make. Then, even if he cannot see the bird in the tree, he will know which bird is near him. There are fantastic audio-cassette tapes of bird songs. These may be available from your library, or from a science or nature store, or a store that sells bird seed and other bird supplies. Also, members of your student's family may be able to help him identify certain bird calls that are familiar to them.

Most major metropolitan areas have a branch of the Audubon Society. If your student shows a continuing interest in birds, you may want to contact the local affiliate and arrange to go on a "birding" field trip or visit an area bird sanctuary. Most Audubon Society affiliates have excellent libraries of resource material and carry on wonderful educational programs for those interested in learning more about birds.

Science: A Naturalist is Patient

Many people who walk through woods, gardens and parks every day may be largely unaware of the variety of animals and plants around them. They may be even more unaware of the habits and characteristics of these living things. (Even people who live in cities may miss noticing or learning about the insects, tiny plants, and large trees, pigeons and other birds, etc. that live in these busy places.) Help your student develop the attributes of a true nature-lover or naturalist. Take him on outings where he is able to spend time observing the phenomenon around him. The ability to take time and quietly, patiently watch the things of nature provides rich rewards.

In order for your older student to begin to make his own discoveries in nature, he should take the time to watch a particular area (an old log, or a small portion of a field, even several feet of sidewalk) and write or draw the things he sees in a notebook. Inexpensive blank books are great for this nature exercise. He might begin with as little as ten minutes of observation time. Just as one reading of a story does not bring out all the aspects of that story, watching a certain place for one interval does not provide the time necessary to make observations, comparisons, and discoveries. It would be excellent if he could make his observations in the same exact location each day for a week, for at least ten minutes a day and add to his notes new things he notices. Each day the things that took him time to notice at first, he will see quickly. Then he will look for different subjects of interest in the same area. In this way your student will discover more with each viewing. He may find topics he wishes to research just from his own observations. For a budding nature-lover, the movie *My Side of the Mountain* may be of interest. It is about twenty years old and tells the story of a young boy's scientific observations of nature. This movie should be available at any larger video rental store.

For your younger student, take walks with him and point out different things that *you* see. As a teacher, *your interest* makes a significant difference. When you are interested and excited about what you see, much of that excitement will be caught. If you happen upon an ant hill, study the sections of the ant's body, how many legs it has, what the ants are carrying and where they are going, etc. Or, study a bumblebee in a flower. Notice the full pollen sacks on its legs. Follow a turtle on his way to the mulberry tree as he searches for juicy berries and notice how his toes point inward and how he hides in his shell if your shadow comes across him. Watch the geese at the pond, which one seems to be the leader? Is there a watch bird that sounds an alarm? What are they eating, etc.? Take time to watch the activity of nature and you will begin to notice things that you never even considered before.

Watch until your student is no longer interested. It is amazing how many facts he can discover just by his own observations about the habits and characteristics of the plant and animal life around him. (Someday when he reads in a book what he has already *personally observed* and found to be true, he will feel great satisfaction and encouragement!)

Teach your student how to use binoculars (especially how to use the strap so they are not dropped!) Let him try to keep a robin in sight until it pulls a worm from the ground! What kinds of things does he observe about this robin finding a worm that he has never noticed before? Is it a tug of war? Does he notice the white circle around the robin's eye and how the robin looks at the ground? How does the robin turn his head to see?

Both your younger and older student will benefit from such exercises by developing patience, quietness and various forms of self-control. In *Owl Moon* it taks patience, persistence, a refusal to complain, and quietness on the part of the father and his child to gain the reward of seeing the magnificent sight of the owl in the night.

Science: Moon

The Bible says the moon is the *"lesser light to rule the night,"* and that it was created with the sun and the stars to be *"for times and seasons."* Man has looked at the moon and speculated about its make-up and its relation to the earth for thousands of years. On July 20, 1969 the United States astronaut, Neil A. Armstrong, actually stepped on the moon!

The definition of a moon is: a natural satellite revolving around a planet. Some planets in our solar system have more than one moon. (Jupiter has sixteen satellites.) The earth's moon is its closest neighbor in space. It has no light of its own but reflects the light of the sun. It is approximately 235,000 miles from the earth and is about 1/80 the mass of earth. The moon makes a complete cycle around the earth about once every 27 1/2 days.

In the story *Owl Moon,* we see the moon lighting up the snowy evening. The moonlight casts deep shadows, and makes the clearings of snow look *"whiter than milk in a cereal bowl."*

If you can, watch the moon with your student, noticing its different phases and perhaps have him draw them in a nature notebook or journal. [**Teacher's Note:** The eight moon phases include: new moon (<u>not pictured</u> *which rises with the sun and sets with the sun*), waxing crescent, first quarter (*moon rises around noon each month during this phase*), waxing gibbous, full moon (*moon rises at sunset and sets at sunrise during this* *phase*),waning gibbous, last quarter (*moon rises in the middle of the night*), waning crescent].

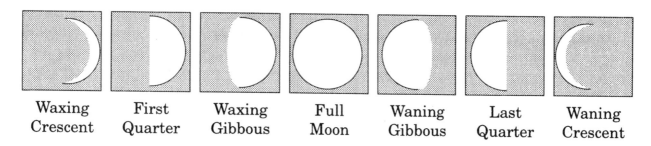

| Waxing Crescent | First Quarter | Waxing Gibbous | Full Moon | Waning Gibbous | Last Quarter | Waning Crescent |

Another interesting thing about the moon is that it rotates once on its own axis as it circles the earth which always keeps the same side facing the Earth. If your student has interest in this subject, books from the library, videos and encyclopedias offer information and pictures at various learning levels. An evening *"field trip"* with a pair of binoculars can turn your backyard into a wonderful observatory which is truly inspirational!

Locate the book *The Moon's the North Wind's Cooky*, edited by Susan Russo. ISBN: 0688418791. This is a delightful volume of poems pertaining to the moon and to other nightime subjects, such as sounds of the night, etc.

Science: Tracks

In the illustration opposite the first page of text, when the owl seekers begin their search, they leave behind footprints in the snow. These are such tiny dots on the page. Surely the artist could have left them out and no one would have noticed. But the artist knows that when someone walks in the snow they produce footprints and he has recorded them accurately. The reader who notices such detail rejoices in the fact that they were *not* left out!!

A wonderful footprint story came from A. A. Milne who wrote, "In Which Pooh and Piglet Go Hunting and Nearly Catch a Woozle," in his book *Winnie the Pooh*. In this delightful story, Pooh goes tracking something. Soon there are two "somethings" and the story continues as Pooh travels in circles and thinks each set of additional tracks that appear are other animals chasing him. He does not catch on that he, himself is making the tracks!! There are also footprint-tracks in Ezra Jack Keat's book *The Snowy Day*.

"Our feet crunched over the crisp snow and little gray footprints followed us," the young story-teller explains. Ask your student to tell how the gray footprints follow the squirrels. (They left their tracks in the snow.) Tracking animals is great fun and helps increase your student's awareness of his natural surroundings. Tracking can be done where there is dirt, dust, mud or in the snow. The edges of ponds, muddy creek banks and dirt roads are good places to look for animal tracks. You can even find the twisted slithers of a snake's path, or the toes-curved, tail dragging-journey of a turtle. In the meadows, woods, and even your student's own front yard, tracks can be found in dirt and snow. (Birds, squirrels, sometimes mice, cats and dogs often leave visible tracks.). Help your stu-

dent keep a record of what he sees. Encourage him to include the date, drawings and other observations. If he continues to observe and journal, he will accumulate for himself much information about the world in which he lives.

(**Teacher's Note:** In order to help you gain information on this subject, an excellent book on tracking animals is *Stokes Nature Guides: A Guide to Animal Tracking and Behavior,* by Donald and Lillian Stokes, Little Brown & Co., Publishers. Also excellent: *Stokes Nature Guides: A Guide to Nature In Winter* by Donald Stokes, Little Brown & Co., Publishers. A good book for your student is *Crinkleroot's Book of Animal Tracking* by Jim Arnosky. This book is available at some bookstores or through Greenleaf Press Catalog.)

Science: Woodland Habitat

Take a large sheet of paper or poster board. With your student make a woodland habitat poster. Include as many animals, plants, water sources, etc., as you wish. You may want to have a pine woods, oak woods, or a woods made up of pines and hardwood trees. Use encyclopedias and books from the library or information from your conservation department to complete the poster. In the northern pine woods of *Owl Moon,* there are owls, rabbits, fox, birds, mice, raccoon, opossum, and deer. Some of these animals are nocturnal (more active at night) and some are diurnal (more active in the daytime). Some are camouflaged (blend in to their surroundings) more than others. The owl practically looks like tree bark from the back! There are many facets of science to explore in this topic. (There is also reference to the meadow in this story. There are some subtle differences in the animals one could find there. You could happen upon a family of skunks, rabbits, voles, moles,mice, and hawks, etc.You might even find beavers which turn a wooded creek area into a marsh. Eventually, this marsh becomes a meadow after the beavers move on.)

Science: Shadows

"Pa made a long shadow, but mine was short and round," observed the young owl searcher. Ask your student if he can tell you why one shadow was long and thin while the other is short and round. Spend some time looking over the shadows in the illustrations. Notice the composition of the owl's shadow on the dedication page. Many pages have shadows. Talk about what makes a shadow. Review what you covered in *Three Names,* and see if your student can name the light source of these illustrations. (In *Owl Moon,* the light source for the illustrations is the moon.) Can your student find the direction from which the light is coming in some of these illustrations?

A NEW COAT
FOR ANNA

Title: *A New Coat for Anna*
Author: Harriet Ziefert
Illustrator: Anita Lobel
Copyright: 1986
Summary: In a post-wartime era, resourcefulness, sacrifice, love and care
                  result in a new coat for Anna.

Social Studies: Geography - Setting of Story

Although the exact country is never revealed, this story takes place in Europe soon after World War II. An older student may want to be a detective and try to narrow down the countries where this story might have taken place. He could include a look at the clothes, carts, and architecture for clues. With your help he could even research the countries of Europe that actually sustained bombing damage. If there is interest, this could be a good springboard for further study of World War II and Post-World War II Europe. By not designating a specific country, the author, Harriet Ziefert, shows the general devastation and shortages brought on by the war over many parts of Europe.

Place the story disk on a country of Europe that sustained damage in WWII or on Europe, in general.

Social Studies: Reactions Following Wartime

The aftermath of war can be a very sad time. There is this sadness in *Grandfather's Journey, FIAR* Vol. 1, p. 59, and the sober illustrations after the war in *They Were Strong and Good, FIAR* Vol. 2, p.64. Things look different. Familiar places are gone or closed. Familiar people have gone away. It can also be an extremely frustrating time because people may not be as able to obtain food and the basic necessities as they were before the war began.

Some people become angry and bitter about these kinds of hardships, but Anna and her mother seem to react in another way. They remain calm, try to enjoy each day and find alternative (other) ways to obtain the things they need. They are what we call *cheerful* and *resourceful*. Can you or your student think of a time when you or someone else you know has been able to get things done in times of hardship or sorrow? They were probably able to think creatively and find special ways to do things that some people thought were impossible.

There have been, even in the past few years, serious floods, earthquakes, hurricanes, and wild fires in addition to areas at war. How do people help each other? The periods after any war, as well as after any natural disaster are times when many people make sacrifices and work together to help each other out. Anna's mother shared the Christmas meal with the people who had helped them. There wasn't as much food as before the war, but in the atmosphere of friendship, appreciation and generous sharing the "not much" became "richly enough."

Social Studies: Pride in Work Well Done

There are several people involved in making Anna's new coat: the sheep rancher, the spinner, the weaver, the tailor and Anna's mother who sacrifices her special possessions and dyes the wool scarlet. Each one seems to do his job carefully and well. Because of their care, the wool is a good quality, thick and warm. The spinning is even and consistent, the yarn is well-dyed– not streaky. The cloth is woven straight and tight. The tailor carefully measures, cuts and sews the coat together and finds the beautiful buttons. Each person that works on the coat does his best and each one can be proud of his work.

Discuss the importance of taking pride in our work and doing our very best. Remind your student of a time you were particularly proud of him for doing his very best. Perhaps you can share a personal story about a time when you took pride in a project, and did your very best and what the results were like. This is a great time to just spend a few minutes sharing along these lines. It can make a lifelong impact on young learners!

Social Studies: Barter - Trade

Barter (trading goods or services without using money) is a good word to know. Many children enjoy trading some of their possessions and bartering has been used throughout history by people to obtain both the necessities and the luxuries of life. Talk about the trading posts of the western expansion where furs were often exchanged for goods. Discuss how doctors and other "service" people would take eggs, hams, grain, etc., in exchange for their help. Each time Anna's mother says, *"Anna needs a new coat. I have no money but..."* [I have something to trade], she is **bartering**.

Have your student look for examples of bartering in other stories, television shows or in his own family life. Perhaps you have a personal anecdote (story) about a successful barter that you've made in the past. Maybe you can arrange a barter with your student; exchanging something he wants, in exchange for a service he can perform. Of, if you have several students, help them negotiate one or more barters among themselves. They can exchange goods or services for something each one wants.

Social Studies: Relationships - Patience

Anna has patience. Talk about that virtue; the decision to be patient, waiting cheerfully when there is something that you want immediately. Anna wanted and needed a coat, but the circumstances of a post-war economy prevented her mother from buying one in a more traditional manner. So, Anna waited cheerfully for her coat for a long while. Ask your student if he thinks this was easy for Anna or if it would be easy for him.

When waiting cheerfully seems impossible, remember that patience is a *decision*. Actually, it is a decision of love because it fosters a peaceful environment, not only for the patient waiter but for all those around him.

Language Arts: Memory and Comprehension

How did Anna's mother obtain the wool?
(She bartered a gold watch for the wool.)

How did Anna's mother get the wool spun into yarn?
(She traded the spinning lady a beautiful lamp for the spinning.)

How did Anna's mother get the wool dyed a beautiful scarlet red?
(She and Anna picked lingonberries, made the dye from the berries and dyed the wool themselves.)

How did Anna's mother get the dyed wool woven into warm cloth?
(She gave a garnet necklace to the weaver.)

How did Anna's mother have the bolt of scarlet cloth made into a coat?
(She bartered a porcelain teapot to have the tailor make the coat.)

How did Anna and her mother give extra thanks to all the people who helped make the coat?
(They invited them to a Christmas party.)

Who did Anna thank last?
(The sheep!!)

If your student enjoys this sort of quiz, try it on a Tuesday and then again on a Friday and see if your student can remember more of the answers! Let him see he is improving.

Language Arts: Informative Story

The story *A New Coat for Anna* tells how a coat is made in a step-by-step process even includes the timing (sheep are sheared in the spring). Have your student choose a subject. It can range from how to make Jello®; to how to clean a room or give a dog a bath; build a train layout, etc. Have him write or dictate on a tape recorder an informative, step-by-step procedure. Your bold, older writer may want to actually write a story that has an informative theme to it such as Harriet Ziefert has done in *A New Coat for Anna*.

Language Arts: Literary Devices - Repetition

Ask your student if he has noticed a repetitive phrase (a sentence or piece of a sentence that is used over and over again) in *A New Coat for Anna*. (Anna's mother says repeatedly, *"Anna needs a new coat. I have no money but......"*) Repetition ties the story together and creates a familiar interest. If you haven't worked on **repetition** before in an earlier story, or if you'd like to review the concept with your student, have him write or tell a story using repetitious phrases.(See **Repetition** in Index of Volumes 1 and 2.)

Art: Scenes of Wartime

Look at the picture before the dedication page. You see a scene of a war-torn street with a little girl in the center. She is in a coat that is too small and is waving to her mother. The buildings are broken down from the bombing. People are huddled together. Some are moving their possessions with carts. What else can you see?

Turn to the title page. The mother and daughter look out the window. What expression is on the mother's face? She seems sober and even a little wistful. She is probably wishing that things would return to normal, missing the life she had known before the war.The pictures on the page where the story begins and the facing picture show a little worry on Anna's mother's face, shortages, an injured person and shops or businesses that are closed. The artist, Anita Lobel, has worked closely with the author's text to give a visual feeling of the street scenes and the emotions involved in this period of time. Encourage your student to be looking for detail in actual photographs of history books, magazines, etc.

Art: Weaving

Weaving, taking threads of yarn and interlacing them in such a way that strong cloth for a garment can be made, is an amazing process!! (**Teacher's Note:** There are special words used in weaving: the *loom* (a frame that allows yarns to be woven together at right angles), the *warp* (threads that run lengthwise in the fabric), the *woof* (threads that run crosswise, at right angles to the warp threads), etc. A weaver must think about which colors that will well together, the pattern of the weave and the method of weaving loosely or tightly, to create a variety of fabrics.)

For younger children, make placemats with large pieces of construction paper. Use two contrasting colors and cut one sheet into parallel one half inch vertical strips. Take the other sheet and draw parallel one half inch horizontal lines across the , *but leave a one inch border all the way around uncut!* Cut the horizontal cuts, being careful to *not cut through the border area.* Now have your child "weave" the vertical strips in and out of the horizontal cuts alternately, making a woven placemat. Older children can weave pot holders on the simple square loom. Maybe you know of someone with an actual loom who would allow your student to to try a larger weaving project, like a placemat, scarf, etc.

Art: Before and After Pictures

In the front of the book there are pictures of Anna in a blue coat; both a back view and a front view. At the very back of the story there are pictures of Anna in her new red coat; both a front view and a back view.

If your student would like, have him try to draw a simple subject with a definite front and back, perhaps a small simple toy or even his own house! Now have him draw both the front and back again *after* certain changes. Perhaps *after* the house has been painted, or *after* the toy has been assembled.

Art: Understanding From Expressions

A good artist will "tell" their part of the story in different ways. One way is by expressive features on the faces of the characters. We can "read" a lot from these expressions. Look from the beginning to the end of the story at Anna's expressions. Discuss the feelings the artist is portraying.

Now look at the expressions on Anna's mother's face from the beginning of the story to the end. Finally, look at the faces of the people who help make her coat. How do they look at Anna? What name would you give that feeling? (compassionate, kind, happy to help) What feelings do their faces express while they do their work? (intense, careful)

Take a look at a variety of other paintings or photographs from books, galleries, magazines, etc., and ask your student to interpret the various expressions on faces. See how many different emotions he can find as you explore facial expressions together.

Math: Linear Measuring

(**Teacher's Note:** If it is easily available, it would be fun to have on hand for this lesson, a cloth (or soft plastic) tape measure, a steel tape measure and a yardstick.)

The tailor takes a tape measure and measures Anna for her new coat. If you have a tape measure, help your younger student to measure the length of the room. Just count how many total tape measure lengths the room is. Have your student measure the room using a steel tape measure, a ruler and a yardstick. It's all good practice.

For your older student explain how many feet (and/or inches) a tape measure is, and measure a room's length with one. Do the same with the steel tape measure and again with the yard stick. Now do the multiplication to find the room's measurements in yards, feet, inches, etc. Perhaps you'd also like to use the metric system and measure objects in meters, centimeters, and millimeters.

Ask your student why he thinks the tailor uses a soft tape measure rather than the steel tape measure or the yardstick. Let him try to measure around your waist with all three and figure it out for himself. (It would be difficult to bend a steel tape measure around arms, legs, and waist!) Your student may think that the cloth tape measure isn't very handy in measuring the length of a room either. Remind him that the steel tape measure is used in many building applications and comes in mighty handy to hang pictures, too. The steel tape measure or the yardstick probably would be the best choice for measuring room lengths.

Math: Patterns

Tailors use *dressmaker patterns* to make the correct size (patterns for garments usually come in sizes) so the garment will fit. A pattern also makes it possible to make identical garments.

The actual word *pattern* means either an artistic or decorative design. Show your student the pattern on dishes, fabric or wallpaper. Some patterns will be random and some may be repeating designs. Templates or paper forms that you trace around can be used to make the same shape over and over. Take some cardboard and cut out geometric shapes. Allow your student to trace around them with colored pencil or marker. He can make his own designs and patterns. Remember, patterns will show up over and over again in either random or specific spacings.

If you sew or know someone who does, let your student see how a garment is made. Let him see the pattern pinned to the fabric and watch it cut out. Later he can see and examine the finished product.

Science: Lingonberries

The lingonberry is a small, dark, red berry related to the cranberry. Other names for it include bog cranberry, and partridgeberry. It grows in the cooler, mild climates of Canada and Scandinavia. Perhaps you can find lingonberry syrup at the grocery store or a specialty food shop nearby. Serve it on pancakes you make with your student.

While you're at the store buying lingonberry syrup, look at the other varieties of berries. These may include: blackberries, gooseberries, cranberries, raspberries, mulberries, strawberries, etc. You'll find them fresh, frozen and canned and your student will be amazed at all the varieties.

Science: Sheep

If there is sufficient interest, there is a vast amount of information about sheep to explore, including: their care, shearing, where they are raised, and different breeds (which, by the way have different types and lengths of wool coats). The *World Book Encyclopedia,* as well as many library and reference books, could be used by your older student interested in sheep. You may want to go back and re-read *Wee Gillis, FIAR* Vol. 2, p. 30, for additional information and ideas about sheep.

Science: Dyes

(**Teacher's Note:** Dyes are used to create a permanent color in fabrics, furs, leathers, etc. Dyed fabrics need to be light fast as well as water fast (able to resist fading due to the ultraviolet rays of sunlight as well as from washing). Fabrics have been dyed for several thousand years in natural dyes. These were made mostly from plants and animals. Today most of the dying processes are done with synthetic dyes. Besides the berries, bark, onion skins or whatever is used to create the color of a natural dye, a *mordant* is added to help set the color and cause it to penetrate deep into the fibers. Tannic acid is a common mordant. Others include soluble compounds of metals such as aluminum, copper or tin. Prepackaged synthetic dyes are complete and ready to use.)

There are library books on making natural dyes if you have a budding chemist or artist. But you can also use a packaged dye to try tie dying a tee shirt or 16 inch squares of cotton for dinner napkins. For those students who are budding nature lovers, try gathering a variety of natural "dyes" such as blackberries, blueberries, rose petals, tea bags, etc. These natural ingredients can be used to dye several small swatches of white cotton or wool fabric. Try several different ingredients and then compare the results? Which treasure of nature makes the best dye?

Science: Health - Staying Well

Ask your student why he thinks Anna's mother is willing to sacrifice (give up) precious, special things like a gold watch, teapot, etc., to obtain a coat for Anna. It seems the coat cost Anna's mother a great deal! Use this question to check your student's inferred comprehension skills. **Inferred comprehension** is an important reading skill which every child needs to learn. We generally make certain inferences from our reading on the basis of what is said explicitly in the text, but some material must be inferred, or deduced on the basis of what is not said or is said implicitly rather than explicitly. In this case, we can infer why Anna's mother might have been willing to trade such valuable possessions for a new coat. If Anna had not had a new coat that fit her and was thick and warm, she would have been cold. When we get cold, sometimes germs and bacteria are able to cause sickness, whereas they would not be able to harm us if we kept warm. If Anna had become very cold she might have become very sick. Anna and her health were more important to her mother than the things (lamp, tea pot, etc.), even if they were special treasures. Your student may be able to understand (infer) the mother's feelings, even though they were not expressed in the text.)

Talk about ways to prevent illness: wearing warm clothes in cold weather and cooler clothes in hot weather, washing hands before eating, putting uneaten food away properly, getting exercise and plenty of rest, etc. This is a great time for a Health Habits Review! Make a poster or a booklet on all the health habits you can think of together.

Title: *Mrs. Katz and Tush*
Author/Illustrator: Patricia Polacco
Copyright: 1992
Award: 1993 Honor Picture Book: Jane Addam's Children's Book Award; also a Reading Rainbow Selection
Summary: A young boy learns compassion and finds a lifetime friendship.

Social Studies: Relationships - Loving Our Neighbor

Larnel doesn't know Mrs. Katz, but his mother visits her every other day. Ask your student why she does this? (She visits because she knows Mrs. Katz feels sad and lonely after the death of her husband and because Mrs. Katz has no children. Many Jewish people have a strong sense of family and so this is a great sadness to Mrs. Katz.) Larnel gives her a kitten. Does it help her? (Yes, she gives her love to the kitten and it keeps her company.) Ask if it looks like fun when Mrs. Katz and Larnel dance the Polish dance? Larnel learns to care for his neighbor by the example that his mother and father model before him. His mother is willing to give up some of her time and spend it with Mrs. Katz. It is Larnel's father and two other neighbors who search for Tush and bring her home. Good neighbors are a blessing. Talk with your student about chances to be a good neighbor. Soon he will be looking for such opportunities. (Remind him to follow his parent's safety rules when visiting others, etc.)

When Larnel follows the example set by his mother and father and spends time with Mrs. Katz. He, too, begins to receive special benefits. He makes friends with another person who loves him. He learns about Poland and about being Jewish. His friendship lasts a lifetime, till Mrs. Katz dies. Larnel, through his concern, receives the gift of knowing *"Mrs. Katz, our Bubee...such a person"*!

If you are fortunate enough to be near a good Jewish Delicatessen, take your student. Let him see the different kinds of foods, smell the smells of meats and cheeses, pickles, and breads. Try some kugel or a pastrami sandwich, listen to the voices and enjoy!

Social Studies: Persecution of Minorities

In *Mrs. Katz and Tush*, you will learn more about the persecutions which have followed the Jewish people throughout history. From Pharaoh's enslavement of the Hebrews to Hitler's holocaust, unto the present day, Jews have been persecuted. An interesting discussion might be to explore your feelings and your responsibilities when you see persecution happening. Are you to simply look the other way, pretending you do not see?

If history teaches anything, it's safe to assume that there will be groups persecuted again during your lifetimes; perhaps Jews, Blacks, Christians, Asians, Hispanics or some other group. How will you react if you see persecution taking place? Obviously, this is a *heavy* subject to be handled delicately with young students. However, it may not be too early to plant a *seed* about the importance of righteousness and humanity in the governments of the world. You can begin to introduce the concepts that will result in future concern for these ideals, as well as model these ideals yourself.

Social Studies: Geography

We don't know the exact city setting of this story, although New York would be a safe guess. Mrs. Katz is originally from Warsaw, the capital city of Poland. You may want to put the story disk on Poland and say each day, "This is the country Mrs. Katz lived in before she came to North America." There is also a brief mention of the Catskills, an area of low mountains along the Hudson River in New York. It is one of the most beautiful natural areas in the state of New York and there are many parks and resorts there.

Social Studies: Immigration

Mrs. Katz immigrated to North America from Poland. Immigration is moving into and settling in a country that is not the country of your birth. People immigrate for different reasons. Some are fleeing persecution for religious or political reasons. Some want land or a different job or are following a spouse or other family. Talk with your student about how he would feel if he moved to China tomorrow. Ask him how he thinks he would adapt to the strange food, language, and customs. Does he think he would miss his homeland? Many immigrants are homesick and feel lonely when they come to this country. They often have the added handicap of not being able to speak English and be understood. That is one reason why people from the same countries tend to live next to each other, forming small communities such as Chinatown in New York, or Little Italy, etc. In this way they can share memories, celebrations and customs of their homeland, and continue to converse in their native tongue. These communities provided some sense of security in an often frightening new enviornment.

You can begin to make rich discoveries when you and your student research his family and trace the origins of his ancestors. Make maps and trace routes from the native lands to America. Photocopy pictures of ancestors, cut them out and paste them on the maps to make them come "alive" with real people. Use symbols that represent people (coat of arms, symbols of their occupations, etc.). Learn the customs of the represented countries (the foods, music, etc.). These studies will help your student establish memorable ties to his generational past.

You may wish to make a short unit on immigration for your older student. Include such topics as immigration during colonial times in America, or the Great Immigration from 1830-1850, or the second wave of the Great Immigration from 1860-1890, Ellis Island, immigration laws, citizenship, illegal aliens, deportation, refugees, the Irish immigration, etc.

An older student may also wish to pick from lists of famous immigrants. (See *The World Book Encyclopedia* at the end of the article on immigration. Follow up with biographies of some of these people and their experiences leaving their homeland and making a life in a new land.)

The American Girl Series includes a story about a young girl named Kirsten who immigrates from Sweden. *Meet Kirsten* by Valerie Tripp, is the first title. These books are usually available at the public library.

Social Studies: History - Jewish Exodus From Egypt

You will Patricia Polacco's explanation of Passover on the page where Mrs. Katz and Larnell visit the delicatessen. Your older student may want to research the historic event of Moses leading the Hebrew people out of Egypt. The account is found in the Bible in Exodus, Chapters 5-11. What convinced Pharaoh to let them go? (The last of the 10 plagues sent by God.) Read the story of the Passover in Exodus Chapter 12. Using the card file or computer index at your public library, you and your student will be able to find age appropriate books concerning the topic of the Jewish exodus from Egypt.

Language Arts: Reading Comprehension

The title picture after the copyright page, shows Mrs. Katz gazing into a picture. After you have read the story several times, ask your student what the picture might be. In order to be able to give several answers to this question, your student will need to understand and remember the many relationships of Mrs. Katz. See how many possibilities he can think of. (Answers could include Myron (her husband), Larnell, Tush, Larnell's baby, scenes from Poland, or the Catskills Resort, etc.)

Language Arts: Yiddish

Yiddish is a language (derived from a dialect of German) which is over a thousand years old, older than modern English. Yiddish is approximately 10% Hebrew, 20% Slavic and 70% older German in origin. It is spoken mostly by the Jews of eastern and central Europe and their descendants. It is written using letters of the Hebrew alphabet. It used to be spoken by the majority of the world's jews, between eight and ten million Jewish people. With the destruction of more than 6 million Yiddish-speaking Jews during the Holocaust in World War II, today the language is spoken by less than 1 million people. Many of them are religious, or Chasidic (Ha-seed-ick) Jews.

Many Yiddish words have become common or "borrowed" into the speech of Americans. These provide even more gradations of meaning to our already colorful language. (It seems as if Americans, as a people, have always loved to add what they learn from others to their own language. Americans have incorporated a wide variety of French, Italian, German, Spanish, Scandinavian and Yiddish words to their everyday language.) The wonderful Yiddish words in this story include:

bubeleh   (bubble-uh) darling one or little one

kugel   (koo-gull) pudding made of noodles, potatoes or matzoh

tush   (tush) buttocks; Mrs. Katz named her cat Tush because it had no tail.

borscht   (borsht) soup made from beets; in this story a *borscht resort;* a hotel which caters to Jewish vacationers with kosher foods, etc.

kaddish   (cod-ish) prayer for the dead

shalom   (shuh-lome) literally means "peace;" also used for hello and goodbye

kattileh   (cot-ill-uh) small cat or kitten

bubee   (bub-ee) grandmother

Mazel-tov   (Mozzle-tauv) congratulations, or good luck

chuppa   (hoo-pa) a canopy used in Jewish weddings

Hannukah   (Hahn-uh-kuh) eight day festival commemorating the victory of the Maccabees over Antiochus Ephiphanes in 165 B.C. and the rededication of the Temple at Jerusalem. It is also known as the Festival of Lights or the Feast of Dedication.

Passover   (Pass-over) eight-day Jewish holiday commemorating the story of Exodus 12, the escape of the Hebrews from Egyptian slavery.

Art: Design, Patterns and Texture

In the picture where Mrs. Katz is knitting and playing with Tush, enjoy the variety of color and texture in the knitted scarf, the fabric on the chairs, the wall paper, Mrs. Katz' dress, the rug, the wood grain, etc. You can find similar variety on many pages of this story. If your student enjoys color and detail, he will love searching the pictures for variety. You may ask him what he sees and then follow up by asking, "And what else?"

Have you ever noticed a picture done by your student that shows a variety of pattern and design? If so, bring the art work out and review it with him. Look for other artists work using designs, and textures. Some artists excel in detailed designs. Let your student appreciate the works of such artists and illustrators. Possibly by pointing out to him colorful patterns in dresses, scarves, rugs, wall paper and pottery, more of this love of design and texture will appear in your student's future pictures.

Art: Expression and Action

Spend a moment and look at the expressions on the faces of Mrs. Katz and Larnell. Notice how they look into each other's eyes, especially the scenes opposite the sewing machine, and Larnell's face on the last page.

Look also at the movement, the action in the figures of Larnell, Mrs. Katz and Tush. Notice the expressive hands of Larnell. Whether the hands are open or clasped together he seems so alive, so real. When Mrs. Katz and Larnell dance together it is such a free, wonderful time of friendship, celebration and memory that you may wish you could join them. Notice the cat is as joyfully abandoned as the rest in this time of fun!

Larnell goes with Mrs. Katz to say kaddish (pron. cod-ish) for her husband Myron. Mrs. Katz face is full of memory and Larnell is so serious and respectful as he carefully sets the rock on top of the headstone.

The expressions when Mrs. Katz and Larnell find Tush missing are fully expressive in their faces and hands. You can sense the sorrow and surprise. The hug Mrs. Katz gives Larnell when he asks if he can have Passover dinner with her is a real hug that you can almost feel. Doesn't Tush look completely glad to be home? There is intense action in the scene at the delicatessen, and a calmer action as the Passover cloth is spread and the dishes set. Then rapture sets in as Mrs. Katz realizes Tush has had kittens. And at last she experiences a much deeper love, as Larnell brings his own baby to visit her. She has found happiness, even a family in her good neighbors!

Art: Detail

On the first page in the book, Mrs. Katz is looking out her window. Ask your student what *he* sees outside. (wash on the line, fences, buildings, etc.) Compare this to what else he can see through the windows in Mrs. Katz' house and to the street scene where they hand out the lost cat notices. Have your student look out a nearby window and draw the things he sees there. Encourage him to include specific details.

Math: Counting Skills

In nearly all the illustrations, Mrs. Katz has some sort of polka-dot or repetitive pattern on her dress. Select one or more illustrations and count the repetitions. Find a piece of fabric, clothing or wallpaper that has a repetitive pattern and count again. For older students, explore the use of multiplication to count the patterns more quickly. For example, there are four hearts across the width of the scarf, and ten rows of hearts down the length of the scarf. We can multiply 4x10 and conclude there are 40 heart designs in total. Now let your student *prove* the problem by counting them one by one.

Younger student may enjoy counting the various baked goods in the delicatessen display shelves. He'll find bagels, white bread, whole wheat bread, fruit cakes, black forest cakes, cheesecakes and challah (hahl'ah–the twisted or braided loaves near the bagels).

Math: Cats Multiply!

Tush has four kittens. Invite your older student to calculate how many grandchildren, great-grandchildren and great-great-grandchildren Tush might have if each offspring has four kittens. (16 grandchildren [4x4], 64 great grandchildren [16x4] and 256 great-great grandchildren! [64x4])

Science: Cats and Kittens

The fat cat that slept a lot is going to have kittens. Look at the warm basket Mrs. Katz provides for Tush and her kittens. (Cats usually find quiet dark places to give birth.) Tush has four kittens. Is this a normal litter for all cats? (Cats usually have three to five kittens but there have been cases of more than ten.) The gestation period (the length of time a kitten grows before it is born) for a cat is about nine weeks. The kittens are born with their eyes closed and their ears sealed. They cannot see (their eyes open in about ten to fourteen days) or hear when they are born and must depend on their mother for care.

Your student may also be interested in knowing that the origin of the name Katz, means "cats." Mrs. Katz is literally, *Mrs. Cats!*

Science: Chemistry in Cooking - Yeast

Yeast is a tiny one-celled plant that grows in things containing sugar. Talk about the properties of yeast, the way it can be killed by heat, the way it causes dough to rise by creating gas bubbles in the bread, etc. (Yeast has other applications besides bread making.)

The bread of Passover contains no yeast so it is flat—more like a cracker than a loaf of bread.

Make a recipe of bread using yeast and a small recipe of bread without yeast. Let your student watch the two kinds of bread and observe the difference between the one that rises and the one that does not. Bake them both and let him taste them.

MIRETTE ON THE
HIGH WIRE

Title: *Mirette On the High Wire*
Author/Illustrator: Emily Arnold McCully
Copyright: 1992
Award: Caldecott Medal
Summary: A young protegee of the famous Bellini ends up encouraging her
                    teacher.

Social Studies: Geography - Paris, France

"One hundred years ago in Paris," begins the story of *Mirette On the High Wire*. If
you have already studied *The Giraffe that Walked to Paris, FIAR* Vol. 2, p. 12, then you
may have explored this famous city in France. Also in the story *Madeline, FIAR* Vol. 1,
p.23, there is a geography lesson on Paris, France. Remember that *"old house in Paris
that was covered with vines?"* If so, then use this lesson as a review. To these previous
lessons, add the new information gleaned from the text of *Mirette On the High Wire*.

In this story by Emily Arnold McCully, the city of Paris is seen as a famous gathering place for the authors, playwrites, artists, dancers and musicians of the world. Ask
your older student if he knows of such places in the United States. (Hollywood, California
or New York City, etc.). Place your story disk on Paris, France.

Social Studies: Geography - Map-Making

Also mentioned in *Mirette On the High Wire* are geographic locations such as
Moscow (as in *Another Celebrated Dancing Bear, FIAR* Vol. 1, p.71), Niagara Falls (located
on the border between the state of New York and Ontario, Canada), Barcelona (a city in
Spain) with a picture of a bull ring like in *Ferdinand, FIAR* Vol. 2, p. 80), Naples (a city in
Italy), and the Alps (Europe's largest mountain range. The Alps range across France,
Switzerland, Italy, Austria, Germany, and five other eastern European countries.)

With your older student, try drawing a world map. Include the places mentioned in
this story and trace Bellini's career. Labels you may want to designate on such a map
include Niagara Falls, Barcelona,Spain, Naples,Italy, the Alps, the Seine River that flows
through Paris, etc.

Social Studies: Discovering Gifts, Talents and Abilities

Mirette discovers she has a desire to walk on the high wire. She pursues this desire with much practice and discovers she has the necessary talent to perform. Her fine sense of balance and the fact that she does not fear height, along with her ability to concentrate, helps her to succeed.

One of the wonders your student will experience is learning which things hold special interest for him. He will discover what activities or interests he cares about enough to invest long amounts of his time in study and practice. Ask him what kind of things make him especially happy when he does them. What kind of things does he want to spend a lot of time learning? Maybe he will have a ready answer or perhaps you will just encourage him to be looking for those special activities or interests.

One important goal of *Five in a Row* is to provide many opportunities for exploration of the rich and diverse universe of topics and activities available to your student. Always watch for subjects or activities in which your student shows a particular interest. Never be afraid to spend additional time and resources learning more about these subject areas. Perhaps one of them will become a lifetime interest and open a career path uniquely suited to your student's gifts and talents!

Social Studies: Boasting

Bellini sharply scolds Mirette for boasting she,"...*will never, ever fall again.*" Ask your student if he can tell from the entire story why Bellini might have been so harsh? (Is it possible he once made the same boast and then had a fall which scared him badly? Maybe he does not want Mirette feeling so secure that she is no longer careful.)

Discuss some of the reasons for boasting. Sometimes it may occur when one feels invincible (unable to fail). Another reason someone might boast is to raise his feelings of self-esteem. If a person cares too much about what other people think of him, sometimes he boasts about what he can do or about things he has done. He thinks that people will like him better. Ask your student if he has noticed anyone boasting and if it caused him to think more or less of that person. It is better to let *someone else* boast about you!

Social Studies: Not Giving Up - Or Practice Makes Better!

Both Bellini and Mirette, when they began to walk the high wire, practiced a lot because they wanted so much to walk the high wire. They did not give up, no matter how many times they fell. Ask your student if he remembers other characters from *Five in a Row* stories that practiced a lot until they were a success. He may recall *Lentil* (Vol. 1) and his harmonica, or the juggler from *The Clown of God* (Vol. 1). Does your student have something that he practices? Does he want to succeed so much that he doesn't want to give up?

Social Studies: Occupation - Keeper of Boarding House

Madame Gateau (pron. Gah toe) is the keeper of a boarding house. A boarding house is like a hotel or an inn. It also serves meals (or board) as a part of the prearranged daily cost of lodging. The saying "room and board" means a person receives a room with a bed to sleep in along with daily meals. In earlier American history, school teachers often were paid a salary plus "room and board" with various school families.

Discuss with your student the attributes an innkeeper should have. (They would certainly have to like a variety of people. That means they would need to be sociable, being good listeners and conversationalists. And they would need to have a heart to serve their boarders.) In this story you read, *"Madam Gateau worked hard to make her guests comfortable and so did her daughter Mirette."* Mirette demonstrates expertise at various cooking and cleaning duties and proves that she is a good listener. These kind of skills show a heart to serve people well.

The proprietor of a boarding house should also be a good business person. Think of how many details need to be handled, from how many pounds of potatoes are needed and how much potatoes cost, how much to charge for the rooms and food, hiring other people to help, to what to do if the people get angry and begin to fight, and much more.

Ask your student if he would like to be the keeper of a boarding house, hotel or lodge. Listen to the reasons he gives why he might or might not like that. Perhaps your student would rather work in a boarding house than run one. (Some people enjoy serving more than administrative details or having the total responsibility for a business.)

Try play-acting the events of running a boarding house, the same as you would play store. You could pretend that you are receiving new clients, as in the picture of Bellini arriving at the boardinghouse. You might learn to make a perfect bed, decorate seating cards for guests at the table, create and cook a meal to serve (either real or imaginary), figure the rates and take the money for the boarding.

Look for opportunities to use "innkeeper skills" with your student. Perhaps you have friends or family coming as guests for a holiday. Perhaps you have neighbors coming over for dinner. There are lots of opportunities to use hospitality skills in our every-day lives.

Social Studies: Occupation - Agent

An agent is someone who represents another. There are insurance and real estate agents who represent the business interests of others. There are ticket agents who sell airline or railroad tickets, representing the airline or railroad. In this story, an agent is someone who represents a person of talent and sets up bookings (setting the dates of a performance and contracting the amount to be paid for the performance), makes travel and accommodation arrangements, and promotes the act (advertises and finds new places to perform). An agent is a salesman and administrative person who handles countless details for his client. Having an agent handle the necessary details, allows the actor, musician, performer, professional football player, etc., the time to practice and perform.

Being an agent carries important responsibilities. We must always act in the best interests of the one whom we represent. Discuss situations where we act in the capacity of agents for others. (delivering a message for someone, answering the family telephone, etc.)

Language Arts: Vocabulary

boardinghouse   (compound word) like a hotel but providing room and meals (board)

protegee   originally, a woman or girl whose care or career is promoted by an influential person; today we do not distinguish female *only*. (The spelling for a man or boy is *protege.*)

agent   one who represents another; in this case, one who handles the booking details of a celebrity

stupendous   fantastic! (The word stupendous appears in the last illustration.)

feats   notable acts of courage; great deeds of strength or imagination

salute   a gesture of hand to face performed to show respect, as in the military

hemp: tough, coarse fiber of the cannabis plant used to make cord (Bellini's high wire was hemp with a steel core.)

winch   a machine that helps pull cord or cable tight, by winding the cord around a drum; also used to hoist heavy items

recline(d)   to lie back or lie down; to assume a prone position

devoure(d)   to eat up greedily or quickly without leaving a trace

vagabond   a person without a permanent home

retired   no longer working at one's occupation

omelette   a French egg dish made with eggs and cheese in a round frying pan and folded over (Try making one for lunch!)

trance   In this story, it means having intense concentration, and closing out the distractions of one's surroundings.

Language Arts: Compound Words

Mirette on the High Wire has several compound words in its text. Let your reading student search for them and talk about their meanings. Remind him that each of these combined words is spelled as a single word: boardinghouse, overhear, afternoon, court-yard, windmill, cannot, bullring, spotlight, something, skylight, daylight, and tightrope.

Art: Drama

If your student enjoys acting, place the following phrases on pieces of paper and place them in a basket or hat. Let him pull them out of the container one at a time. Have him read each phrase, or you read it to him. See if he can act each one out. You may need to explain a word or two to him so he can understand the meaning:

"Mirette turned and ran to the kitchen as tears sprang to her eyes."

Pretend to walk the high wire (especially with intense concentration)

"Bellini paced his room for hours."

"She stretched her hands to Bellini." (She was trying to encourage him to come toward her. Her facial expressions showed excitement and encouragement.)

Art: Performing Artists - Tightrope Walkers

The category of performing artists includes, dancers, actors, musicians, mimes, circus type performers (jugglers, acrobats, tightrope walkers, clowns, etc.), comedians, singers, etc. In the story *Mirette on the High Wire,* the fictional character Bellini is based on the life of a real performing artist named Jean Francois Gravelet known as the "Great Blondin." He was the first of many to cross Niagara Falls on a tightrope. He actually toasted the crowd with champagne. In other attempts, the Great Blondin traveled across Niagara Falls on a bicycle, pushed a wheelbarrow and actually cooked an omelette on the high wire! Your older student may want to research Blondin.

Art: Medium - Watercolor

Emily Arnold McCully won the coveted Caldecott Medal for her watercolor paintings in *Mirette on the High Wire.* Spend a few minutes just looking through the paintings. Enjoy the rich colors, the shadows, the yellow light coming through windows in the dark, the colors of the shutters, roofs, and the vines on Madam Gateau's house (like in the story *Madeline, FIAR* Vol. 1). There is a wonderful orange cat that your student can search for which appears in many of the story's pictures.

Art: Viewpoint

Beginning with the illustrations on the title page, copyright page and continuing throughout the story, examine the viewpoint into each picture. In some, you are looking slightly downward, onto the characters. In others, Mirette or Bellini is up high on the wire. In another, you look way down on Mirette on the white and black checked floor as she scrubs it bright, etc. There is an up and down motion throughout the story as the illustrations reflect the emotion of the text. The building views are sometimes from an aerial perspective, while at other times we look up at them.

Again, how does the artist create the illusion that the viewer of the picture is down on the ground looking up, or that the viewer is up high looking down on the scene? What particular object does the illustrator use to show how extremely high Bellini was over Niagara Falls? (the large ship, drawn very small; the people below appear small as if he is a great height)

Have your student try drawing a picture of someone overhead on a tightrope, or looking down from the tightrope to the crowd below.

Art: Detail

In the picture where Bellini is walking the wire with the laundry sheets blowing below him, notice the methods the artist uses to gain the effect of waving cloth. Notice where the cloth is highlighted (lightest part) and where the artist uses shadows and dark places. Notice the artist's use of color such as pink, green and blue on the white sheets!

In the same picture, Mirette is holding a laundry basket. Look carefully at the way the artist darkened the inside of the basket to make it appear deep, while leaving the edges lighter. There is a highlight on the right side of the basket. Ask your older student if he would like to try drawing a basket or bucket or similar object and use shading to make it look deep. Remember it may be easier for him to draw while looking at a real object or a photograph. You may also draw (or trace) such an object for your younger student and just have him try shading.

Remember the lesson on complementary colors, using the color wheel? (*FIAR* Vol. 1, p. 80, and the color wheel in the Index) In brief, the complementary colors are red and green, blue and orange, and yellow and purple. The use of blue color next to orange creates strong contrast and brightness. Mirette's hair and her blue dress (as she gazes over the balcony watching the famous boarders talk at dinner) is an example of the use of complementary color. In fact, blue and orange is a common color theme throughout this story's illustrations. With your student, find some additional examples. (Look for the orange cat next to the blue can, etc.) Try coloring a picture which has some blue and orange combinations for contrast.

Art: Action and Expression in Figures

Because walking the high wire is an athletic endeavor, there is much action drawn in the illustrations of Mirette. Mirette herself is portrayed as an active young person with many expressions. (Notice her arms and legs in action in many pictures. Emily McCully paints illustrations vibrant with action to compliment the text of her story.

The first color picture on the title page shows Mirette coming out of a doorway. The next page shows her skipping down the street. Look at the man and boy opposite her. Ask your student if he thinks the trunk is heavy based on the expression of the boy's face. Now, look at the man in the black suit and hat. What is he doing? (He is intently trying to read a piece of paper.) Who is this man? Is he the man with a top hat (you may need to explain what a top hat is) pictured on the first page of text? (That man does not have black pants and his coat is rather brown. But, turn the page and see the man bowing with his hat in his hand and the trunk beside him!! This could be the same man.)

Art: Circus Posters

Circus Posters (or posters of special performances) are an art genre in themselves. Some people have made large collections of them. The artists that illustrate the posters use color, action and words to make the event sound exciting. Look at the poster on the last page and read it again. Did Emily McCully use color, action and words to show the excitement of this event? What else did she use on this poster? (portraits of Bellini and Mirette and fancy print for the words, etc.)

Does your student remember the poster in *Another Celebrated Dancing Bear, FIAR* Vol. 1) that made Boris want to be a dancing bear like Max? If you still have access to the book, look at that poster and see if it contains action, words, color or pictures.

Have your student watch for giant circus billboards that still appear today whenever a circus comes to town. Do these posters look exciting?

If he would like, your student could design his own poster of an exciting event. It could be an imaginary event, or it might be something as simple as tonight's dinner. But remember, using the circus poster style, even tonight's dinner can be made to sound exciting! Remind him to think about using color (complementary colors are exciting), action, pictures, persuasive language and include the time and date, and price (if any), of the event.

Math: Counting

There are lots of counting opportunities in Mirette. Your young student can count windows and doorways in many of the illustrations. He can count the buttons on Mirette's shoes (on the book cover), or the black and white floor tiles, the arches in the Barcelona bullring, etc. Make counting games fun!

Math: Geometry - Lines and Points

In many pictures of Mirette, the high wire is stretched tight from one place to another. Take a piece of paper and make two dots at least a few inches apart. Now, ask your student to connect the dots in the shortest distance possible. They probably drew a line with his pencil. If it is indeed the shortest distance, the line will be a *straight* line. The shortest distance between two points is *always* a straight line! A line connects at least two points, which define the line's ends. These are called the endpoints.

Look at a map. Any map will do. Now have your student select two points on the map. Perhaps the points are two interesections, or two cities, or two countries. Now lay a ruler along an imaginary straight line between those two endpoints. This is the shortest route. But can we usually travel in a straight line cross-country? Only if we're flying! Have your student find the shortest route using streets and highways between the points.

Science: Metal - Copper

In the picture with the first page of text, you'll find a kitchen with a soup pot on the stove and many pans hanging from the ceiling. These pans have an orange tint and are made of a metal called copper. Attractive pans, such as these, are popular in France. They are made of copper because this metal conducts heat so well. Copper is a metal ore, mined from the earth. The ore is crushed and heated until the metal becomes liquid. It can then be formed into a variety of shapes. If you can, show your student a copper cooking pot or look for an illustration of one in gourmet cooking catalogs. Help your student make a page for the science section of his notebook. Include facts about copper, illustrations from magazines or catalogs of things made of copper, the Cu sign for the element copper (found on the charts of elements), pictures of old pennies, etc. Your fact sheet might look something like this.

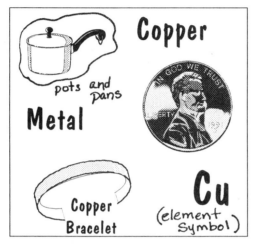

Copper turns from its bright, shiny, natural orange color to a dull green when it oxidizes. (Oxidation is caused by exposure to oxygen in the atmosphere.) Find several pennies which are made of copper. Some will be brighter than others. Even a dark, green, oxidized penny can be made bright and shiny again when it is polished. Using a metal polish, the oxidation, or tarnish is wiped away, which allows the pure copper to show once more. Let your student polish several pennies using various combinations of metal polish, toothpaste, lemon juice and salt, purchased copper polish, etc. See which ones work best. Now compare the shiny copper of a polished penny to other household metals such as steel, stainless steel, iron, aluminum, silver, gold, and bronze (a mixture of copper and iron).

Science: Physical Education

Your student may want to try the skills involved in walking the high wire. You can stretch a cord tightly along the floor. See if your student can place one foot in front of another, keeping his eyes straight ahead and standing tall.

If you have access to a low balance beam, that would also be fun and a way for your student to improve in balance, posture and concentration. Your younger student can enjoy walking along a chalk line on the sidewalk, driveway cracks or even a narrow board placed on the ground. If the weather is nice, take a break and go outside for a walk on the "high wire!" Encourage your student to use his imagination as he looks down at the Niagara River hundreds of feet below.

THEY WERE STRONG
AND GOOD

Title: *They Were Strong and Good*
Author/Illustrator: Robert Lawson
Copyright: 1940
Award: Caldecott Medal
Category: Classic
Summary: The narrator shares his family tree, introducing his ancestors with pride and a touch of humor.

(**Teacher's Note:** This particular book selection has a long list of activities. There are probably far too many to be explored in a single week and still keep the warm, light-hearted, learning adventure enjoyable. If you feel the material is valuable, use the book for another week at the end of *FIAR* Vol. 2 and try some more of the activities.)

Social Studies: Geography

They Were Strong and Good has three countries and four states within the United States showcased by the various members of the family. They include Scotland (my mother's father), Holland (my mother's mother), England (my father's father), and New York, New Jersey, Minnesota, and Alabama. You may want to make extra story disks from the blank circles to represent these places. Or you can place your story disk on New York, the state where the narrator was born. If your student is young, just mention these places and it will set the stage for geography lessons in later years.

For your young student give a brief introduction to the directions north, south, east and west. Show him that from England, Scotland and Holland people usually traveled west to reach the United States. Mention that Alabama is a southern state, Minnesota a northern state and New York and New Jersey, eastern or northeastern states. Teach your older student to use a compass. Look at various maps together and remind him that north is often at the top of a map, but not always! Finding the map key or legend will settle that issue. You may have to give your student a lesson in using map keys or legends.

Social Studies: Geography - Islands of the Caribbean

Point out the name Caribbean Sea, and if you wish, use a blank story disk to label it. On a map, trace the route that the Scotch sea captain sailed in the brig *Eliza Jane Hopper*. He sailed from New York to Puerto Rico, Cuba and the Isthmus of Panama. Your older student may want to research Puerto Rico (finding that it is a U. S. protectorate), or Cuba (learning of Fidel Castro and the Communist government there), or the Isthmus of Panama (tracing its history, the canal, and present political status). Your young student might enjoy learning about the wide variety of things which come from Panama. These include monkeys, parrots, sugar cane and, sometimes, Panama hats, etc.

Social Studies: How Cities Change

"My mother's mother," as the book says, *"lived on a farm in New Jersey."* With your student, look at the picture of the farm and list as many details as you can. Then turn back a page and look at the city of Paterson. Isn't it amazing how a geographic area changes over time?

Ask your student in which setting he would have liked to live: the modern city of Paterson or the earlier rural farm? Discuss with your student the city, town or farm area in which he lives. What did it look like 50 years ago? 100 years ago? 200 years ago? What causes a rural (country) area to become an urban (city) area? (an increase in population, the agricultural base changing to industry as more factories and businesses move in, a new train running through town, etc.) Conversely, sometimes a city will cease to exist. The booming mining towns of the west became "ghost towns" once the gold, silver, copper, lead, etc., ran out. Ask your older student if he thinks all such mining towns are doomed to the same fate. (Anything mined will eventually run out. However, often a mining town has a second or third industry, special crop, or livestock operation that can keep it going, even after the mines are finished.)

Social Studies: Education - Schools

In *They Were Strong and Good*, the girl from Minnesota finds life around her to be too frightening. So, she is sent to a convent school as a girl. You may want to explain that this is a boarding type school for girls, run by Catholic nuns. It generally provides a peaceful atmosphere for learning. Ask your student if he remembers what the girl learned at the convent school. This portion of the story could also be a springboard for an older student to explore the history of education and the options available. (There are parochial schools which include convent and other Catholic schools as well as Protestant and non-denominational schools. In addition there are private secular schools, and public schools, home schools, and schooling with a tutor or a governess. Some students in remote areas receive their schooling through ham radio school classes, and others through correspondence courses.)

Social Studies: Occupations

Ask your student how many different occupations are mentioned in this story that he can remember. What does he think are the enjoyable and the difficult parts involved in such jobs? Occupations might include sea captain, lumberjack, preacher, farmer, shopkeeper, etc. For example:

sea captain   He was able to sail to interesting places, see many things and be in charge of his ship, but he also had to stay awake for two days straight in charge of a ship in danger!

Each occupation has different rewards, excitements, dangers, and disappointments. Talk about the different facets of occupations. You can list them with pictures for each occupation and have your student think about what he might like to be! You can also talk about an occupation being a way that each of us is productive (giving) to our society (the people among whom we live). We seem to place most of our emphasis on occupations as the way we make our money. Providing for one's self or family certainly *is* a very necessary aspect of occupations. But, maybe we have lost sight of another facet of occupations, which is taking the talents and gifts we've been given and being able to use them to make a productive contribution to our society. Since we can't do everything, we find we need each other and the collective contributions we each can make. You might remember a similar lesson in *FIAR* Vol. 1, p. 89, from the story *The Clown of God* where the juggler realizes that his contribution is making people smile.

Social Studies: Genealogy

What is a family tree? (If you can obtain a copy of *They Were Strong and Good* that is a twelfth edition copy or earlier, there is a double yellow page at the front of the book with a drawing of a large tree. In its branches are the portraits of the "mothers and fathers." This picture provides a wonderful *graphic* illustration of a family tree.)

Using this story of ancestors and relatives, begin to talk about your student's family. If he is interested, let him begin to ask questions about where family members came from, what their occupations were. You could make story disks with copies of old photographs and place them on the areas of the map from which the ancestors came.

Show your older student the different ways people research genealogies and ways to graph or interpret their findings using brackets or different types of tree illustrations. As your student becomes interested in his family and ancestors, incorporate history and geography lessons related to their lives. Your student can write his findings as a writing lesson. He can also create an art lesson as he decides how he wants to express the family tree and the decorations and illustrations he might use. Many libraries will help you with genealogical research and most counties have a historical society which may be a wonderful resource in learning more about genealogy.

Social Studies: History Topics

There are many history topics introduced in *They Were Strong and Good* that could be expanded for your older student: Indians, Indian Wars, land grants, treaties, and Civil War (including Yankees, Rebels, deserters, generals, captains, guidon bearer, artillery, ammunition, cannon battery, or slavery). Slavery was mentioned in *Who Owns the Sun*, *FIAR* Vol. 1, p. 36, and will be re-introduced in *Follow The Drinking Gourd*, *FIAR* Vol 2, p. 142.

Social Studies: Family Relationships and Family Pride

Consider, with your student, the institution of a Family Day; a day once a year to celebrate being a family. Let him collect family stories from parents, siblings, relatives or friends, and make a *Family* notebook. You might use a tape recorder to interview family members, etc., and record their stories. Family stories are ties of love and of *place*, both geographical place and *place* in history. Later, your older student can transcrib them (possibly with your help) and place them in the Family notebook.Consider making a *What Our Family Stands For* list or a *This Is What The Smiths Do* list. Your student may also want to make a family crest, or a family flag to be flown on Family Day.

Have him consider with his family what makes his family special, what special giftings and talents they have, what kind of work they do and what kind of things they do together. Then, talk about special foods and events that could become traditions for his Family Day. (Such as: On our Family Day we *always* have a giant bowl of spaghetti for dinner and chocolate chip cookies for dessert, and we play baseball together, or we go to the park, or to the movies, etc.)

The forward in *They Were Strong and Good* admonishes us to *"guard well the heritage left us."* We've talked about finding the distinct qualities of a family and the suggestions for Family Day, etc. These are the things that make us proud of our families. This is the right kind of pride; not that we're better than others but that we know who we are as a unique family. Knowledge like that can be a deterrent to juvenile problems. If there is the right kind of pride, a young person does not want to let his family down. On the other hand, when people feel unimportant or without value to themselves and to others, they often become a problem. So how do we guard the heritage? You could begin to teach that you guard it by virtuous living. Your student will find that what he chooses to do, *does* make a difference. His choices, for good or bad, doing the right thing or the wrong thing, count!! He needs to know that there is room for a mistake or a stumble, but what he is proud of, he will want to protect.

Social Studies: Relationships - Emotions

This story includes a wide array of emotions to explore. Consider the Scotch sea captain's temper, and his anger when the Panama straw hat is destroyed. Look also at the the preacher who fights evil, the heroism and bravery shown by the soldiers and especially by the young flag bearer. Notice the pride that same young man showed as he holds the ground for his company until they have to retreat. There is the pride the narrator shows in his ancestors and in his heritage. Consider, too, the fear and discomfort of the young girl in Minnesota who eventually finds peace and contentment in the convent school. Can you find other examples of emotions from the text and the pictures? Discuss them and offer examples from your own and your student's own memories.

Language Arts: Vocabulary

brig a two-masted boat (Three-masted vessels are not brigs.) Point out to your student the masts to which the sails are attached.

battery a set of guns or other heavy artillery; an artillery unit

Language Arts: Thinking Skills - Similar Themes

If you enjoy comparing books, find a copy of *Ox-Cart Man* written by Barbara Cooney. If, after several days of reading *They Were Strong and Good*, you read *Ox-Cart Man* to your student, he may recognize a similar scenario. In *Ox-Cart Man*, food is grown and products packed into a covered wagon to take and sell in the town. This is the same scenario that the Dutch farmer from New Jersey undertakes in *They Were Strong and Good*. The ability to recognize the same scenario, or to see similarities of theme in different stories is a valuable thinking skill.

Language Arts: Punctuation - Italics

As in several stories from *FIAR*, Vol. 1, where the names of ships or boats appear in italics, we have in this story the name of a brig, the *Eliza Jane Hopper* which appears in italics. Perhaps, by this time your student will notice the unusual print and know from the context that you are reading about a ship. If not, then continue to make brief mention of the different print called italics and that it is used to show several things, including the names of ships and boats. Be sure and remind your student that when he writes his own stories by hand, italics are shown with underlining.

Language Arts: A Good Title

The title of this story is powerful. What words make it powerful? (Words like *were*, *strong* and *good* are powerful words. If the story were entitled *"They Seemed Soft and Warm,"* the feeling of strength would not be there. Try thinking of other words that make you think of strength: oak, marble, power, solid, great, mighty, elephant, bull, granite. Let your student try telling you, or writing, a descriptive sentence using strong words. Also, try a sentence with gentle sounding words.

Does your student wonder who "They" are in the title. Sometimes words like that make you want to read the story to find out "who."

Language Arts: Recognizing Latin Influence

In the section of the story called "My Father," we read about two hound dogs. They were named Sextus Hostilius and Numa Pompilius. Do these sound like strange names? The "-us" endings on these names are typical of Latin word endings. They remind us of names like Julius, Augustus and Marcus Aurelius. Latin was the language spoken in Rome over five hundred years ago. An older student may enjoy being introduced to the influence of this language on our own. Many, many English words have their origins in Latin, since all of the romance languages (French, Italian, Portuguese and Spanish) developed from Latin during the Middle Ages. Most English words that name abstract ideas have their origin in Latin; words like charity, virtue, power, independence, liberty, spirit, etc.

Art: Illustrations Full of Contrast and Strength

One of the choices an illustrator makes is to find the medium that best represents and enhances the story. Ask your student if he likes the black and white illustrations and let him show you a favorite picture or two. Black and white are high in contrast. Each emphasizes the other because they are opposites. Since this story is about being strong, these illustrations not only seem fitting but tend to extend the author's message in a bold, strong way.

Find some rubber stamps or make potato carvings and let your student try some black ink printing. Your younger student may simply enjoy random black designs on white paper, but your older student may want to make patterns, repeating a stamped design in evenly spaced increments to make a placemat border, bookmark, etc.

"My Mother's Father," page shows a very strong face, made even more dramatic by the use of black ink. Try choosing a strong subject such as a stone building, or an elephant, etc. After you've drawn it, let your student fill in some spaces with black marker to make it look extra strong!

Art: Illustrations - Symbolism

On the title page, beneath the title, is a collection of items: a cannon, a plow, a book, a spinning wheel, an anchor and a cradle. Can your student match the items to some of the people in the story?

What collection of items could describe your student's family? In one family there might be a horseshoe if the mother loved horses, and a basketball if the father was a basketball star. Perhaps your student would include a piano or flute for a musical sister, a cozy fireplace to represent their home and a train for a little brother who wants to be an engineer, etc. Each member of your student's family could choose a picture symbol to represent himself. Make a collage or drawing of the composite family symbols. Your student may want to use this design for the title page of his Family Day book (see: *FIAR* Vol. 2, pp. 66-67).

Math: Counting

Have your student count all the animals in each illustration from the beginning of the story to the end. (There are over forty-five.)

Math: Hexagons and Octagons

The bees in the hives at the convent gardens make honeycombs that have storage spaces with six equal sides in which to deposit their honey. Draw a hexagon and let your student examine it. Does the shape look familiar to him? Look at several pencils. Some are formed into a six-sided (hexagonal) piece of wood. This is a creative idea that helps prevent pencils from rolling off tables and desks! A stop sign looks similar, but actually has eight equal sides which makes it an octagon. Take cardboard and make templates of different sizes of hexagons and octagons. Let your student use the templates to make designs and draw around them with markers or colored pencils. If you made a geo-board (FIAR Vol. 1, pp.35 and 46)), allow your student to make hexagons and octagons on his geo-board.

Math: Subtraction or Multiplication

When the young guidon bearer stands proudly beside the guns in the battery, he stands by four cannon at first, then later only three, then two and finally there is only one. After the battle at Atlanta there isn't even one. For your young student, introduce the concept of subtraction by using four objects to count. Remove one and have him count the results. Then, you can write the facts in numbers. Show him how these facts correspond to your groupings of objects.

For your older student, subtract 1940 from the present year date to find how many years ago Robert Lawson wrote this book. Also, do some simple multiplication with the cannon battery as the subject. If you had three cannon in each unit how many cannon would be in the general's battery if he had two, three, four, five, etc., units?

Science: Bees and Beekeeping

The girl from the Minnesota woods attended a convent school where there were lovely gardens. In these gardens she learned to grow flowers and care for bees. Through this senario of *They Were Strong and Good,* there is an excellent chance to introduce a most valuable member of the insect community–the honey bee. There are so many facts and subject areas related to the bee that can be covered it is sometimes difficult to narrow them down. But, you may find books at the library appropriate for the age of your student and see what facet of the world of bees is most interesting to him. If possible, visit a flower garden. Watch the bees at work, or visit an apiary (pron. A' pee air ee), a place where bee-hives are kept and bees raised for their honey. The type of hives that are drawn by Robert Lawson are seldom used today. Instead, white boxes called standard hives are what most beekeepers use. There are probably good videos on Beekeeping that can be requested and borrowed from your library. At any rate, enjoy the adventure of research and discovery, and have some bread and honey for a snack!

Science: Ecology - Pollution

You may or may not have talked about industrial city pollution while reading the story *Grandfather's Journey, FIAR* Vol. p.62. In either case, the picture of the city of Paterson in *They Were Strong and Good* provides another chance to introduce the topic or to explore the actual pollutants. Find what can be done to steward our natural resources (including the air we breathe). Have your student look for examples of clean industry, as well as factories that may need to improve their methods of operation.

Title:	*Babar, To Duet or Not to Duet*
Author:	The original characters of the Babar stories were created by Jean and Laurent de Brunhoff. This book, using those characters is based on a story by Elaine Waisglass, adapted to an animated series *"Babar."*
Copyright:	1991
Summary:	Learning to curb an over-active ambition, father and son overcome a problem which they both share.

(This book is not in print at this time. The book, however, is well worth the search due to the story content and the introduction to music and composers. Many libraries have this volume or can order it easily from another, nearby co-operating library, using the Inter-Library Loan System–ILL. There are additional titles added to FIAR Vol. 2, in case you would prefer to use an alternate story.)

(***Teacher's Note:** The **original** Babar stories are excellent examples of writing in the present tense. Example: "Babar *is* going to see Pom," etc. When you need to teach a lesson on present tense verbs, remember original Babar stories provide good examples. As stated previously, *To Duet or Not to Duet* is **not** an original de Brunhoff story, **nor** does it follow the present tense verb form.)

Social Studies: Geography - Setting

The setting of this story is the fictitious city of Celesteville. If you would like, you can place your story disk on an designated spot (a land of make believe) on your literary map. Many stories have fictional sites that have become famous such as Celesteville, from Babar stories and Never-Never-Land from the story of *Peter Pan*, etc.

(***Teachers Note:** Here is a brief background to provide details, if you or your student are not familiar with the Babar story characters which have been enjoyed since l931 when the de Brunhoffs first created them. While young, Babar has many adventures and learns about civilization. Later, he builds the city of Celesteville in the jungle and becomes King of the Elephants. King Babar and his wife Queen Celeste have three children, Pom, Flora and Alexander. Babar also has special friends, Arthur, Zephir the monkey, Cornelius who is old and wrinkled, and the Old Lady, of whom Babar is very fond.)

Social Studies: Relationships - Making Yourself Vulnerable

Talk with your student about the problem that Babar's son Pom faces. (He has chosen something very difficult and has not been able to accomplish it.) Ask your student why he chooses such a project. (Because he wants everyone to admire him.) Ask your student how Babar helps his son learn to choose a project he could do and to do well. (Babar wisely and compassionately decides to share a personal incident of his *own* past. Babar makes himself vulnerable and gives Pom time to make the decision to confess, on his own. When Pom's guilt is removed by his confession, Pom is able to think of a more appropriate science project. Ask your student if he would appreciate older people in his life sharing with him the way Babar does with Pom.

Babar, instead of scolding, identifies with Pom. He explains how to handle his problem in a different way. This is the same theme as *Katie's Adventures at Blueberry Pond* by Josh McDowell which you may want to search out, or review if you've already read it. When we make ourselves vulnerable to others, and are willing to share our own experiences truthfully, we make it easy for them to be honest too. Our tendency is, too often, to be self-protective and concealing. If act as if we have never made a mistake, it compels the other person to act out the same pretense.

Social Studies: Relationships - Telling the Truth

To Duet or Not to Duet provides a living picture of the consequences of a lie. Talk with your student about how a lie can grow, as more and more lies become necessary to cover the first one. Discuss how difficult it is to confess, especially when the lie has continued. With young Babar, the lack of peace he experiences even leads to bad dreams. Note that the confession brings him back into fellowship with everyone.

You may want to have a conversation about how important it is to tell the truth. Truth-telling results in a reputation for honesty. People will believe an honest person when he speaks, instead of always mistrusting him. A good reputation is hard to win and easy to lose!

Social Studies: Relationships - Listening to Advice

Highlighting pp. 11, 36, and 39, talk about how the Old Lady gives Babar good advice. Ask your student to explain how he respondsto that advice. Later in the story, the Old Lady hears the truth and graciously takes pity on Babar, even though he has paid no attention to her advice. She teaches him a simple piece to play with the Great Leopold. Talk about difficulties in taking advice (being humble), and the importance of learning to consider what other people may have to say *before* making up your mind.

Social Studies: Relationships - Discipline

Each goal that is set takes work, time and discipline to accomplish. Babar (as he reveals in his childhood experience) tries a short cut and ends up at a dead end! There is a saying: *"There is much drudgery between the first enthusiasm and the achievement."* It may not be entirely drudgery but there is certainly much hard work required to accomplish anything worthwhile. Starting out with a realistic goal helps, but what is it that keeps one going during the dry stretch when it seems as if the end is not in sight?

Talk with your student about tasks or goals that you have been excited about and then struggled to accomplish. Be honest! Share some examples where the goal was not met and some where the struggle was worth the effort. Ask him for any examples of his own, or that he has witnessed in others. Have him look for struggles that take persistence and end in triumph! A part of learning discipline is understanding the rewards.

[**Teacher's Note**: The author of *FIAR* was in part inspired by *To Duet or Not to Duet* to continue to work and complete the first volume of this curriculum. The task of writing the book was very exciting but also extremely difficult. The author seemed to find many things to do (like working in her garden, or reading, or many other little time-consuming jobs) and she might not have completed the volume without this helpful lesson from *To Duet or Not to Duet*. From Pom and Babar she learned that if she is to accomplish a difficult goal, she must work day by day and be careful not to be sidetracked by unnecessary distractions.]

This might be a good time to re-tell the fable *The Tortoise and the Hare*. As you remember, it's the story of a fast rabbit and a slower, but more diligent turtle who eventually wins the race. Your older student could do a report comparing Babar and Pom's adventures in *To Duet or Not to Duet* with this ancient fable.

Social Studies: Relationships - Respect

The Old Lady demonstrates her respect for Babar, because he is the King, by cheerfully arranging music for him. She does this even though she believes the piece is too difficult for him. Her advice has been ignored, but she is still friendly and helpful. Can your student imagine how difficult maintaining this attitude would be? Respect often means honoring another's request, even when we don't necessarily agree with it, or even understand it. (Obviously, your student must learn not to follow someone's instructions if these instructions are against the law, his parent's rules, etc.)

Language Arts: Title - Play on Words

After reading the story at least twice, ask your student about the title *To Duet or Not to Duet*. Does he understand the meaning of the word "duet" and how it relates to the story? Ask him if the title sounds like something else. (to *do it* or not to *do it*) The word *duet* is so close in sound to *do it,* that the play on words gives a humorous effect. You may want to add *Play On Words* as it relates to the title, to your on-going list *Choices a Writer Can Make*. When your student has an assignment to write a story or wants to write a story on his own, he can consult the list and bring to mind many techniques and literary devices other authors have used. Out of this list, he may be inspired by one or two that seem to fit his idea for a story.

Language Arts: Formal Speech - Manners

Page 8 says, *"...the Great Leopold, accepted an engagement to play in a concert in Celesteville."* This is certainly different from a modern slang approach where a performer agrees to "do a gig." Formal speech, like neat handwriting, tells something about the person who is speaking or writing. For one thing, it shows that the person has accepted the discipline of learning. Proper speech and attractive handwriting take time to learn and lots of practice. It also shows that the person has a respect for those around him. He desires to be graciously understood when he speaks, and desires people can easily read what he has written. There are times that are more appropriate for formality and times when a more relaxed informality is fine. Remember, a soldier cannot stand at attention all the time!

Find a book of manners and practice the most kind and gracious methods of answering the telephone, introducing people to one another, greeting a guest, answering a greeting, or visiting a person who is ill. Also, practice adding extra graciousness to existing habits of table manners.

Your older student might also write a play and act it out with your help. This could be quite a creative venture. He can use any subject to act as situation and setting, for a play centering around formal manners and speech. Some examples could be: the coronation of a king, the respect shown an elderly person or a war veteran at a banquet, a knighting ceremony, visiting the queen, or an extremely formal party, etc.

Language Arts: Vocabulary

[**Teacher's Note**: You do *not* have to use every word. Just select a few that you think your child is ready to learn. Work with those words for this lesson. Different words are appropriate for different ages!]

splendid	wonderful, p.7.
entry	the piece of work that is entered in a competition, p.7.
mysterious	of unknown origin, p.7.
occasions	at such times, p.9.
inspired	guided by; literally means "breathed into," p.11.
compliment	to give praise or positive remarks about; used in this story to mean as a way to show honor, p.11.
miracle	something that seems impossible, p.14.
astonishing	unbelievable; amazing, p.16.

illusion	an incorrect perception of reality; something that looks like a certain things but is really different, p.17.
courage	strength or bravery.; In this story young Babar plays the stereo to give himself the strength to begin to practice, p.17.
extract	to take from; In this story Babar could not get the right notes to come out of the piano, p.18.
remarkable	wonderful; worthy of being spoken of or remarked upon, p.18.
disastrous	terrible; as if from a disaster, p.22.
broadcast	send out or communicate by radio or television, p.22.
fabulous	incredible, wonderful, p. 23.
affectation(s)	behavior that gives a false impression, p.25.
modest	not overly praising one's self; modest, p.25.
etiquette	good manners, p.32.
regulations	rules, p.33.
scandal(ous)	improper behaviour that shocks others, p.35.
audience	the people who watch a performance of music, play or game, p.35.
applaude(d)	to clap as in appreciation, p. 39.
genius	someone with outstanding abilities in a particular field, p. 42.
limitations	where one must stop, boundaries, p. 42.
ambition	the desire to do great things, p.42.

Art: Line Drawings

The illustrations for *To Duet or Not to Duet* are line drawings, blocked out much like a coloring book. There is very little evidence of shading (here or there on a pillow or the sheets and other objects. The characters are generally a solid color. Ask your student if he likes these illustrations. They are more simple than many he has studied. Ask him if the colors seem pleasing. Does the broad expanse of bright color perhaps balance the fact that the figures are simple line art?

Art: Music Vocabulary

pianist   one who plays the piano, p.8.

engagement   performance date, p.8.

concert   a performance of music, p.8.

duet   two musicians playing (or singing) together at the same time, p.27.

symphony   an extended piece of music, in three or more parts, written for the symphony orchestra. p.40

keyboard   the black and white keys of a piano, organ or synthesizer, p.14.

stereo   a sound system for listening to music that makes one feel as if he were seated in the middle of the performance; the music comes from speakers on each side of the listener and is recorded in a special way to produce this type of listening sound, p.17.

variations   tunes or themes which are repeated with changes in either rhythm or harmony, p.41.

embellishments added decoration or extra detail

ovation   a round of applause following a performance. A standing ovation means the audience stands as they clap, showing even more appreciation for the performance, p.4.

orchestra pit   an area where the orchestra is seated below and in front of the stage; notice the picture below the stage on p.40

Art: Potato Print Notes

Cut a potato in half. Trace an eighth note (drawn as large as possible) on the raw potato half. Either you or your older student, if he can, carefully carve the areas that are **not** eighth note away. This will leave an up-raised eighth note form. Dip the potato stamp in different colors of poster paint or ink and press to make a free-form picture. Or draw a musical staff on a large sheet of paper and "stamp" a tune! The staff can even be curved as on p.17.

Art: Promotional Poster

On p.27, there is a poster showing the upcoming concert. In this poster there are different styles of printing, a circle to enclose the picture, etc. Have your student choose an event, either real or imaginary, and create a poster announcing the occasion and giving information such as what, when, where, who, cost, etc. Encourage creativity with colored pencils, colorful markers and other helpful art aids such as compasses, triangles, stencils, and different kinds of paper or poster board. You may want to take more time with this lesson and find a book of posters, old circus posters, current sports or musical event posters and examine what eye-catching techniques the artist has used to capture the viewer's attention. (There is also a promotional poster illustrated in the story *Another Celebrated Dancing Bear*, FIAR Vol. 1. Remember that the poster filled Boris with excitement and caused him to want to dance? Also, there is a promotional poster in the story *Mirette on the High Wire*, FIAR Vol. 2) Posters have been used to herald such a variety of historic, artistic, and sports related events that you can experience many enjoyable (and educational) lessons by taking the time to research posters.

Art: Orchestra

An orchestra consists of a large group of musicians and instruments (sometimes one hundred or more) drawn from four groups: strings, woodwinds, brass, and percussion. There are good picture books in the children's non-fiction section of the library that show the varied instruments of the orchestra and the basic seating arrangements.

A marching band differs from an orchestra by not including stringed instruments. This would be an interesting point to bring up, not by teaching it directly, but rather by finding pictures of bands and orchestras or reading stories that include them. Let your student discover for himself the difference.

(**Teacher's Note**:You'll love this wonderful book called *The Orchestra*, by Mark Rubin, 1984, Firefly Books, ISBN 0920668992. Also, an unusual book called *Orchestranimals* by vanKampen shows the orchestra portrayed by animals that have distinct personalities. You may want to preview this book before you use it.)

Art: Musical Composer - Haydn

On p. 40, the Old Lady teaches young Babar the first few bars of *Baa, Baa, Black Sheep*. This happens to be the same first few notes as Haydn's *Surprise Symphony*. Franz Joseph Haydn was an Austrian **composer** (a writer of musical pieces), born in 1732 and died in 1809. (For "timeline" purposes, Haydn lived during the French and the American Revolutions.) Haydn knew Mozart and taught Beethoven for a brief time.

The *Surprise Symphony,* also known as *Haydn's Symphony No. 94 in G Major*, was written in 1791. It's called the "*Surprise Symphony*" because of the loud chord which suddenly bursts into the slow movements. If you can find a recording of the *Surprise Symphony*, listen to it with your student. Can you find the notes that sound like the music for *Baa Baa, Black Sheep* which Old Lady taught Babar? Listen, also, for the loud "surprise" chord.

Math: Days of the Week

On p. 7 we read *"...for <u>over a week</u>, Pom, the son of Babar and Celeste, had been building a model balloon...."* See if your young student knows the number of days in a week and how many days would be "over" a week. Have him name the days. Your older student should spell them. You may want to continue with the number of days (and weeks) in a month, in each of the four seasons, in a year, until his birthday or some other special event.

Math: Fractions

Music is a wonderful way to continue the subject of fractions. The whole, half, quarter, eighth, and sixteenth notes make a good study. Look at the various musical notes and discuss their meaning. Try using pennies, toothpicks or some other small item to group sixteen items into halves (two piles of eight), quarters (four piles of four), eighths (eight piles of two and sixteenths (sixteen piles of one). Your older student may be ready to add or subtract fractions.

Math: Geometric Shapes

The wide, box-like drawings of this story contain many shapes such as circles p. 17, ovals p. 11 and 20, triangles p. 22, stars p. 16, rectangles p. 17, squares p. 9 (down low), diamonds p. 32, half circles p. 15, trapezoids p. 14, and maybe more. There are also cubic shapes, such as a pyramid p. 18 (the top section of the metronome), spheres p. 43, cylinders p. 41, rectangular boxes p. 22, etc. Depending on the age of your student, you can search these illustrations for many examples of geometric shapes. Use familiar items and have your student draw examples of these shapes for his notebook. Your older student can write definitions and applications for the different shapes. (Spheres can be a ball, an orange, a moon, etc.)

Your student can make a chart of shapes and their names (and uses) to include in his notebook. He can also make abstract pictures using templates of the shapes and different colors and even textures.

Science: Sound

Musical instruments make their notes and sounds in a variety of ways, but vibration is a part of all musical sound. In fact, vibration is a part of every type of sound. Our ear drums *feel* the vibrations as they are transmitted through the air around us. Whether the sound is the violent banging of a bass drum, or the delicate sound of a harp's string, all sound is created by vibration.

For your young student, you may want to merely mention that the human ear is able to hear volume (loudness), pitch (intensity) and tone (quality).

Lessons for your older student might include a study of sound frequencies and the sounds that a human can and cannot hear. You might want to research the hearing of certain animal species such as dogs, bats and whales.

Have your student make notes about sound and hearing and illustrate them, when possible. He should in-clude these pages in the science portion of his notebook for reviewing later.

Science: Human Body - Ear

Because music is enjoyed by hearing sounds, you can use this opportunity to study the ear. Your young student may begin with the lesson of the anatomy of the ear. It consists of the outer ear, middle ear and inner ear. For your older student you may wish to include information about the outer ear (pinna), the auditory canal, the middle ear (the ear drum, and the three bones–the hammer, anvil, and stirup), and the inner ear (the cochlea, semi-circular canal and the auditory nerves). An older student may also be interested in the ability of the human ear to keep equilibrium and provide the balance necessary to move and bend without falling down.

By using the encyclopedia and books from the library, your student may find topics of interest that will lead to positive learning experiences. Begin with simple books on the subject and continue to increase their level of difficulty, until your student's level is reached, and then continue from there.

Have your student make a picture of the parts of the ear he has studied. Include it along with any other information in his notebook to be reviewed later.

See the simple drawing of the human ear in the Appendix.

Science: Animals - Elephant

In the story of Babar, *To Duet or Not to Duet*, the elephants are personified (made to be like people). They talk and wear clothes and have human feelings, etc. Yet through the inspiration of this story, your student may have a genuine interest in the true elephants of the wild. If so, take this opportunity to study the subject of elephants; the different kinds, where they live, what they eat and how they act. There are two types of elephants: African and the Asian (or Indian) elephant. Elephants are the largest living land animals. They eat plants, are mammals and have one to two babies after a twenty to twenty-two month gestation period. There are many other interesting facts about elephants to explore. If you have a zoo nearby, consider a trip to see elephants first-hand.

You may also want to look into the subject of elephant training and how elephants are used to help people work and to provide entertainment like in a circus. In fact, a trip to the circus is a wonderful way to see live entertainment and a wide variety of amazing animals, including elephants, tigers, etc.

Title:	*The Story of Ferdinand*
Author:	Munro Leaf
Illustrator:	Robert Lawson
Copyright:	1936
Category:	Classic
Summary:	Every bull might not be alike, but Ferdinand has to go to such lengths to make his point!

Social Studies: Geography - Spain

The first phrase of the first sentence sets this story in Spain, a country in Europe. Spain presents a rich variety of architecture: castles, farms, and cities with tall buildings. There are stone and brick streets; special kinds of music made with guitars, castanets, and tambourines; special foods like paella (several kinds of fish with rice and saffron); and different sports like bull fighting, etc.

Your older student may learn that Spain, along with the country of Portugal, occupies a portion of land called the Iberian **Peninsula** (a piece of land that projects into a body of water and is connected to the mainland by a narrower strip of land called an isthmus). Spain nearly touches the continent of Africa. They are separated only by the **Strait of Gibraltar**, the natural opening that allows travel from the Mediterranean Sea into the Atlantic Ocean. Spain was conquered and settled by different peoples, including the Romans and the Moors. And both Spain and Portugal were involved in exploring and trading by sea. Columbus sailed from Spain when he discovered the New World in 1492.

At the library, you may wish to locate books with good pictures of Spain, a Spanish cook book, travel videos that give you a homeside tour of Spain, or even audio tapes and compact disks of Spanish music and Spanish language. Preview these before using.

If your student is making a flag for each new country, have him include the flag of Spain, and place the story disk on this European country.

You may also decide whether to teach only the "Spain" represented in Lawson's illustrations, or have your older student research and discover the "Spain" of today.

Language Arts: Animal Fantasy Story

"Once upon a time..." Ask your student if he thinks this is going to be a true story. Generally, this opening phrase signifies fiction—in this case an animal fantasy with talking animals and imaginary items, like the corks tied on to the cork tree. (See **Science** section of this lesson plan for information on cork.)

Have some bottle corks on hand (you can find them at a craft or dime store). For fun, tie or glue them together on a leaved twig for your student's amusement on the last day of your story.

Language Arts: Including the Reader

Munro Leaf includes the reader in *The Story of Ferdinand* when he asks the reader questions: *"Well, if you were a bumblebee and a bull sat on you what would you do?... Then came the bull, and you know who that was don't you?"*

Add this technique to your list of *Choices a Writer Can Make*. Then, have your student try a short story (either written or dictated to you) in which he includes the reader into the story by asking a question or two.

Language Arts: Repetition

Remind your student that *repetition* is the use of words, phrases or ideas more than once in a work. Ask him if he can hear some repetitive phrases in *The Story of Ferdinand,* or have him find some if he is a reader. A few repetitive phrases and ideas are:

"run and jump and butt their heads together"

"sit quietly and smell the flowers"

"his mother who was a cow"

"even though she was a cow"

Language Arts: Interjection

An *interjection* is a part of speech that usually expresses emotion or surprise and can stand alone, such as "Great!" or "Oh!" Have your student hunt for the short word that is followed by an exclamation point on the page that show the hoofs of Ferdinand and the bee. (You may need to explain what an exclamation point is.) The passage reads: *"Wow! Did it hurt: Ferdinand jumped up with a snort."* "Wow!" is the interjection. With your student, make up some sentences that contain interjections. Add this term to your list of *Choices Writers Can Make.*

"Boy! Did you see that comet!"
"Great! Thank you for your help."

"Oh! I didn't know you had arrived!"

Remind your student that if he chooses to use dialogue in making up stories, and in writing about his adventures, that interjections often add a sense of excitement to dialogue.

Art: Humor

Art, in all its form, is a wonderful vehicle for expressing and experiencing emotion. Whether we're talking about drawing, painting, singing, acting, dancing or sculpture, art can help us experience sadness, joy or laughter. Robert Lawson has used his drawings to help us laugh.

Ask your student to show you his favorite "funny" or humorous picture in *The Story of Ferdinand*. Share yours with him. There are many to choose from such as the entire bee sting series that portrays powerful emotions. Notice also, the troop of bull collectors–the five funny men with their accumulated features, expressions, costumes and hats!! (Which hat is your favorite?) And, when you turn the page and view them from the back, they are still funny! There is also the picture of Ferdinand coming out into the bull ring–or not coming out, but rather peeking out! Notice the small person hiding behind the door. Or consider the picadores (pron. pick uh door' ehs) who are stamping mad, and the matador who cries because he can't show off while Ferdinand sits primly smelling the flowers in the center of the ring, as well as other funny pictures throughout the story.

Art: Drama

Your young student may want to act out the *"sitting on the bee"* scene. Include the sitting scene, the facial expressions of the bull (or the bee!). He could include the jumping up and running around, puffing, snorting, butting and pawing.

Art: Symbolism

Symbolism is an important aspect of art. With your student, notice the position of Ferdinand in the cart as he is taken to Madrid. He looks down, and has his back to the driver *and* to the sign of Madrid. Now, look at the second cart ride as he is taken home. He sits beside the driver, looking up. He is facing home with his back to Madrid. Either way, coming or going, the artist pictures Ferdinand with his back toward Madrid. This posture subtly symbolizes his distaste for Madrid and its bull-fighting.

Art: Size and Distance

Robert Lawson, in his illustrations for Ferdinand (possibly done with brush and black tempera) created the illusion of distance in some of his pictures. Together, look at the picture of Ferdinand's mother ("...who was a cow...") as she looks at her son sitting on a distant hill under a cork tree. Ask your student how Mr. Lawson drew these characters to make Ferdinand look like he is far away. (Ferdinand's mother, is large and in the right side foreground of the picture. Ferdinand, however, is smaller in size and is elevated to the upper left hand corner on a little hill, under a tree. The reader can tell the tree is large in comparison to Ferdinand, but the tree itself is still small in relation to the mother cow.

The size of the two characters and the elevation of Ferdinand to the upper part of the page work together to give the effect of distance. Let your student try drawing a simple picture. Using the same strategy, he could place a large bull ring in the foreground and the outline of a small town and a cork tree in the uper corner.

For your younger student, or one not yet proficient in drawing, make a cut-out of the bull ring and the town with the cork tree (just simple outlines). Let your student glue them to a piece of paper. Place with the bull ring in the foreground and elevate the town to a corner of the paper. Then, rough in the horizon line and the road. Step back to look at your work. Does it give the impression of depth and distance? Now, look again at the picture of Ferdinand and his mother for the illusion of distance. Watch for pictures in books, magazines, billboards, and works of art, that demonstrate how the size of different elements in an illustration helps create the feeling of distance.

Art: Line of Design

Pictures created by artists can follow different lines of design. Some pictures have a circular line, some a triangle form, some a serpentine line or "S" shape line (forward or reversed), etc.

For an example of the triangle line of design look at the first page of the story. The line of view rises from the giant black "O" to the peak of the castle-like buildings, and down to the cows on the hillside and back to the "O", to complete the triangle design line that your eye follows as you look at the picture.

The serpentine line can be seen in the third picture of the story. The little bulls, who run and jump and butted their heads together, are strung out in a backward "S" shape from the top of the page to the bottom. This line of design provides variety from the traditional straight horizon pictures. If you'd like to give your student some hands-on experience with this type of design line, take a piece of paper and very lightly draw an "S" shape (or reverse "S") like this picture in the story. Then, let him draw on the line, any kind of objects or figures (or use cut-outs from magazines). Remember to place larger figures in the foreground and smaller ones higher up to show distance. Afterward, he can add details or background to complete his picture.

The circular line of design is roughly shown in the picture of the banderilleros, picadores and the matador. All of them are hopping mad because Ferdinand will only sit and smell the flowers. This illustration shows five men surrounding the bull in a circular pattern. (If you still have a copy of *Mike Mulligan and His Steam Shovel,* by Virginia Lee Burton, *FIAR* Vol. 1, look again at the illustration of the circular cloud of dust as Mary Anne, the steam shovel, digs hurriedly.) If you like, you can help your student create pictures showing both the triangular and circular lines of design. Create these in the same way that you made the serpentine line of design pictures.

Art: Balance

Robert Lawson demonstrates his skill as an artist, in the pleasing balance of his illustrations. In the first illustration, Lawson has created horizontal balance. He uses the clouds to balance the tall buildings and the "O" to balance the cows. There is vertical balance in the illustration of Ferdinand after the bee sting; the clouds above balance the bull below.

There is diagonal balance in the picture of young Ferdinand walking toward his *"...favorite spot out in the pasture under a cork tree."* The young bull is on the lower left page, with the cork tree in the upper right of the page.

There is almost an hourglass type of balance in the illustration following,*"So they took him away for the bull fight day...."* The cart and team stretch out across the bottom of the page with the bridge and mountains across the top, while the gorge connects the top part with the lower portion of the picture.

Notice the illustration opposite the text, "They had a parade into the bull ring." Ask your student what detail in this picture balances the horse's head and the bugle-like instrument? (the grand sweep of the horse's tail) Search for other examples of balance in this story and in other pictures and illustrations that you see. Remind your student that balance is another factor that an artist considers when composing a picture.

For your older student, take a piece of construction paper. Give him three (or five*) various size leaves from a tree or houseplant. Let him arrange these leaves in several different ways to create balance. (Remind him of the various types of balance including: horizontal, vertical and diagonal.) If he desires, after he has considered different balancing arrangements, let him find his favorite and glue the leaves on the paper. He might label his composotion with the type of balance (horizontal, vertical or diagonal) his has chosen to employ. Then, he can file this page in the art section of his notebook for review.

*Artists often use an **uneven** number of objects in their compositions.

Math: Measuring in Feet and Inches

"As the years went by Ferdinand grew and grew until he was very big and strong." The picture that follows this text shows Ferdinand staring at a growth chart carved on the tree stump. Is there a growth chart in your student's home–a place where he can see his own progress growing up? If not, help him make one. Then, based on skill level, have him

determine how tall he is in inches, then in feet and finally in yards. If there is sufficient data, let him make a notebook page showing height, weight at birth, 6 months., l year, 2 years, 3 years, etc. Have him place the page in the Math section of his notebook.

Math: Counting

Your young student may enjoy counting the corks on the "cork tree", or the flowers on the front and back covers.

Science: Cork Oak Trees

Cork comes from the bark tissue of the *"cork oak,"* (Quercus suber). This is an ever-green tree native to the Mediterranean and cultivated in Spain and Portugal as well as India and the western United States. Although the leaves look more like an elm, this tree has acorns like other oak trees.

Cork from the cork oak, (Quercus suber) is a hollow celled structure that is buoyant (floats in water), insulates because it is a poor conductor of heat and sound, is waterproof and resilient (springs back after compression). Cork would be an interesting topic to research for your older student. Students of any age will enjoy demonstrating some of its properties (buoyancy, resiliency, and insulation, etc.). There is also another tree that is actually called a "cork tree" (Phellodendron amurense) which is found in Japan and China but we do **not** get cork from this tree.The so-called *"cork tree"* in *The Story of Ferdinand* was probably the cork oak that grows in Spain, although it does not grow "corks" on it as the pictures so humorously suggest.

Science: Vultures

Robert Lawson has drawn a vulture, sitting atop the growth-chart tree. Vultures are fascinating birds because they are the only birds with "naked" heads. The tops of their heads are featherless! Vultures eat the bodies of dead animals, serving a useful purpose in nature by getting rid of decaying corpses that might otherwise spread disease. Every-where in America, you can see one or more of the six species of New World Vultures as they circle in slow, lazy circles in the sky. If your student shows an interest, he will proba-bly look for vultures. You can also often find them sitting or roosting in trees, particularly near water. Lawson's illustration is surprisingly accurate, capturing the bald head, s-shap-ed neck, and large body of a type of vulture which lives in Europe.

Science: Clover

Robert Lawson has also created a wonderful illustration of clover. It is shown in the illustration of the bee, just before Ferdinand sits down on it. If it's an appropriate season, go out and pick some large red or pink clover. With your student compare the clover with Lawson's illustrations. They're wonderfully accurate and detailed! Clover is used to feed animals, to enrich soil, and is a valuable crop to farmers. Clover is actually a legume, or a member of the pea family and is a favorite flower of bees. Purchase some clover honey at the store and share it with your student on some buttered toast!

DOWN DOWN
THE MOUNTAIN

Title:	Down Down The Mountain
Author/Illustrator:	Ellis Credle
Copyright	1934 by Thomas Nelson & Sons, copyright renewed 1961 by Ellis Credle
Summary:	The wisdom of Granny sends Hetty and Hank on an adventure that reveals their industriousness and generosity.

(**Teacher's Note:** This book is currently out of print, as of December 1994. It should still be available in most libraries, either on the shelves or through the Inter-Library Loan System—ILL. If you cannot find a copy, there is an alternate selection to replace this title called *When I Was Young in the Mountains*. These lessons begin on p.153). The decision to use the out-of-print title *Down Down the Mountain* is based on the excellence of story and the warm illustrations. It is too special to leave out.

Social Studies: Geography - Blue Ridge Mountains

According to *The World Book Encyclopedia*, the Blue Ridge Mountains are eastern ranges of the Appalachian Mountain System. The mountains extend from southeastern Pennsylvania across Maryland, Virginia, North Carolina, South Carolina, and northern Georgia. Their name comes from the blue tone that the forested slopes of the mountains display, when seen from a distance. The Blue Ridge Mountains are famous for their beautiful scenery. (Lois Lenski wrote a wonderful children's book called *Blue Ridge Billy* that you might use as a read-aloud or have an older student read for himself.) Place your story disk anywhere on the eastern Appalachian region.

Social Studies: Appalachian Culture

The story *The Rag Coat* by Lauren Mills, was featured in *FIAR* Vol. 1, and your student may remember from it some aspects of Appalachian culture. After reading *Down Down the Mountain* several times, it would be fun to re-read *The Rag Coat*, and compare the various aspects of Appalachian culture found in each book. Your older student could make an Appalachian Culture page for his history notebook. Encourage him to search both books for details of mountain life and list as many of the combined details as he can. He could also add to this page as he discovers more facts about this mountain region in other books or magazines that he reads. (Find *Appalachia, The Voices of Sleeping Birds*, by Cynthia Rylant, copyright 1991, at your library or bookstore. Excellent for this study!!)

As you begin the story, you see a log cabin up the hill from Hetty and Hank. The building is made of logs, and has a stone chimney and fireplace. Thus, this log cabin home is made out of the native, natural resources available. (For your older student, have him compare this method of building with what we have today. Today, there are many synthetic [man-made] materials, as well as native stone, wood, etc., that may go into the building of a home.) When English colonists came to the east coast of North America, they did not know how to build log cabins. They used other types of shelter until they could make the familiar frame houses that were familiar to them in England. The knowledge of log cabin building came with colonists who immigrated from the forests of Germany, Switzerland and Scandinavia. The first log cabins built in America were built by Swedish settlers in Delaware in the early 1600's. Once the knowledge of how to build a house of logs became widespread, it made it easy for many settlers to build homes that were strong and solid using the natural resources plentifully available. (**Teacher's Note:** If you have access to *The World Book Encyclopedia*, there is a wonderful picture showing the different parts of a log cabin under the entry: **Log Cabin**.)

In *Down Down the Mountain,* notice: the foods cooked by Mammy in the cabin, the table made of planks, the butter churn and kettles, the strings of shucky beans, bunches of peppers and ears of popcorn, etc., that hang from the rafters. This is their place to store things. Then, look at Mammy washing clothes by the creek or river (and see where she dries them!) Also, notice the friendliness of the mountain people, the lady that gives directions to Hetty and Hank, and the different jobs such as: driving turkeys to town, cutting sugar cane, and soap-making. Any of these activities could be discussed. Notice, too, that Granny smokes a corn cob pipe. Can your student spot another woman who does, also?

Finally, Hetty and Hank watch the thundering train with round eyes. Ask your student why. (Maybe by living in an isolated home the mountains, they had never seen a train before.) Talk about the factors of isolation. For example, the mountain people have to make many of life's necessities with their own hands. As Pappy says, *"We've everything we need right here in these hills."* They either grow what they need or barter (trade) among themselves. They also have a close community life and rarely mingle with the people from the lowlands. This is because there are differences in the mountain and lowland cultures. For instance, town children all wear shoes, but Hetty and Hank have never even owned a pair of shoes. See how many of the hill people your student can find in the illustrations that do not wear shoes. There are also differences in food, music, education, etc. Their ways of living were different and differences tend to separate people and keep them apart.

Social Studies: Family Relationships

Ask your student if he felt that Pappy is unfair when he tells the children they cannot have shoes. You might discuss that in the culture in which Hetty and Hank live almost no one wore shoes. What the children are asking for is more a *desire* than a *need*. Also, point out the page where it says, *"Pappy laid the bag proudly across the gray horse's back..."*. Discuss the fact that he is extremely proud of Hetty and Hank for working hard for what they wanted and raising such fine turnips. Also, talk about Granny who has the wisdom to know how Hetty and Hank can obtain their heart's desire. Many older people have the kind of wisdom that only comes from life experience. From this story, your student may begin to understand that grandparents and older people help us in many ways.

Language Arts: Vocabulary

cozy snug, comfortable and warm; Even though Hetty and Hank's home is small, it is still comfortable–lovingly warm and cozy.

planks trees roughly cut into boards; The old plank tables were rough and not nicely finished like many tables today.

tilted slanted or inclined because one side is raised higher; The children planted their turnip seeds in a tilted field–a field with a steep slope. For inferred reading comprehension, ask your student why the children's turnip field is tilted and see if he knows it is because they live in the steep mountain hills.

fetch to get or bring; Pappy says the turnips will "fetch" a good price in town. That is they will "receive" a good amount of money for them.

boost to help; Pappy gave the children a boost up on the horse. He helps them get up early in the morning when it is light, but before the sun has risen.

groaning In this story, the word means the table is so full with food (heavy with food) that the table is groaning from the weight. This is a form of per--sonification as if the table is groaning like a person weighted down.

examine look at closely

(judge)ing a person deciding which entry is best in a contest

shucky beans beans you take from their skins, like limas, red beans and pintos; They are strung while still **in** their skins and hung up to dry.

Language Arts: Making a List of Foods

Make a list of all the foods you can find in *Down Down the Mountain*. Would your student like these foods? (You can have a snack of hot cornbread and honey for a surprise treat, as your student makes his list. Your older student may like to make the cornbread. Try using one cup cornmeal, one cup flour, four teaspoons baking powder (**not** soda), one-fourth cup shortening (oil, margarine, butter, etc,), one-fourth cup sugar **or** a little less than one fourth cup of honey, one egg and one cup of milk. Stir the first three ingredients together, and add the rest. Mix **only** until moistened and pour into an 8" x 8" greased square pan. Bake 15-20 minutes at 400 degrees Fahrenheit. A toothpick that pulls out clean means the cornbread is done. Serve with butter and honey.

Language Arts: Alliteration

After reading the story a few times, ask your student if he likes the sound of the names Hetty and Hank. What if they were named Hetty and Ben? The "h" sound which begins both the names H̲etty and H̲ank is poetic alliteration. The same beginning sound in two or more words is called **alliteration**. This is a poetic device that makes words sound interesting to your ears. With your student, try writing some alliterative phrases: A̲llison A̲lexander, S̲amuel S̲mith, h̲aving h̲ardly enough h̲am. Alliteration can be used in writing poems or prose, giving the writing a more poetic sound.

Language Arts: Onomatopoeia

Remember the *"creaky-squeaky"* shoes? Both *"creaky"* and *"squeaky"* imitate the sounds they describe. This literary device is called **onomatopoeia** (pron. owna-mat-uh-pee-uh). *"Creaky"* sounds like something creaking. *"Squeaky"* sounds like something squeaking. Also, the horse goes clippity, cloppity. The words actually remind you of the sound a horse's hooves make. The lady's horse splishes and splashes. There isn't a big lesson here, just the introduction to the knowledge that an author or poet can make use of words that not only describe something but actually *sound like* the thing they are describing! For fun, you might try thinking together of sounds associated with trains, or planes, or crickets, etc.

Language Arts: Poetry and Prose

In *Down Down the Mountain,* Ellis Credle writes a prose story that has within it pieces of poetry. Did your student notice or comment on this poetry? The poems that she writes for this story are rhyming poems. The first piece of poetry is when the children plant their turnip seeds in the tilted field next to Pappy's corn patch. Credle writes: *"Our fields are high up in the air, We wouldn't dare plant pumpkins there, for pumpkins grow so big and round, They'd break right off and tumble down."* This four line stanza is followed by a second four line stanza.

Later, Granny tells them how to find the town. *"Just keep to the road, it will lead you down. Sometimes it's steep--just like the stair. Sometimes it's narrow--like a hair. It turns and twists and winds around, but at the end you'll find the town!"* The author uses the poetry to make an enjoyable break from her prose writing. It may be intriguing for your student to discover that when he writes a story, he may also include bits of poetry to make it more interesting. (The *Frances* books like *Bread and Jam for Frances,* by Russell Hoban, along with *The Merry Adventures of Little Brown Bear* by Elizabeth Upham are some other stories that use verse [in the form of songs] throughout their prose writing.)

Language Arts: Themes

Down Down the Mountain showcases two important themes. A theme is the main idea behind a story. The theme may not be stated explicitly. Often the characters and events portray the theme of a story. For instance, in a book where the words *loving kindness* are never actually mentioned, the characters may demonstrate so much love through their kind acts that it becomes apparent that *loving kindness* is one theme of the story.

In this story by Ellis Credle, the children consistently demonstrate generosity and industrious hard work through their actions. You might begin to explore with your student, the word *generous*. Generous is usually considered *more than fair*. For instance, if your student were to split a candy bar with a friend and he divided it so both halves were even, that would be considered fair. But if the candy bar broke with one end larger than the other, and he gave his friend the larger piece then that is considered generous. Generosity is giving more than someone would expect. The opposite of generous is stingy. That is keeping things for yourself, hoarding or taking the best part. Yet, Hetty and Hank are not stingy. The children meet many people on their way down the mountain. Without thinking that they should save every turnip for their own shoes, they continue to give the vegetables away as they see the needs of others.

Discuss with your student the advantages of living a generous life. Tell him of examples from your own life and ask him to share times when he has done a generous act. Ask him how he felt afterward. Talk about the emotions that Hetty and Hank feel when they discover they have given away all but one turnip. How do they handle these emotions? Are they angry at the people who received the turnips? What do they do? How do they finally get their special creaky-squeaky shoes? The list of things they purchase for their family in addition to their shoes is another example of their generous hearts. Can your student tell from memory the items Hetty and Hank purchase for their family and to whom each item goes? (The yellow hat is for Pappy, the sash is for Mammy and the red handkerchief and the package of needles are for Granny.) Generosity, then, though not directly mentioned, is an underlying theme of *Down Down the Mountain*.

Hetty and Hank exhibit also exhibit great industry when they plant, tend and harvest their turnips, and then go down the mountain to sell them. This is a second theme which underlies the text of the story. As you discuss topics such as generosity and industry revealed in a story, your student will be learning to distinguish story themes whether or not you actually call them *themes*. They will learn to understand the point an author is making with a story. Eventually (when you want to introduce the name of the concept) you can let them know that these ideas are called a story's theme.

Language Arts: Backtracking

As Hetty and Hank go down down the mountain, they pass pink laurel flowers, cross a little stream and go underneath the tall pine trees. Conversely, as they start off from the store where they buy their creaky, squeaky shoes, they go up up the mountain past the pink laurel flowers, along the little stream and underneath the tall pine trees. This re-tracing of their path gives a feeling of reality and completion to the story. They aren't instantly back at their cabin. Rather, they follow home the same path from which they came. Writing in this realistic fashion is logical, comforting and interesting. The repetition is also fun. Just point this out briefly and remind your student that this type of backtracking might be something he would like to keep in mind for his creative writing. Backtracking will give variety, repetition and a feeling of reality to his stories, too. Add this concept to your list of Choices A Writer Can Make.

Language Arts: Drama - Acting out Words

Find the illustrations where Hetty and Hank go into the general store. Look at the picture on the left side page. Can you tell looking at the children's backs that they are excited? As you re-read the paragraphs by this picture, have your student point out the action words (*dashed*, *ran*, *skipped*, *dodged*, *raced*). Read just the action words again and have your student do the actions, each for a short length of time. Include the concept of *being out of breath,* and have him act that out also. It is good exercise and you will quickly know if he understands words like *skip, dodge* and *dash*. Acting out words helps your student remember the meanings.

Art: Perspective

Find the first page of the story. Look at the picture of the log cabin to the left. Using a ruler, measure the lower portion of the path to the cabin, at its widest point. It should be approximately three inches. Now, measure the width of this path at the steps of the cabin. This width should measure approximately one half inch. Your student may be surprised at the difference, but you can help him see that artists use this technique (one element of perspective) to make paths seem to disappear in the distance. In this case it look as if the path goes a distance up to the cabin. Paths are often drawn wider in the foreground of the picture and narrower as they move (sometimes meandering) toward the background, horizon, or between two hills, etc., to give this feeling of distance.

Art: Two-Color Ink

Ellis Credle has used two-color ink printing for her illustrations. This is more color than the black and white work of Robert McCloskey (*Lentil*, *FIAR* Vol. 1) or Robert Lawson (*They Were Strong and Good*, *FIAR* Vol. 2), but not like the full color illustrations of Roger Roth (*The Giraffe That Walked to Paris*, *FIAR* Vol 2). If you have these books available, you might look through them again, noting the differences in the use of color. Your student may already be appreciating the variety of color from full color to monochrome that artists use in story illustrations.

Remind your student that a good illustrator integrates (brings together) the feelings, subject matter and words of the text with the medium, color and design of the drawings or paintings. Does your student think Ellis Credle chose the colors and style of drawing wisely for this story? It seems as if the limited use of color, the rounded figures and warm, friendly drawing style illustrate the expression of the mountain people. Maybe Credle used limited colors because the mountain people are very private. Rather than see them in "full color" we only catch a glimpse, as if we are looking at them through the pine trees. Maybe the illustrator thought the use of a *simple,* two-color style better illustrated the *simple* life of the mountain people. It is enjoyable to see the different ways that illustrators treat the subjects of their stories.

Art: Making Composite Illustrations

Find the description of Hetty and Hank's mountain cabin opposite the picture with the fireplace and kettles, etc. There are many things listed in the description, but not all of them are in the picture. Have your student draw *his* rendition of the cabin and put in as many of the details from both the text and illustration as possible. He might want to include items mentioned in other places of the text, such as Pappy's fiddle (which could be propped in the corner, or perhaps he could include a quilt on a bed, etc.) Also, let him decide whether to use full color or a limited palette for his picture.

Another idea for your older student is to draw a picture from low on the ground, looking up at the things hanging from the rafters. This type of drawing takes a lot of planning and thought, but if the student is interested it can be an enjoyable challenge.

Math: Playing Store - Working with Money

When Hetty and Hank reached the general store they had a five dollar gold piece to spend. Your older student might enjoy the following exercise reminiscent of Hetty and Hank spending their prize money at the store: If the shoes are $1.00 a pair, the yellow hat for Pappy cost 75¢, the bright sash for Mammy costs $1.25, the big red handkerchief for Granny is 25¢, and the needles are 25¢, how much did they spend? And how much did they take home? (Maybe they bought more turnip seeds!!!)

For your young student, play store (appropriate to his skill level) and try using pretend items that could have been in that small town store; crackers, cheese, sacks of grain, a new fiddle, a hoe, etc. Have fun thinking of items that might have been included and what price they might have been. (Remember the poem *General Store* by Rachel Field? [not a FIAR title] It begins: "Someday I'm going to have a store with a tinkly bell hung over the door, with real glass cases and counters wide and drawers all spilly with things inside...." This poem continues by naming the items. It can often be found in older collections of children's poetry. You could also look at your library for a collection of children's poems by Rachel Field. *General Store* is included in *The Golden Book of Poetry*, Edited by Jane Werner, copyright 1949, Golden Press, New York. It is worth the search!

Math: Counting

Try counting the number of people in *Down Down the Mountain*. You can decide whether or not to count people as they appear over again in the story. Or count first, each individual person, and then count every person on every page, even if they have appeared before. Your older student can then subtract the larger figure from the smaller one.

Science: Gardening

Chances are, that this is the time of year for gardening! Your student may already be an experienced gardener or it may be just the right time to introduce him to the wonder of growing things. Even a city apartment can have a patio tomato plant or a string of peas climbing up the balcony. Inside at a sunny windowsill a sweet potato will vine, and scarlet runner beans climb!

Potted plants and vines are fine, but if there is space, a larger garden provides a wealth of learning (by doing) experiences. If your student loves gardening, he will begin to learn the science of gardening. This includes such topics as: weather (and how much water plants need to grow), the soil, types of seeds (hybrids, etc), germinating (sprouting), insects (both beneficial and pests), amount of sunlight necessary, the how and why of weeding, and the actual processes of how a plant grows. Gardening might also have the added advantage of encouraging the development of new food tastes, like tomatoes or even turnips!

Maybe if your student is a second grader or older, he would enjoy *Linnea's Windowsill Garden* by Christina Bjork. This book is available from most libraries. Your young student might appreciate the boy's determination in *The Carrot Seed* by Ruth Krauss. This classic children's story is also available at most libraries.

If at all possible, let your student grow some turnips (usually considered an early spring crop). Or purchase some and try cooking them. They could be prepared like this: Peel two medium turnips, and slice thinly. Place the turnips in a microwave dish with a tablespoon of water and cover with plastic wrap. Cook them on high for 3-4 minutes or until tender. Drain the water, and add a teaspoon of butter or margarine. Lightly salt and pepper the cooked turnips. (You can also cook them on the range top with a little more water in a pan with a lid.) Cool slightly and let your student sample. Some families like a turnip dinner with crisp bacon crumbled on top served with hot cornbread and honey.

Your student may enjoy growing flowers, rather than vegetables. Giant sunflowers are fun. There are even newer varieties that are full sunflower heads on foot-tall plants! And there are many things to learn in flower gardening, as well. Some gardeners mix a few rows of flowers with the rows of vegetables in the garden so that there is something for the eyes as well as for the table!

Science: Botany of the Blue Ridge Mountains

The pink mountain laurel and the tall pine trees are the kind of plants that grow in the cool mountain region of the Blue Ridge Mountains. Find a library book about the Blue Ridge Mountains that has good color pictures of the plants of the region. See if you can find a picture of mountain laurel. Notice the other types of plants, flowers (possibly azaleas, and rhodedendrons) and trees that grow in the region. It is interesting for your student to know that in each region of the country and climatic regions of the world, there are different types of plants and trees. Add to your student's science notebook section with maps showing various growing regions or zones.

Science: Night Birds

Down Down the Mountain mentions the whippoorwills, the owl, and the sounds they make. The whippoorwills begin their calls at dusk and continue into the evening. Whipporwills are interesting birds because they do no perch upright like robins, blue jays, etc. Instead, they sit flat against a tree branch or on the ground.

It is usually after dark that you hear owls, although barred owls are heard in the daytime, also. If owls are an interesting topic for your student, let him explore as far as he desires, using videos, tapes of bird sounds, picture books, etc. He may wish to make sketches of these birds or find magazine pictures and add them to his science notebook. *The Moon's the North Wind's Cooky,* selected by Susan Russo, Wm. Morrow Pub. ISBN 0688418791 is a book with special poems about night sounds and sights. Try it!

MAKE WAY FOR DUCKLINGS

Title:	*Make Way For Ducklings*
Author/Illustrator:	Robert McCloskey
Copyright:	1941
Award:	1942 Caldecott Medal (Remind your student what the Caldecott Medal is—an award given to the most distinguished American picture book for children, published in the preceding year. Let your student know also that a large gold sticker, marked *Caldecott* is evidence of this award. There are also Caldecott Honor books with a silver sticker.)
Category:	Classic (This story is over fifty years old!)
Summary:	Parents need the right place for raising their families, although these duck parents have to negotiate a busy city to care for their young.

Social Studies: Geography - Boston, Massachusetts

Boston is a multi-harbor city in Massachusetts, which is part of the New England region. Find Massachusetts on your map and place the story disk there. Some areas of Boston still look very much like Robert McCloskey's pictures in *Make Way For Ducklings*. You could still visit Beacon Hill (north of Boston Common) and Louisburg Square. The Charles River is an actual river and Mt. Vernon Street and Beacon Street are real streets. But, today you would also see tall modern buildings. There is more than one public park in the city of Boston, but west of Boston Common lies the formal Public Garden where people can still ride in swan shaped boats during the summer months. If you can visit the Boston Public Garden, you will also see an amazing sculpture of Mrs. Mallard and her ducklings! (**Note for the Teacher:** In the text of *The World Book Encyclopedia*, see **Boston.** This article is fascinating, and can yield a multitude of history research topics for your older student.)

Also, with your student, enjoy the wonderful aerial views of Boston created by Mr. McCloskey. The illustrator has drawn his aerial scenes to represent the mallard's point of view.

Social Studies: Family Relationships

Mrs. Mallard is choosy about a place to nest because she has an instinctive desire to protect her babies. Mother cats and dogs try to find a private, quiet, warm place to have their litters. People do not rely so much on instinct, but on learned behavior. People have the ability to reason and to make choices. Most parents want the safest possible environment for their children. They work hard to provide for them, protect them, and teach them.

You may want to continue exploring the topic of family relations with conversations about how a mother and father prepare a room for their baby. What kinds of things would they like to have ready? (diapers, crib, clothes, blankets, etc.). Does your student have any younger brothers or sisters? Can he remember the preparations his parents made for the new baby and its arrival?

Social Studies: Relationships Between Man and Nature

Compare and contrast the boy on the speeding bicycle and his lack of concern for the ducks with the protective concern of the policemen who work together to stop traffic for the Mallard babies. Ask your student if he has seen examples of both types of behavior. Talk about organizations that work to protect wildlife such as the Conservation Commission, etc.

Social Studies: History - Finding Clues to the Past

Most students enjoy hunting for clues. Have your student look for clues in this story to life in days past. For instance, in searching the illustrations he might find an unusual looking baby carriage, different from today's modern strollers. He might notice a tricycle (most recently replaced by Big Wheels®), or an old-fashioned looking bicycle. The cars do not look like the cars of today, nor do many of the clothes. (ladies' hats, shoes, etc.) Do these various objects look "funny" to your student now? Does he think today's styles, fashions, automobiles, bicycles, etc., will look "funny" to others fifty years from now? Why? Why not? Maybe your student can begin to understand the concept that today's objects will always look familiar to him, since he grew up with them. Perhaps he will even understand how things that seem old-fashioned to him seem so natural to grand-parents or great-grand-parents, since they grew up with those "old-fashioned" objects.

Social Studies: Map-Making

Help your student draw a map of the route the ducklings take to the park. Re-read the story for details to include on your map. (For extra help look in *The World Book Encyclopedia* under **Boston.** You will find an excellent map called "Downtown Boston." On it, your student can trace the path of Mrs. Mallard and her brood from the Charles River, up Mount Vernon Street to the corner of Beacon Street and on to the Public Garden.)

If your student enjoys drawing, have him draw a map of his house and neighborhood. Be sure he includes the route to the grocery store, the library, the fire station, etc. Have him practice the concepts of left and right as he thinks about corners, turning toward the park, etc. Move small toy cars and trucks around your map as you discuss the directions: north, south, east and west. Put a map legend in the corner to show which direction north is on your map. (North is generally at the top of a map, but many maps are tilted or turned so that you need to designate (or read) each map's legend for clarity.)

Social Studies: Being Appreciative

What a great picture of the policemen waving goodbye to Mrs. Mallard and the ducklings! All eight of the ducklings happily and greatfully quack "Thank you" back to the men! Ask your student if he has had the privilege of helping someone recently. Ask him if it felt good to help, even if it was difficult. Also, ask him if he has been helped by some adult, a teacher, policeman, fireman, medic, or older friend. Did he give his "Thank you" as happily and gratefully as the young ducks do? Gratitude is an important concept to teach children. We want students to understand that thankfulness is an essential heart-attitude. It is something that is always worth expressing to others.

Social Studies: Relationships - Not Too Quick to Take Offense

Mr. Mallard quacks "Good morning" to the enormous, strange bird. He decides the bird is too proud to answer. After several readings, ask your student why the bird does not reply. This scene is meant to become humorous when the reader realizes that the bird is not too proud. It isn't even alive. The bird is a part of the wooden boat!

Many times things are not what they seem at first. This is especially true when a person faces a new situation or unfamiliar territory. The person needs to be patient and find the truth. It is helpful to wait, watch, observe, and ask questions, rather than be quick to take offense. In this case Mr. Mallard thinks he has been snubbed or ignored, when actually he has not. If Mr. Mallard had carefully observed for a time, he might have reached a different conclusion. Teach your student to have patience, be gracious and observant. Also remind him to extend mercy to others. These are important lessons at any age.

Language Arts: Vocabulary

Boston	the capital of Massachusetts
cozy	snug, comfortable, warm
molt	as it applies to this story; a period of time when a duck loses his older feathers and grows new ones; Until the new ones grow back in, the duck cannot fly.
incubate	to warm the egg until it hatches, whether by mother duck or by an incubator machine; (This word is not in the text of the story, but it is used in the explanation of the life cycle of a duck.)

Language Arts: Rhyme

What makes a rhyme? Two words with similar ending sounds such as *cat* and *mat* are said to rhyme. A poem rhymes when the words that end the lines have similar sounds: The black *cat*, upon the rug *sat*, But the sleepy *dog*, was in a *fog*. Ask your student if he knows what part of the story *Make Way for Ducklings* has rhyming words? (The names of the ducklings, Jack, Kack, Lack, Mack, Nack, Ouack [pron. wack], Pack and Quack.)

With your young student, make rhymes whenever you have extra minutes. Rhyme words with cat, rag, dig, sing, long, fine, etc. You may even find a made-up word or two! Your older student can work on short poems that rhyme. Give him a subject to begin with: *A lively old man* or *a slow poke dog*, etc. Ask him to recall some of his favorite poems that have strong rhyme. Encourage him to look for others. As he can tell from *Make Way For Ducklings,* authors can use poetic elements in their stories, and your student can decide to use elements like rhyme in his stories as well. Add rhyme to the list you are keeping called Choices Writers Can Make. Rhyme is also listed in the Literary Glossary in the Appendix.

Art: Caldecott Medal

It was pointed out in the introduction that Robert McCloskey won the 1942 Caldecott Medal for his 1941 book *Make Way For Ducklings.* This is an award given for the best illustrated children's book published in the preceding year. In his acceptance speech for this award, McCloskey said, *"When we first heard about this Medal, Mrs. Mallard said she should be allowed to wear it around her neck because she raised the ducklings, and Mr. Mallard thought he should wear it because he was the head of the family, and Jack, Kack, Lack, Mack, Nack, Ouack, Pack and Quack all thought that they should take turns wearing it. But we finally compromised and pasted it on the book jacket, and we all are very pleased, and we all thank the A L A.* [American Library Association] *very much."* McCloskey's acceptance speech quotes from *Caldecott Medal Books:* 1938-1957, edited by Bertha Mahony Miller and Elinor Whitney Field, Horn Book Papers, Vol. 2, page 84.

Art: Medium

McCloskey made lithographic drawings on zinc plates for this story. The subtle shades of brown ink were well chosen. They create a soft, warm, monochromatic effect that is in keeping with the text of the ducks' nurturing family life. Your student may want to try a simple sketch with a brown pencil. Suggest that he draw from a model of something real, such as an apple on a plate, or a set of blocks or books. Again, remind him to try to draw what he *actually* sees, line for line. He will need to draw slowly and watch how each line connect with the others. As he practices in this way, he will become more satisfied with his finished products.

After several readings, ask your student if he minds the lack of bright color in McCloskey's illustrations. As he has seen before in *Lentil, FIAR* Vol. 1, illustrations of one color must have a great deal of personality and life in them to be interesting. Ask your student if he feels the pictures in *Make Way For Ducklings* are interesting. What about the picture of the swan boat and all the different people on it? Look at the boy who nearly runs over Mr. and Mrs. Mallard with his bike—not to mention the look on the faces of the ducks! And don't forget the expression of Michael the policeman as he rushes to help the ducklings. Mr. McCloskey may use only one color for these illustrations, but his variety of figures, expressions and use of action scenes keeps the reader watching each page.

Look, too, at the front cover picture. Notice the turn of Mrs. Mallard's head, and the variety of eight ducklings, each in a different pose, especially the one about to step off the curb! Bravo, Mr. McCloskey!!

Art: Speed Lines

Ask your student if he remembers the discussion and examples of lines that give the illusion of speed in the story *Papa Picollo, FIAR* Vol. 1, p.80. These lines show the kittens moving so fast they are a long blurred line. In *Make Way for Ducklings*, the scene with the large picture of the boy on his bicycle shows his hair and tie streaming back, due to the forward motion of the bike. There are also lines behind the boy's figure that give an indication of movement and speed. The lines around Mr. Mallard give the impression that he falls back hard. There are also tiny lines by the bike's tires that show it hitting a puddle or throwing up dirt because of its speed. As you look through the illustrations, you will see speed lines by the cars as they appear to move by quickly.

If your student would like, have him draw something in motion: a spinning top (remember to blur the pattern or colors), an animal or a machine. Encourage him to try adding lines to show speed. These lines are subtle in form and color. They just give the *impression* of movement. Sometimes photographers use a fast shutter speed to "stop the action" when they are taking action pictures. But, other times they do not and the resulting picture is blurred with the motion of the subject. Look for examples of these blurred "action" pictures in magazines and talk about the photographic effects of action shots. Compare these effects to the drawn and painted artwork of the illustrators that you study. Place some of these magazine pictures in the art section of your student's notebook.

Art: Lines Indicating Water

Does your student remember the lesson of *Ping, FIAR* Vol.1, p.14, about drawing water? Have him look for lines in the illustrations of Make Way For Ducklings that give the indication of water. There are the broken circular lines around the island, the squiggly trailing water lines behind the ducks as they swim, water lines around the base of rocks, and wavy reflections and shadows on the water. In each picture where there is water, ask your student what the artist did to give the impression of water, rather than land. Your student is welcome to compose a picture and try any or all of these techniques. Remind him that practicing is fine—it's what artists do! Each picture does not have to be finished or be hung in his home. It is also good to make many sketches as he experiments with the various techniques. He may be ready for his own sketch book, a more private place to "try" his ideas.

Art: Shading

Make Way For Ducklings has illustrations that make great use of shading. Shading is an artistic element that provides contrast. It shows the source of light, while it provides depth and roundness.

The policeman, Michael, *"planted himself in the center of the road and raised one hand to stop the traffic."* In this picture, have your student notice the light areas of

Michael's body and the darker areas of ink. See how dark the ink is on the upper right shoulder (as you face him)? This makes the line of Michael's neck more definite and makes it stand out so you can see it. The dark area where his coat and pants meet shows the shadow cast by the coat. The dark line at the top of the pants causes the coat to stand out and be more visible. Notice the difference between his dark shoes and the lighter pants cuffs. There is also an example of the use of shading for rounding effect along the sleeves and on the front of the coat. The cars opposite Michael have shading that makes the fenders rounded looking.

Learning about light and dark values helps one understand how to *do* shading. See the work sheet on Values and Shading (an activity for your older student) in the Appendix. After he has completed the worksheet, then have him try drawing a simple object—an egg or an apple, or a ball. Shade under the object as well as experiment with some shading for roundness. Have your student look at the shading in McCloskey's work and see what areas on his own work could use more shading.

Art: Research and Preparation

Robert McCloskey, in his acceptance speech for the Caldecott Medal said, *"When I started making the final sketches for this book, I found that in spite of my various observations of mallard duck anatomy (the body structure) and habits, I really knew very little about them."* He then explains going to a natural history museum and studying stuffed mallards, as well as visiting a museum library and discovering valuable information on the molting and mating habits of mallards. But, he said he still needed models. At a city market he purchased two pair of mallard ducks and took them to his studio home. Amid their quacking and squawking, he followed the ducks around making sketches of them in every different pose. He even sketched the ducks as they played in the bathtub. In his own words, *"All this sounds like a three-ring circus, but it shows that no effort is too great to find out as much as possible about the things you are drawing. It's a good feeling to be able to put down a line and know that it is right."* (The acceptance speech quotes from *Caldecott Medal Books* 1938-1957, edited by Bertha Mahony Miller and Elinor Whitney Field. Horn Book Papers, Volume 2, p. 82-84.)

Discuss with your student Mr. McCloskey's comments. Talk about the importance of preparation for any task we undertake. Even an accomplished artist like Robert McCloskey spent hundreds of hours preparing to draw his subject. Whatever we set out to do in life, whether it's drawing or anything else, patient, disciplined preparation is important. Share a personal story with your student about a time of preparation in your own life. Encourage him to talk about his own goals. Discuss what preparations might be necessary to accomplish those goals.

Math: Multiplication or Grouping

If Mr. Mallard had to find two snails for each of her babies, how many would she have to find? She has eight ducklings, so your older student could set up his multiplication problem to solve two times eight. He could continue with an infinite variety of problems from the eight tables. If Mrs. Mallard found six peanuts for each of her babies, how many peanuts would she have? Or five bugs, etc.

Your young student can work the same problems, by using *grouping*, rather than multiplication. Cut eight yellow ducklings out of construction paper. Lay them across a table. Use pennies for the snails and ask your student, "If Mrs. Mallard wants to feed her babies two snails each, how many snails would she need to find?" Your student would then place two pennies beside each duckling cut-out. When he is finished, have him count the pennies. Then he can answer the question. (Mrs. Mallard would need sixteen snails.) You can then use real peanuts (or beans to represent the peanuts) and have him figure how many Mrs. Mallard would need if she wants to feed her babies six peanuts each, etc. Continue your grouping problems in this way. As a pre-multiplication lesson you do not need to use the word *times*. But, after your student has counted the grouping, remind him that eight *groups* of two equals sixteen, or eight groups of six equals forty-eight, etc.

Math: Counting Practice

Count the total number of automobiles in this story. This is fun because your student must look through all the pictures hunting for them and keeping track of the count.

For more advanced counting practice, have your student count the windows in the Beacon Hill/State House aerial view, double picture. (There are, also, tiny cars in this picture! Have your student check the other aerial views for small cars he may have missed.)

Math: Converting Days to Weeks

Duck eggs, depending on the variety of duck, hatch in twenty-one to thirty days. Have your older student figure the number of weeks that is. When converting from a smaller unit (days) to a larger unit (weeks), the problem needs division. The number of days in one week is seven, so that number is used as the divisor. Either twenty-one or thirty days is the dividend. The quotient is either three (weeks) or four with a remainder of two (four weeks and twodays).

For your younger student, use blocks or beans for the counting items. Arrange twenty-one beans in groups of seven. Count the number of groups which represent the number of weeks.

Science: Animal Parenting

Some animals have parenting responsibilities after their young are born and some do not. Owls, bear, deer, birds of many types, dogs, cats, etc., care for their young, sheltering, protecting them, providing food, and teaching them skills for survival. Make a list or chart of animals that care for their young and the different ways they do this. An opossum has a different kind of responsibility than a moose, for example. Animals such as snakes, turtles, lizards, some types of fish, etc., do *not* care for their young once they are hatched or born. You might have your older student research some of these types of animals and explain how their young mature.

The ducks in this story search for a safe place for their nest. They care for their young ducklings, and teach them the skills they need to survive and grow.

Science: Development of a Duck Egg

Duck eggs, like the eggs of other birds, are fertilized in the oviduct. This produces an embryo which develops through many cell divisions before the egg is laid. Once the egg is laid, it must be kept at a constant temperature of approximately one hundred degrees Fahrenheit until it hatches. Duck eggs take between twenty-one and thirty days to hatch. They can be held in commercial incubators, or in a nest beneath the hen. Some domestic chickens may lay eggs year-round. However, wild birds (like ducks) normally lay their eggs in the spring months. Your older student may want you to help him research why this is so. The discussion of egg development and embryos may lead to questions about human embryos and the development of human babies during pregnancy, etc. Be prepared to deal with these types of questions beforehand and you'll feel much more comfortable when the time comes to talk.

Science: Conservation

The concern shown by people for the ducks in *Make Way For Ducklings* may be used as a springboard for discussions of conservation, environmentalism and good stewardship. Information about these topics can be found in encyclopedias, libraries, and from your state conservation department. In fact, writing to your state conservation department may yield a wealth of informational posters, pamphlets, etc., that could come addressed to your student. Protecting our environment, wildlife, wildlife habitat and natural resources is an important responsibility. Explore these topics with students of all ages. Be sure to include field trips and hands-on activities. Children love nature and most will jump at the chance to learn more about any of these related topics.

A great companion book for *Make Way for Ducklings* is *The Secret Place* by Eve Bunting, 1996, Clarion Books, New York, ISBN 0-395643-6708. A young boy finds a place rich with wildlife in the midst of a busy city. The book will appeal to young naturalists and conservationists alike. They'll enjoy the wonderful colorful illustrations of Ted Rand and appreciate the idea that some special places might best be kept secret. Too good to miss!

THE TALE OF
PETER RABBIT

Title: *The Tale of Peter Rabbit*
Author/Illustrator: Beatrix Potter
Copyright: 1902
Category: Classic
Summary: Disobedience leads to some harrowing adventures for Peter Rabbit.

(**Teacher's Note:** You might consider trying the Social Studies lesson on *Relationship and Trust*, as well as the lesson on *Setting Rules* at the end of the week after your student has had time to think for *himself* about the consequences of disobedience and the benefits of mutual trust. It will be even better if your student actually brings up parts of these lessons himself during the reading or discussions.)

Social Studies - Relationships Based on Trust

In Peter Rabbit's family, his mother is raising four bunnies by herself. What happened to Peter's father? Ask your student if he thinks this should have been a good warning to Peter? Ask him what kind of relationship he thinks Peter has with his mother? If a good relationship is built on mutual trust and concern for each other, what seems to be missing in this story?

Social Studies - Setting Rules

Ask your student why the story says Flopsy, Mopsy and Cottontail are good little bunnies. How was Peter different? (While his mother is purchasing good food for her children, Peter runs straight away to the place he was asked *not* to go.) Contrast the picture on p.16 and on p.19. Hold the book so that your student can see both pictures at once. These illustrations faithfully follow the story. While Peter is supposed to be with his siblings, he is instead off by himself in a place where he should not be.

Ask your student why Mrs. Rabbit does not want her bunnies to go to Mr. McGregor's garden. Does your student think she was a wise mother? Ask your student to name some rules he is to follow.

Recall any special or difficult rules you had to follow when you were a child, and tell your student of your experiences. Acknowledge the difficulty and temptations these rules may have created. Also, talk about the consequences, as well as the feelings of conscience, you may have experienced. Use this opportunity to discuss a list of rules your student may have. Talk about the rationale behind those rules; the reasons why Mother or Father have made the rules. Discuss the consequences when those rules are not followed and what the dangers are.

Social Studies - Relationships - Encouragement

There is a right word at the right time. Peter has given himself up for lost and is sobbing when he is *"...overheard by some sparrows who flew to him in great excitement and implored him to exert himself."* Peter gives one last effort and escapes just in time. Can you think of a time when someone has just about given up? A well-placed word can make the difference. Knowing that someone cares can often give extra energy for effort. Can your student think of a time when someone greatly encouraged him at a crucial (difficult) moment? Do you have a story to share with him? Encouraging one another is very important. Words of encouragement can often bring *life*!

Social Studies: Geography - Setting

Beatrix Potter was born and raised in England and wrote of the country life there. The setting for *The Tale of Peter Rabbit* is the English countryside, a country field and a cottage garden. Certain details are typical of England, including the neatly trimmed English hedges around the garden areas and the misty, cloudy look in many of the pictures. Peter Rabbit's home looks simple and country-like, not modern or elegant as a city home might be.

Look at the shoe on p.28. It doesn't look much like an American sneaker does it?. Also, the robin in the same picture is an English robin. It is smaller and shaped differently than our North American bird. These English robins (as well as hedgehogs) in text and illustrations will tip you off to an English author in many story books like *The Secret Garden* by Frances Hodgson Burnett, etc.

Place the story disk on England, a group of islands on the west coast of Europe.

Language Arts: Onomatopoeia

Whether or not you think it important for your student to learn this word, it is still fun for them to know that words can sound like the thing they are describing. Page 49 has "the noise of a hoe—*scr-r-ritch, scratch, scratch, scritch.*" You can "hear" the hoe with these words. If the author had said, *"Mr. McGregor was hoeing in the garden,"* the words would not be onomatopoetic. Then you would lose some of the interest gained by words that sound like what they describe. Think, together, of other onomatopoetic words. (Splishing and splashing of raindrops, humming of the sewing machine, slam-banging of the door, etc.) Your student can see that the use of these kind of sound describing words in his writing will make his work more interesting and noisy!! Like the other literary devices they should not be overused. Have him include onomatopoeia in his list of Choices A Writer Can Make.

Language Arts: Descriptive Language

The passage on p. 46 is well written in descriptive language. This passage reads: "*A white cat was staring at some gold-fish, she sat very, very still, but now and then the tip of her tail twitched as if it were alive.*" Has your student ever observed a cat showing this kind of behavior? Those that are well-acquainted with cats will quickly recognize this description. Your older student may want to imitate this type of passage using a subject which he has observed in detail. Your younger student may choose something that is alive to observe for a period of time. He will notice things about his subject that he did not already know. If he would like, he can then dictate a descriptive passage to you.

Language Arts: Animal Fantasy Story

The Tale of Peter Rabbit begins *"Once upon a time"*. This is a typical imaginary tale beginning. It contains such elements as talking animals who are acting like people and dressed as people would dress. The picture on p. 8 shows natural looking woods and fields with cotton-tail rabbits. But, when you turn the page the imaginary animal tale begins and the rabbits are dressed and talking. Does your student think rabbits really talk and dress and walk about? That's what an imaginary story is all about. It's a fun, fantasy story in which we learn *life lessons* through imaginative stories, often including an entire make-believe world of creatures and customs.

Language Arts: Vocabulary

implored	begged
exert	to try hard; put forth effort
sieve	a device to sift and separate large particles from small; The sieve is probably used by Mr. McGregor to sift a light layer of compost over his seeds. This makes it easier for them to sprout.

Language Arts: Noticing the Details (Text and Illustrations)

With your student, make a list of the things that happened to Peter. Pay close attention to the illustrations, the expressions, etc. and use the illustrations as well as the text. For instance:

p.22-23	(look at Peter's expression) He eats too much and feels sick.
p.26-27	(look at Peter's expression) He is chased by Mr. McGregor.
p.28-29	He is most dreadfully frightened, and he loses his shoes.
p.30-31	He gets caught in gooseberry net.
p.32-33	He gives himself up for lost, and sobs big tears.
p.34-35	He is nearly trapped under a sieve and loses his new coat.
p.36-39	He has to hide in a watering can and becomes cold.
p.40-43	He is almost stepped on! He is frightened and lost. (Peter's expression on p.43 is different from the one on p.19).
p.44-45	He can't get out the door and cries again.

| p.46-47 | He becomes more and more puzzled. |
| p.56-57 | Peter is sick and has to drink camomile tea. He misses the bread, milk and blackberries that everyone else has for dinner. |

Last of all, look at the picture to the left of the title page. Does it look like Peter enjoyed his outing to the forbidden garden?

Art: Naturalist

A nature lover, or naturalist, is a person who loves and studies nature. He may appreciate all the aspects of creation, including trees, plants, animals, insects, rocks, shells, stars, etc. Beatrix Potter, the author of this story, loved animals and the nature around her in the English countryside. She learned to observe (wait patiently and watch) the animals and the plants, the weather and the people that were around her. Then, she accurately captured their likeness on paper with drawing pencils and later watercolors. She included many natural details. Notice the moss on the rock, and the holly at the gate of p.19.

Beatrix Potter actually owned rabbits, a hedgehog*, birds, sheep, cats, dogs and many other types of animals that appear in her stories. By caring for them and watching and sketching them many times, she became knowledgeable of their characteristic movements and habits, as well as their physical form. In her stories, both animals and plants are painted in naturalistic style. That is they are drawn with correct details. The rabbits are even drawn with some of the correct mannerisms. (Beatrix Potter does personify the rabbits with some clothing and movements, but their bodies are drawn accurately as they appear in nature. They do not look like a rabbit cartoon or a rabbit caricature.)

(*Hedgehogs live *naturally* in England, not in the United States–although, pet stores in the United States are beginning to import, raise and sell these animals as pets.) Have your student watct for stories with hedgehogs, like *The Tale of Mrs. Tiggywinkle*. He will find that often these animals appear in stories written by English authors.)

Your student might like to know that one of the farms where Beatrix Potter lived in England has been made into a museum. Many of her original watercolor paintings for the Peter Rabbit Books are there for public viewing.

(**Teacher's Note:** If possible, locate a copy of *Country Artist, the Life of Beatrix Potter,* by David Collins. This is a quick sketch of her life. You will learn facts to share with your student and enjoy a glimpse into the life of this famous lady. You might even find it appropriate to read all or part of this book aloud. If you want to know more, there are other excellent detailed biographies with many pencil sketches of her famous animals. (One such biography is *Beatrix Potter, Artist, Storyteller and Countrywoman* by Judy Taylor. This includes many of Beatrix's sketches, and colored journal pictures from the early age of nine). Sometimes it is amazing to students that an artist can spend so much time in making many sketches before deciding on one to use in a story! (If the subject of pre-sketches for a book fascinates your student, another good reference is *The Pooh Sketchbook,* by E. H. Shephard, edited by Brian Sibley. This book contains the preliminary sketches for the *Winnie the Pooh* stories set alongside the actual finished illustrations.)

Art: Medium - Watercolor

The paintings in *The Tale of Peter Rabbit* are a gentle rendition of woodland and garden life, showing a typical day in the English countryside. How does the artist achieve this gentle quality? (The characters are drawn in rounded figures and the artist uses soft, subtle colors.) Find the page where your student thinks the artist uses the strongest color (perhaps p.15 where Mrs. Rabbit's shawl is dark. Or maybe p.11 with the bunnies little red capes.)

Set against the soft colors of the illustrations is the intense text of the escape of Peter from the garden. It is as if he alone is out of sync with his surroundings. Maybe your student can think of a reason why. (Perhaps because he is not where he is supposed to be or doing what should be doing.)

Art: Details - Movement

Page 23 shows Peter at the edge of the cold frame (a covered place where young seedlings are put while it is still too cool at night to plant them out). When you turn the page, he has walked along the front of the frame and reached the corner at the other end.

It is interesting to see the movement conveyed by showing part of the structure in one picture and the other part in another. An ambitious art student might like to try this idea. Your student can show the back half of a car, wagon, or bicycle along with a person or animal in one picture. In the next picture he can draw the front portion of the vehicle. The person or animal is now drawn ahead of this vehicle. When viewed after the first picture, a forward movement of the character is perceived, while the background remains fixed. A similar senario might be a picture with a person or an animal walking toward the woods. The second picture could show the person or animal actually in the woods, etc. The idea is to make two or more pictures which give the appearance of forward movement to the characters or animals.

Art: Drama - Acting Out the Story

Your student may be a budding thespian (actor), or he may be extremely shy, so choose this lesson with care, remembering it is supposed to be a lot of fun.
Suggest that your student act out a part of the story. He may have a particular part in mind and already "see" the performance in his imagination. Let him loose and enjoy!! For another student it may be helpful to suggest a part and maybe to play along with him. For instance, place a board or pillows across two chairs to create a hole or space underneath.

Have your student act out the scenario on pp. 49 and 50: Pretending to be Peter, your student, could act out being startled by the extremely close scritch-scritch, scratch of the hoe (show by facial expression), and scoot beneath some nearby furniture, then come tentatively back out and climb up on a chair (to replicate the wheelbarrow) and peep over the back. All of a sudden the gate is spied (which is the hole you made with the pillows or board over chairs) and Peter makes a run for it, safely slipping through the hole and running home.

Math: Figuring and Grouping

Mr. McGregor was planting a garden. In order to plant a garden and actually harvest produce (crops), one has to know math. Each type of seed and plant has a certain number of what is called "days to maturity." That means the number of days it takes from the planting of the seed to harvesting the first of the peas, beans, etc. In places with a cold winter, if you plant the seeds too late the winter will kill the plants before you can harvest from them. (You don't want to plant them too soon either.) So you have to be able to read the seed packet and calculate the number of days to maturity and decide when your planting date will be. Some peas have a maturity date of 54 days, some beans 60 days, one kind of corn 78 days, etc.

If there is interest, use these dates or find a good seed catalog and design a *possible* garden. If there is a "last date for killing frost" in your area, make sure you plan your garden calendar to plant after that. Then figure when you'd plant each crop (maybe use pictures from the seed catalog or draw the different kinds of plants) and when each would be ready to pick.

Also, for your older student, you could make division math problems from seed packets or their information. For example: If a corn seed takes 78 days to produce an ear of corn, how many weeks is that? (Remember that if you are converting from days to weeks, you are going from a smaller unit to a larger unit and that takes division. Also the "special converting number" is 7 since there are seven days in one week. So you set up your problem with 7 as the divisor and 78 days as the dividend, and let them find the quotient which will be expressed in weeks (eleven) with–in this case–a seventh of a week or one day left over as a remainder. Eleven weeks is a long time and corn in the midwest isn't usually planted till the ground warms up so we see corn harvest in late July or early August. Is it the same where your student lives? (Younger students can count an item such as pennies or dried beans up to fifty-five or sixty, or higher. Then group these amounts into groups of seven and thus find out how many weeks the different plants take to reach harvest)

More math: Flopsy, Mopsy and Cottontail picked blackberries. If there were 30 blackberries in the basket, how many could each one have if they wanted to share equally? If there were 60? If there were 90?, etc.

Personal computer users might be interested in a software product produced by Mindscape. *Peter Rabbit's Math Garden* is designed for ages 4-8 and drills children with math facts hidden under flower pots and other scenarios from the story. A wonderful way to marry math with a great story! *Peter Rabbit's Math Garden is* available for bothWindows and Mac systems. Mindscape also offers a delightful comapnion disk entitled *The Adeventures of Peter Rabbit & Benjamin Bunny*. Filled with fun activities and beautiful art taken from Beatrix Potter's classic books, this program is an absolute delight for chilren from four up.

Math: Fortnight- a Measurement of Days

A fortnight is 14 days, or two weeks. It is a measurement that is somewhat archaic (not often used, gone out of fashion), but necessary to know because it appears in so many pieces of literature.

Math: Graphing

0	10	20	30	40	50	60	70	80	90	100
Radishes
Beans
Corn
Tomatoes

For your second– fourth grade student, this is a wonderful opportunity to do simple graphing, to show the number of days to maturity for the various vegetable crops. Use a seed catalog to graph other vegetables. For example: Radishes- 25 days, Beans- 55 days, Corn- 80 days and Tomatoes- 95 days in the graph below.

Science: Gardening - Details in Text and Illustrations

Make a list of Mr. McGregor's garden. What did Mr. McGregor grow? Listen to the story and look carefully at the pictures for clues. You may find in the illustrations:

cress (watercress) (at the fish pond)
waterlilies   (at the fish pond)
nasturtiums (behind Peter on p. 43, note the rounded leaves and orange flowers)
geraniums   (when Mr. McGregor nearly stepped on Peter, p. 40)
gooseberries (where he loses his coat)

(The following list is included in the text about Mr. McGregor's garden:)

blackberries, black currants, radishes, potatoes, onions, lettuce, french beans peas, cabbage

Ask your student if this is everything that Mr. McGregor grows? (First of all, your student may find some things omitted in this list. Since this is all that is listed in the text, and we have searched the illustrations, this is all we know that Mr. McGregor grows.)

Science: Gardening - Planning the Garden

Mr. McGregor plans out his garden with all the crops we listed in the previous lesson from the blackberries through the cabbage. Now, have your student plan a garden of his own. This can be a pure fantasy lesson where your student can design and color the "garden of his dreams." This may or may not include spinach, you understand, or tomatoes, etc.! It could even include imaginary foods of unknown origin.

If there is interest in a serious garden, good seed catalogs (free by mail) and library books can provide the information necessary to plan a good garden. Just by planning a garden your student may learn about such topics as companion gardening (planting marigolds next to tomatoes for insect control, etc.), which insects are pests and which are helpers, new lessons about weather conditions, etc. Also, consider when planning the garden site the number of hours of sunlight your crops will get. Plan to have the taller plants behind, so the lower plants get plenty of sun. Or plan that smaller plants that need more shade will be planted behind taller, sun loving plants. Your student will learn many lessons as he considers the various apects of planning a garden. This should be an enjoyable exercise for those students that wish to explore a topic to its limits.

You may want to help your student put his ideas into practice in an actual garden. Or, you may wish only to let him sprout some seeds to get an idea of the different germination times, how a plant grows and how each kind of plant is different. You can easily sprout nasturtium* seeds in a pot in the window and let your student compare the leaves and blossoms to the nasturtiums in Beatrix Potter's art work. [*As long as you have not used insecticide on them, nasturtium blooms (Tropaeolum minus and T. majus) are edible (you don't *have* to eat them, but they are safe for decoration) Use the blossoms to decorate for a surprise lunch. Make a "Mr. McGregor garden sandwich!"]

Science: Emotions - Fear

Remember *FIAR* Vol. 1, *Storm in the Night* and *Very Last First Time,* when we talked about being afraid, and how it can make you forget things you actually know? In *The Tale of Peter Rabbit*, Peter becomes so frightened he forgets his way back to the gate. (Peter's fear, in this case, is a direct result of disobedience, but he still needs to do some CRISIS THINKING! He needs to calm down, not panic, be quiet, and think carefully about how he is to get out of the garden.)

Science: Gathering Wild Food

In *The Tale of Peter Rabbit*, Peter's siblings gather blackberries from the woods. Sometimes people do find fruits, nuts, mushrooms, etc., in the wild, but BE CAREFUL!!! There are many things that look good to eat that are poisonous. Even adults who regularly gather wild food are *very* careful. Remind your student to never put anything from the outdoors in his mouth unless his parent or teacher says it is safe. Remember, this story is a fairy tale. In addition, here are a few botanical details from the story: Blackberries have thorns. See them painted on the branches on p.16? Camomile is a very small daisy-like herb used for a calming effect. Parsley is a pungent herb used to sweeten breath and upset stomachs, but more popularly to garnish food.

Science: Natural Enemies

In this story, the cat and Mr. McGregor are the enemies of rabbits, including Peter. The cat is a natural enemy of rabbits, mice, birds, etc. If you have a young nature lover, he may be interested in finding the natural enemies of bears, foxes, deer, raccoon, etc.

Science: Introducing New Species

On p.54 you'll find starlings, a *native* bird of England. Native species are those that have always lived in a certain place. We also have starlings in North America, but this was not always so. Starlings, like those pictured in this story, were released in New York's Central Park after they were brought to this country from England in 1890. Starlings have grown to more than a quarter billion population in less than a hundred years and each year cause massive crop loss because of the enormous quantity of grain they eat. They also spread a disease called histoplasmosis in areas where they roost densely in trees near people.

When we move species from their native habitat to a new location, we often cause problems. Other problems include the Gypsy Moth, accidentally released in this country in 1869, the Canada Thistle (a plant), as well as Zebra Muscle (an animal), which came to this country accidentally when it "hitched a ride" in the ballast of ships from Europe to the Great Lakes. Each of these relocated species has caused much destruction because it often flourishes due to lack of natural enemies in its new habitat. For the budding environmentalist, this kind of information can be the springboard to a whole new area of study. For your own study, look for good pictures of starlings in a bird book. Also, point out a starling to your student when you happen to see one outdoors.

Science: Health - Catching Cold

When Peter chooses to jump in the watering can to hide, he gets wet, begins to shiver with cold and starts to sneeze. Ask your student why it is that when we get damp and then cool, we often catch cold? One reason is that the wet *causes* us to become cooler. The lowering of our body temperature makes us more susceptible to germs and viruses that are always present. These germs and viruses are present but not harmful unless we're vulnerable (weakened) by being colder than is good for our bodies. Discuss with your student prudent measures to keep warm. This may include seeking out weather information and dressing accordingly, wearing layered clothing, quickly drying off if you get cold and wet, warming up with a mug of cocoa or hot tea, taking a warm bath if you've become cold, etc.

Summary

If your student has fallen in love with *The Tale of Peter Rabbit,* there are many auxiliary activity books available. There is the *Peter Rabbit Cookbook* which has easy recipes for children. I have seen, in a large bookstore, a set of masks that several children could use to act out the characters in Beatrix Potter's stories. There are diaries and birthday books (to keep track of everyone's birthday), illustrated with Beatrix Potter's art-work. And there are more stories in the *Peter Rabbit* series, twenty-three in all!

MR. GUMPY'S
MOTOR CAR

Title:	*Mr. Gumpy's Motor Car*
Author/Illustrator:	John Burningham
Copyright:	1973
Summary:	A sunny day, a chance for a drive, and an exercise in cooperation take place in a changeable English countryside.

Social Studies: Setting- Geography

The story *Mr. Gumpy's Motor Car* does not give the specific setting of a country, however there are certain clues that give us the idea that the story is in western Europe, and probably England. Look with your student at the second color picture in the book. Can you see anything about the car that looks different from cars in the United States, other than the age of the vehicle? (A European license plate.)

The animals, the girl and the boy ask for a ride. Mr. Gumpy says, *"All right...but it will be a squash."* This is a more English-sounding phrase. Americans might say, "Ok, but it will be a tight fit." Part of the enjoyment of this story is the unfamiliar wording.

You can research and find that the author John Burningham was born in Farnham, Surrey, England. Also, the copyright page says the book was printed in England, and by the look of the dates, probably before it was printed in the United States. Although the text never says, this story takes place in England, from clues we see it appears to be an English story. So, place the story disk on England.

Social Studies: Being Social

Explore the word "social". In part, it means the enjoyment of people living together or being together. The word implies the friendliness necessary to be together happily. We get phrases like Social Studies (the study of people's relationships to one another and how they live together), and "ice cream social" (a party where people get together and enjoy games, entertainment and dessert).

When Mr. Gumpy fills his motor car with petrol (gasoline), he has planned to take a drive by himself in the country. As he passes the crowd of animals and children, they ask if they can go, too. Mr. Gumpy is quite social when he agrees to let everyone come with him. Discuss some of the social skills necessary to get along happily with others.

(Learning to share, learning to be flexible, letting others have a chance to speak, not always demanding your own way, looking out for the needs of others and caring about them, as well as being honest, etc.)

Look at the expressions on the face of Mr. Gumpy at the beginning of the story and as it progresses. Talk about the way Mr. Gumpy handles the emergency situation and how he remains friendly. He even invites the riders to swim and come back for a ride another day. Mr. Gumpy is being sociable!

Social Studies: Cooperation

When the wheels of the motor car begin to spin, Mr. Gumpy says, *"Some of you will have to get out and push."* Ask your student what the riders say. (They all make excuses why they cannot possibly do it.) Ask your student if he remembers some of the excuses. Does he think these excuses are valid (make sense)? Ask him what happens next. (No one will push and the car becomes hopelessly stuck.) Then all the riders have to get out and push or *cooperate*. (To cooperate literally means to co-operate, or to operate *with* others or work together. Cooperation is important in all that we do.) Earlier in the story, some character might have been the hero for the driving party, by offering to be the one to get out and push the slightly stuck vehicle. Yet, as the story progresses, the car becomes stuck fast in the mud, and requires the cooperation of *everyone* working together to get free. This might remind you of the *Little Red Hen* story where no one wants to help bake bread, but everyone wants to eat it. However, in this case, though everyone wants to ride with no responsibility (a rather anti-social idea) in the end they all have to cooperate to help free the car.

Language Arts: Time Sequence

Some stories may cover a few days of time, a week or many years (as in *They Were Strong and Good*). However, *Mr. Gumpy's Motor Car* takes place in only a few hours. Have your older student try to write a short story that takes place in a few hours time. Discuss this time element with your student. If you have studied the story *They Were Strong and Good*, earlier in Volume 2, compare and contrast the time period of that story to the time span of *Mr. Gumpy's Motor Car*.

One of the most powerful elements of writing or storytelling is to be able to expand or contract time. We can take a story that occurs over centuries and tell it all in a few minutes. Or, we can take a scene that takes only seconds to actually occur, and expand it until the telling or reading may take several hours to cover. Exploring time through writing is a wonderful learning experience for your student. You may want to find simple stories that showcase a variety of time elements. Read and discuss them with your student.

Language Arts: Onomatopoeia

John Burningham has used poetic language as he describes the sounds of the car in the mud. Onomatopoeia (Owna-mat-uh-pee-uh) is a poetic device where the words create the sound of the subject as you say them such as *gasped* or *squelched*. Made-up words like the *clacketa-clacketa* of the flying machine in *The Glorious Flight* (Vol. 1), or *ping* for the sound of struck metal or the *crack* of a book hitting the floor are all examples of use of onomatopoeia. If it seems appropriate, have your student pick a subject and try writing a few sentences about that subject using an onomatopoetic word or two.

Language Arts: Detail

Mr. Gumpy is going for a ride. Ask your student how Mr. Gumpy prepares for his outing. (The picture on the second page shows Mr. Gumpy filling his motor car with petrol (the English word for gasoline). Ask your student if he has ever watched someone preparing his car for a vacation or trip. Have him list some of the things that such a person might check. (A car needs gas, a tune-up, oil, good tires which are properly inflated, window washing fluid, transmission fluid, etc.) Also ask your student what the tire on the back of the motor car might be for. (Your older student will probably know about a spare tire and your young student may need help in figuring it out.) At home, have the student find out where the spare tire is on the family car.

Mr. Gumpy's car has a top that you can put up or take down. What do we call these kind of cars today? (Convertibles. Explain the word convertible and convert, and use the words whenever the opportunity arises, like when you see this type of car on the road, or when you are changing one thing to another, "I'm going to *convert* this check into cash.")

On the page where the riders each give an excuse why they cannot push car, the repetition of *"Not me, said the ___"* gives a rhythm to the text of the page. It again reminds the reader of the *Little Red Hen* type stories.

Art: Drawing Sun Rays

With your student, look at the picture on the page where you read, *"I don't like the look of those clouds."* How did John Burningham draw the rays of the sun in a way that is different from the approach of many other artists? Most pictures of the sun have the rays fanning out like spokes on a wheel from the center of the sun. But Mr. Burningham chose to show the rays in concentric (one within another) circles, using broken lines. You may like this picture, just because it is so different. Maybe your student would like to draw a picture and try a sun in the style of Mr. Burningham.

Art: Making a List of Colors

Make a list of the colors the illustrator has used. There is a rich variety of subtle colors in this story. If your student knows the primary and secondary color names, maybe he can learn the names of several new colors such as moss green, khaki brown, rust, yellow ochre, etc. (See FIAR Vol. 1, p. 79-80 for more help and ideas teaching color names.)

Art: Action

Look at the picture on the page where it says, *"The wheels churned...."* How does the artist give the effect of churning, nearly-stuck wheels? Have your student use crayons, colored pencils or oil pastels and pick a subject that shows mud being thrown about. It could be anything from a tractor pull or dirt bike, a big rock being thrown into a mud puddle to a dog digging in the garden. Notice in Mr. Burningham's picture the fine lines as well as the thick brown lines. Notice, too, the darker "chunk" spots along with tiny amounts of color that go together to make the picture look as if the mud is flying! Also, don't forget the angle at which the dirt is being thrown up. You can see the angle in this picture and the one on the next page opposite where the riders are pushing the car.

There is also action in the picture where the riders go for a swim. The action is in the downward flight of the girl, the dog diving out and down into the water, and the splashing lines. These lines not only go in concentric circles, but also create arch-shaped, outward splashes all the way around, like rings around a Lifesaver® candy.

Action is also portrayed through the motor car in other pictures where you see the car bouncing sideways, tires lifted off the ground, and when the car going downhill with its back tires off the ground, etc.

You can see linear action in the picture where the riders are pointing to each other and giving their excuses. Your eyes dart back and forth across the page as excuses fly!

Art: Textures

John Burningham is an artist who uses line to make many different textures. In the first picture, look at the types of lines he uses to make the roof, the building, and the tree bark. The slanted marks on the gate are different from the rounded lines on the tires and the tree trunk. Look at the trees. How many different kinds are there? How did the artist make each type look different? Remind your student that he can draw a picture with different kinds of vegetation and use different marks for each kind (or at least he can appreciate the fact that Mr. Burningham has done so.)

Look at the picture of the riders finding excuses and accusing each other. With your student, examine the use of line to make the texture of wool on the sheep, the different lines for chicken feathers, and the longer lines for the hair of the goat. Compare this picture of textures with the third full-color picture of the prospective riders. (Look again, at the "excuses" picture. There is a use of surface lines for roundness on the horns of the goat and the steering wheel. Line, here is not just for texture, but also for showing roundness.)

Curly wool for sheep

Overlapped "u" or "v" shape makes feathers

Curved lines on animal's horns for texture and "roundness" perspective

Suggest that your student try a picture of some form of transportation with a large collection of riders all "squashed" together. It could be a hot air balloon, a bus, a canoe, etc. Gently encourage the use of some texture lines to bring variety to the riders who can be any type of people to any type of animals, or as in this story, a combination of both.

Art: Shading - Cross Hatching

John Burningham uses cross hatching in *Mr. Gumpy's Motor Car*. Cross hatching is an artist's technique in which lines and crossing lines are used to show texture. When the lines are very close together, the resulting effect can also act as another method of shading. The figures in *Mr. Gumpy's Motor Car* are line drawings. They are not rounded by the kind of shading as in *Make Way for Ducklings,* but instead cross hatching is used for some shading. The closer together the crossed lines are, the darker the shading. (Contrast the method of cross hatching with the blended type of shading in Robert McCloskey's *Make Way For Ducklings, FIAR* Vol. 2, p. 98. In McCloskey's book the shading is accomplished by light to dark color blended subtly. The darkest color appears under an object making that object stand out more clearly. In Burningham's work the cris-crossed lines (cross hatching) beneath an object cause the object to stand out.)

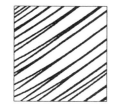  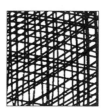

The illustrator of this story uses cross hatching for both texture and shading. The first picture shows the use of cross hatching for texture as you look at the red paint of the car. There is also cross hatching texture on the building. But, in the picture where the riders are pointing at each other and making excuses, look at Mr. Gumpy's hat. The top of the hat is vertical line, yet the brim is cross hatched to show shading underneath. (Look at the picture where it says, "*everyone was enjoying the ride.*" The hat has the same shading in that picture, and there is also cross hatching under the chins of the cow and dog.)

It may be enough for your student just to appreciate a new technique and know that many artists make use of cross hatching. You may want to look for other examples of line drawing in magazines and books. If he has interest, have your student try a simple drawing of an object and use this technique for shading or for texture. If he is keeping a notebook of technique or artists' choices, have him make a page for cross hatching and draw or find a picture as an example. You may also want to keep a chart of these techniques with illustrated examples. If you have a serious art student, he make want to spend extra time just studying the use of line in these illustrations. He may see many new ideas.

Art: Symbolism and Contrast

In the picture opposite the text, "*...and down came the rain,*" the car begins moving downhill. The direction of the car and the rain go together. This symbolizes the downpour.

and acts as symbolic foreshadowing. The events of the motor car and its occupants rather spiral downward from this point, until everyone cooperates and again, the car begins to move "uphill."! You may decide whether this kind of in-depth study is beneficial to your student or just useful just for your own information. If your student does not quickly understand the symbolism or seems uninterested, then this type of lesson is probably too advanced.

Mr. Burningham uses color to show the contrast of situation. With your student, examine the light picture opposite the text, *"everyone was enjoying the ride."* Then look at the darkened contrast in the picture where the riders are making excuses. It is nearly the same picture, yet one is light and airy and the other more dark and troubling. How does the artist create this effect? (In the darker picture, the light area around the car is missing. The bright red of the car's hood is missing. The riders are drawn larger, they are more crowded together and the colors are darker and more somber.)

Next, look at the picture opposite the text, *"Let's take the old dirt road across the fields."* Notice the bright, sunny day. Keep your finger in this place and turn to the picture opposite the words, *"Some of you will have to get out and push."* The contrast (difference) is apparent. Ask your student how the artist achieved the light sunny, effect and what he changed to get the ominous storm effect. (The main difference here is the color used.) Maybe, your student would like to try drawing two pictures of the **same** subject with contrasting backgrounds: day and night, sunny and stormy, wet and dry, or cold and hot, etc.)

Math: Counting

How many riders does Mr. Gumpy take? (eleven) Ask your student to tell you how many riders there would have been if Mr. Gumpy had taken twice (or 2 times) that many? Use blocks for your young student. Pair up the blocks and let him count. (He should count twenty-two blocks.) For additional counting practice, have your student count the total number of people and animals pictured throughout the story.

Math: Multiplication, Twelves and Dozens

For your older student, continue the multiplication practice by asking if one car holds twelve riders, and the same number of riders were in each car, how many riders would there be in two cars, three cars, etc. For your student that loves math and thinks it's an interesting game, teach counting by twelves. (12, 24, 36, 48, 60, 72, 84, 96, 108, 120,132 and 144).

Because this multiplication involves the twelves multiplication tables, you could also discuss the word **dozen** and what kind of things we count by twelves or dozens. (donuts, eggs, inches to the foot, hours, months, and the twelve disciples)

Math: Division

For your older student, use the characters and situation in *Mr. Gumpy's Motor Car* for division problems. For instance, suppose Mr. Gumpy can only carry two riders at a time. How many trips will he have to make to give all eleven characters a ride? (He will have to make six trips, although the last one will have only one rider.) What if he transports three each time? (He will make three trips and the last trip will have two riders.) etc.

Science: Storm Clouds

There are many types of clouds (see *Storm In the Night*, *FIAR*, Vol. 1, p. 103). The clouds which bring storms are usually either nimbus or cumulonimbus. John Burningham draws some of these clouds, as well as some fair weather cumulus clouds in *Mr. Gumpy's Motor Car*. See if you can find them. If your student expresses interest in the study of weather and clouds, set up your own "weather station." Set aside a special notebook section and begin recording daily weather observations. Use library books or encyclopedias, to help your student learn to identify various cloud types. Have him record his observations, perhaps at the beginning of the day, and again at day's end. He may also want to record daily temperatures using either a thermometer or the local weather information. Perhaps you have access to a barometer, which measures the barometric pressure. You can easily make or obtain a rain gauge and record daily precipitation measurements. Soon, your student will begin *forecasting* the weather for himself. He may discover that drops in the barometric pressure usually foretell rain. He can confirm his predictions by observing the changing cloud formations, etc. Weather can become an all-semester project!

Science: Cycles - Water Cycle

Mr. Gumpy has to deal with a surprise thunderstorm. After reading the story, you may want to discuss rain and take time to introduce the concept of the *water cycle*. Where does rain come from? Where does rain go? How does all that water get up "in the air?" Talk about the process. Rain runs off through creeks and streams towards major rivers and, eventually, the ocean. Discuss the process of evaporation, in which surface water becomes tiny, airborne droplets. You may want to talk about humidity if the day happens to be very humid. Consider setting out a container of water and recording how long it takes to completely evaporate. Finally, discuss the process of evaporated moisture *condensing* into rain drops and returning to earth to complete the water cycle.

Science: Friction - Traction

Besides storms and rain, *Mr. Gumpy's Motor Car* provides a chance to talk about friction and traction. You can talk about the adhesion or friction which provides traction. It is the lack of traction which causes Mr. Gumpy's car to slide. What sorts of things work to reduce friction, or traction? (Oil, water, ice and any other slippery substance or surface.) Sometimes, as in the case of our tires on the road, we *need* friction. Other times, such as a door hinge or a fan's blade, we want to *eliminate* friction. To eliminate friction, we must add a lubricant. To get better friction, we must overcome the lubrication. That's why many motorists use snow tires in the winter, to create more friction. That's why we put down sand when we're stuck, to create more friction. Likewise, when we want to eliminate friction, we add lubrication. That's why we oil a troublesome door or a binding fan blade.

ALL THOSE SECRETS
OF THE WORLD

Title: *All Those Secrets of the World*
Author: Jane Yolen
Illustrator: Leslie Baker
Copyright: 1991
Award: Junior Literary Guild Selection
Summary: Janie learns about partings and reunions, closeness and dis-
             tance in *All Those Secrets of the World*.

Social Studies: Geography -
Virginia, Chesapeake Bay, United States East Coast

The setting for *All Those Secrets of the World* is the east coast of the United States, specifically the state of Virginia. We know this because of the reference to Chesapeake (Bay), and the town of Newport News. It is probably enough for young students to put the geography disk on Virginia. Mention that the word "Chesapeake" in the wading scene of the story is actually Chesapeake Bay and show its location on your map.

For your older student, talk about the fact that a bay is part of an ocean or lake that forms an "indentation" in the shoreline, bordered by headlands or capes. According the the *World Book Encyclopedia*, the capes or headlands that form the borders of a bay protect the shoreline within it from the powerful pounding of waves from the sea. This creates a safe, protected haven for boats and ships. Chesapeake Bay is located along the northeast coast of Virginia and divides the land mass of Maryland into two parts. If you have completed *Five In A Row* Vol. 1, you may remember Ungava Bay, Northern Canada from the story *Very Last First Time*. At this time you also may want to mention Hudson Bay, another North American bay that your student will eventually study in his history classes.

Social Studies: Family Relationships

Family Unit: What is a family? Sometimes it's a mother, father and children. But in many cases it looks different. Some families have only one parent with children, or perhaps there is one or more grandparents living with the family. Sometimes an aunt, uncle or cousin comes to live with us and we become one large family. It seems in this story that there were cousins and grandparents all living with a mother and her children. We sometimes call this an "extended family."

Obedience: Heavy moralizing will diminish the enjoyment of this story. However, a brief mention of how Janie and her cousin obey the *"letter of the adult's instruction"* yet clearly miss the *"intent thereof"* might make an interesting topic for discussion. Ask your student what he thinks of the idea that *"no one would know if they waded,"* and that *"wading isn't the same as swimming, they didn't say no wading."*

Saying goodbye: Children have to learn to say goodbye. For some families in which a mother or father works outside their home, each day includes a goodbye and a welcome again. In the *Little House on the Prairie* books, Pa has to go to another town to work and cannot come home for a period of time. Sometimes parents or siblings go on a trip and the separation is a little longer. Some children (and some parents or grandparents who remember when they were children) have memories of separation caused by armed forces leaving during wartime. If your student has such memories, this story will be a vehicle to prompt conversation. Maybe your student's parents or grandparents have stories to be remembered and told. Or, perhaps there is a neighbor or friend who can reminisce about wartime separation and goodbyes. You may find other times in the week to discuss the goodbyes that must be said when a friend or relative moves far away, or a job transfer removes one from family or friends.

Find the "sending them off" picture in *All Those Secrets of the World* to gain a perspective of the large scale farewell which took place as the soldiers left for World War II.

Social Studies: Time of War

There are many avenues of discussion you may pursue, using this story from the WWII era. You may want to discuss any of the wars fought by Americans. An interesting topic of focus could be the soldiers who fought to preserve the rights of the American people and to help protect our allies (friends). Talk, too, about the sacrifices that everyone made to help the war effort. For instance, besides the sacrifice of separated families, there were victory gardens, scrap iron drives, women working the absent men's jobs in factories, victory bonds, etc.

In *Lentil, FIAR*, Vol. 1, you may have introduced patriotism. If so, continue this topic with the added insights from *All Those Secrets of the World*. In Jane Yolen's story you see both the patriotism of the soldiers that are leaving and the patriotism shown by the families that are seeing them off. Remember how Janie waves the flag? Talk about how the flag symbolizes patriotism—loyalty and pride for one's country. At the "sending them off picture" many people are waving American flags. Find other pictures in this story of the American flag.

Language Arts: First-Person Point of View

All Those Secrets of the World is a story told through the eyes of a four-year-old. Yolen uses words like *my, I, me, we* to tell the story. This is called the *first person* point of view. Have your student try telling about a simple event using a first person point of view and illustrating it. For your young student, work on the story together.

Language Arts: Poetic Form

Jane Yolen writes with a poetic prose style. She uses poetic devices such as repetition. (The parting at the beginning of the story, and the reuniting of Janie with her father at the end, repeats the phrase *butterfly kisses and whirling around and around,* and in another place there are two references to *whispering sycamores.*)

She also ends her story with a series of contrasts (or opposites) in a neat parallel construction. Yolen writes that Janie and her father held each other and spun around until they could no longer tell:

> *big from little*
> *young from old*
> *short from long*
> *peace from war...*

With your student, make a list of other contrasting phrases that Yolen might have used: cold from hot, top from bottom, wet from dry, in from out, etc. Just think of opposites.

Language Arts: Comprehension

Learning to read includes learning the letters and the sounds they make, being able to read words together in a sentence form, and understanding the meaning of the sentences. In addition, ideas are sometimes inferred from the reading. In *All Those Secrets of the World* Stevie warns the bad man to stay away from his Mama. Ask your student why Stevie did not recognize his own father. If your student does not know the answer, gently re-read the text of the first page and show the picture of the mother getting out of the car with a small baby. Talk about the earliest memories your student has and help him begin to gain an understanding that a baby cannot remember much.

Language Arts: Foreshadowing

Foreshadowing is when an author gives an indication (clue, hint) of events to come. In *All Those Secrets of the World,* Jane Yolen gives a clue to the final happy outcome of the story when the children hear the bedtime story: *"Once upon a time,"* it begins and *"happily ever after,"* it ends. As the reader turns the page, he sees a happy ending as the father returns home! The ending words of the bedtime story, in this case, foreshadow the actual events in Janie's life.

Some children might appreciate the intriguing idea that authors can drop clues to the events or outcome of a story. They may enjoy watching for foreshadowing in their reading. But, foreshadowing is an advanced subject. It is probably best if you simply note and appreciate it for now. Only if your student that shows unusual interest should he attempt to write a story using foreshadowing.

Language Arts: Vocabulary

jimmies   small, rod-like candy sprinkles placed on top of ice cream

perch   a high place or position (in this case, from which to watch)

horizon   the line where it seems the earth and sky meet

sycamore   a large deciduous (drops leaves in fall) tree with a mottled white trunk

dock   a platform built on or out from the shore where ships and boats can tie up to load or unload

Art: Medium - Watercolor

Ask your student what medium he thinks the illustrator used in *All Those Secrets of the World*. Remind him of the choices: pastel chalk, oil paints, pen and ink, or watercolor. Let him examine the pictures. Look at the illustration when Janie's father returns. Point out the drips and watery places. See if your student can determine the illustrations are watercolor. Look for other pictures in this story with drips and spots. Point out that watercolor almost lets you see the paper underneath so it is called a translucent medium.

Art: Viewpoint

Viewpoint is the position from which you view the subject of the painting. Look at the ship tied to the dock on the second page. The viewpoint, from down underneath the bow, allows the viewer to experience the closeness and astounding size of the ship that is about to take the soldiers away. This picture is unusual because only a portion of the ship is visible. To a young child, it may not even be recognizable as a ship. If necessary, turn two pages to the scene of the ship moving away. Point out the hull and bow, and compare it to the first picture. In this second picture, the people are higher than the ship. This completely changes the viewpoint and shows that as things move away they look smaller. The story is about distance and closeness and the pictures perfectly illustrate that theme as they change from large to small and close to far throughout the text.

Art: Shadows

Shadows fall opposite the light source, both in real life and in artists' pictures of life. Go outside and stand with the morning sun at your right. Observe your shadow to your left. Have your student look for examples of shadows in Leslie Baker's art work. See if he can show in each picture where the light is coming from. Help him if necessary. For instance, the picture where Janie and Michael are eating ice cream cones shows the light coming from the left of the picture. The shadows fall to the right of the objects.

While you're outside, stand in one position. Have your student walk slowly, all the way around you. Encourage him to note, from his perspective, how your shadow and the sun seem to change locations as he moves around you. Keep this exercise fun, but know that he will be learning about shadows. Someday he will find it easy to place shadows in his own pictures. Just remember, where we place shadows as an artist, is determined by where the light source is *in relationship* to our subject!

Art : Distance Perspective

When Janie and Michael are wading in the Chesapeake, Janie sees specks on the horizon. Michael reveals a secret to her and she discovers that the specks are the same gigantic ships she has seen the day before. Ask your student how the artist could show, on a flat piece of paper, both the tremendous size of the ship up close and the tiny specks of the ships far away. (Two of the techniques Leslie Baker used were viewpoint and size. In the "saying goodbye" picture, she painted the people in the foreground smaller than the giant boat, making the boat appear closer and larger. In the picture where Janie sits on Grandpa's shoulders, Baker painted the people in the foreground larger and higher in the picture than the ship, so the ship seems smaller than the first picture. In the wading picture, she painted the children large and the boats as tiny specks on the horizon And she placed these "boat specks" in the background of the picture. This gives the effect of extremely small ships at a far greater distance.

Art: Detail

Look with your student at the picture where Janie and Stevie's father comes home. Did you notice, in the background, the boys playing in front of a tent? Did you recognize the American flag they are carrying? (There is also a flag on the house.) What game are they playing? (Soldier) Another detail is the line of flags on the ship on the sixth page. Ships carry flags for decorations, identification, and to use as messages and signals. If there is interest, an older student might enjoy researching this topic.

What details did the artist use to show how Janie and Stevie have grown up in the two years their father is away? (Two details are Janie's length of hair and her height. Check the first picture and notice her hair and how long her legs are when her father picks her up. Then compare to the picture at the end where he whirls her around under the whispering sycamores. And, Stevie is a baby when the mother gets out of the black car at the beginning of the story. He is walking and talking when his father returns.)

Notice in the last picture how the reader of the story seems to stand along with the Mother, Stevie and Michael looking on and watching the loving scene between Janie and her father. The illustrator has painted an open, inviting pathway to enter the picture and includes you as viewers in a special "close" way.

Remember the lessons from *The Story About Ping, FIAR* Vol. 1, p. 14, about drawing water? Did your student notice the" broken rings" around the ankles of Janie and Michael as they wade in the Chesapeake? This is a technique used by artists to give the impression of water. The second wading picture shows splashes as the waves hit their ankles. These splashes are another technique of illustrating water. There is also a reflection of the waders visible in the water.

Art: Music - Military Music

As the families wave their handkerchiefs goodbye to soldiers during World War II, the band is playing a song called *Over There*. It was was written by George M. Cohan and was published in 1917. That means *Over There* was a song originally used during World War I, which was fought between 1914 and 1918. It was then used *again* during World War II (1939-1945). History discussions of comparisons and contrasts (including the music written and used for each) between World War I and World War II might be interesting for your older student. Just hearing the names of such wars is probably enough for your young student. Perhaps he would be interested in seeing pictures of the "Uncle Sam" posters of the era and learning the lyrics to a song used during the war. During World War II, Glen Miller used his talents to enliven the military music and encourage the lonely troops overseas. Even small introductions to history that are interesting to a child lay a favorable foundation for future studies.

Art: Music - Musical Instrument - Tuba

A tuba is a musical instrument. This instrument can be found in an orchestra or as an instrument of a band. Marching bands often play for military events as the band that played at the dock in *All Those Secrets of the World*.

A tuba is a general name for a number of musical instruments in the brass family. Tuba types differ in size (some are upright, as often used in the orchestra, and some are wrapped around the body such as a sousaphone, used in marching bands, etc.) Tubas also have a differing number of valves, but all have a low pitch, serving as the bass voice in a brass section. They make a deep "oom-pa-pa" sound. Your young student might like to pretend to march in a band making the high sounds of the piccolo and flute, beating the drum, the shrill sound of the trumpet, or the oom-pa-pa of a tuba. Join in with him and have a parade!

Math: Counting by Twos

Stevie is two when his father returns from the war. Janie was four when her father left and six when he returns. The progression of their ages reminds us of counting by twos: two, four, six. Explain to your student how to put 10 marbles in groups of two. Show him how to count 2, 4, 6, 8, 10.

Math: Subtracting Four-Digit Numbers

Let your older student find the beginning or ending dates for the Revolutionary War, the Civil War, World Wars I and II, the Korean War, Vietnam and the Saudia Arabian conflict. Using either the beginning or ending dates of these wars, subtract them from the current year's date to determine how long ago each war was fought. Another subtraction exercise is to determine the length of each conflict in years, by subtracting the beginning date from the ending date.

Science: Chesapeake Bay Beach Scene

Look together at the picture where Michael and Janie are wading in the bay. They are looking down toward their feet. What do you think they could be looking at or looking for? (There are rocks, both large and small in the water, and possibly soft-shell crabs, oysters, eels, bluefish, yellow perch and anemones. Land animals of the region include foxes, snow geese, deer, green-backed herons and white egrets.) This subject could make an enjoyable page in your student's science notebook with pictures from old magazines and sketches from encyclopedias, etc.

Science: Horizon and Old Sea Myths

Before the close of the 1400s, many people thought the earth was flat and that by sailing toward the horizon (where the water seems to meet the sky) they would eventually fall off the edge. By the time of Columbus* more people were theorizing a spherical earth, possibly from watching distant sails rise and fall on the horizon. There are legends that say that one day young Columbus was holding an orange and watched a butterfly slowly appear over the curve of the sphere. Because he could see only a little of the wings and then more and more, he compared the observation to people watching sails appear on the horizon. At first, they see just a little sail and then more and more until the entire ship or boat is visible. Observe this phenomenon for yourselves. Using a ball or melon, move an object from behind it, over the top slowly. Notice how you first see only a little of the object, but as it rounds the top of the sphere, you can finally see all of it.

These kinds of observations may have assured the young Columbus that his belief, that the earth was round like an orange, was indeed correct. As an adult, Columbus was interested then, in using this information to find a shorter sea route to the Indies. (*Educated people of Columbus' day– indeed, a few educated people for many hundreds of years, had believed the earth was round. But, the masses of people were not educated and most of them believed in myths and superstitions.)

Science: Oil on Water

Michael and Janie have been warned not to swim in Chesapeake Bay because it is so dirty with oil. Probably the oil comes from the many large ships docked in the bay. Show your student with some cooking oil how once oil spills into the water, it floats on the surface. If you place the oil and water together in a clear bottle with a lid, you can let your student repeatedly shake the bottle, yet the oil will always rise to the surface. With older students explore the dangers of large oil spills to our ecology.

Science: Sycamore Trees

The large leaves of a sycamore tree make a noise in the wind that Jane Yolen calls "whispering." See if you can find a sycamore tree and listen when there is a breeze. Can you hear the whispering sound? (A sycamore tree can grow to be a towering giant. It is recognized by its mottled white and pale greenish bark, somewhat resembling the bark of a birch tree. Its leaves are large (some five to seven inches across) and the round ball-like-seed pod, covered with spines, is also easily recognizable.

Title: *Miss Rumphius*
Author/Illustrator: Barbara Cooney
Copyright: 1982
Award: American Book Award
Summary: Following in her grandfather's footsteps, Miss Rumphius succeeds in *her* mission and stirs the hearts of the next generation.

Social Studies: Geography - By the Sea

Ask your older student if he think Miss Rumphius lives *"by the sea"* in the northern half of the ocean coast or the southern half? If he has no ideas, look at the illustration across the first two pages. Notice the roofs of the buildings, the winter snow and ice, as well as the girl on the steps in a winter coat. This would seem a northern scenario and probably an Atlantic coast one as well, since the Pacific northern coast is a bit more temperate. There is also a tiny clue in the picture of the young children sitting around the *elderly* Miss Rumphius. See if your reading student can spot it. (The boy on the purple striped pillow is wearing a T-shirt with "Maine" written on it.) Take a chance and place the story disk on Maine!

Social Studies: Finding and Doing a Special Work

Little Alice's grandfather tells her there is something special for her to do; she should "...*do something to make the world more beautiful.*" It may be a new idea to your student that each of us has a special work to do, something to contribute. This could be a piece of music, writing or any kind of helping service. It won't just be a copy of someone else's work or ideas, but something special of the student's own. He'll know it when it is right. Alice's grandfather presents her with a challenge and she continues his tradition, challenging the young children around her to make their world more beautiful.

Social Studies: Not Despising Small Beginnings

Miss Rumphius' garden starts small. With an injured back, she cannot do a lot. However, she does what she can. Eventually, the people of the town are glad that she hadn't thought, "I want a big garden and I can't have it so I won't plant anything at all." She does what she can. Later, when she feels better, she does more until the entire town is filled with blooms.

Discuss with your student the challenge to try things, even if the effort seems small or less than perfect. Help him try some things he's been thinking about doing and encourage the small beginnings.

Social Studies: Changing Times

Point out the differences in the way children dress when Miss Rumphius is a girl and when she is older. Notice the horse and wagon in the street scene of the first picture and the automobile in the third picture from the end of the story. Can you and your student find other signs of changing times? Share with your student (in actual items and pictures, if you have them) what life was like when you were a child. Let him discover how some things have changed. You might talk about the areas of life that have remained the same (people still have to work for a living, there are still mothers and fathers raising their children, people still need places to live, still have pets, etc.) Remind him that he will be able to share *his* experiences with children someday when he is older.

Social Studies: Relationships - Nicknames

Sometimes nicknames can be hurtful because they make fun of someone. What is the hurtful nickname that the townspeople call Miss Rumphius? (That Crazy Old Lady) Why do they call her that? Do they really understand what she is trying to do? Many people make fun of what they do not understand. Ask your student if he has ever had that happen to him, and recount any story that you may remember.

The people change their minds, however. In the spring when the lupines cover the fields, hillsides, and bloom along the highways and down the lanes, the townspeople change Miss Rumphius' nickname. They call her the Lupine Lady. A lovely and not at all hurtful nickname that tells what she has contributed to their town.

Social Studies: Geographical Regions of the World

Adventurous Miss Rumphius travels from her home to far-away places. She goes to a real tropical island, with monkeys, cockatoos, coconuts, grass covered homes on stilts (built in the air to protect them from water), mother-of-pearl shells (see if you can find or borrow one to examine), island natives in native clothes and island hospitality. If there is interest, explore island life and where this island might be. Be sure to look for clues.

Miss Rumphius also visits tall mountains where the snow never melts. Your student may be fascinated by the fact that these are mountains that are so high they have no trees and only a few Alpine-type plants at the top. The line above which no trees will grow is called the *timberline*. There are mountains with snow on the top that never melts in the United States and Canada. Your older student can research this topic.

On her journeys Miss Rumphius goes through jungles and deserts. There are simple children's books about these regions at the library. There are also more difficult volumes on jungles and deserts for your older student. You can sometimes order good videos on jungle or desert life from your local library. If there is a natural history museum near you, it may have room-sized panoramas of each natural region. These panoramas may include actual stuffed animals and representative vegetation, etc. Usually there is either written information at each separate station, or sometimes even audio recordings that explain each region and identifies what you see there.

Ask your student where Miss Rumphius could have seen kangaroos. (Australia)

An older student may have a question about the Land of the Lotus-Eaters. Spoken of in ancient Greek mythology, it was reputed to be somewhere in Northern Africa or possibly islands off the northwest coast of Africa. Supposedly, this land belonged to a race of people who lived on the fruit and blossoms of the lotus (a type of water lily). It is in the Land of the Lotus-Eaters that Miss Rumphius hurts her back getting off a camel. Talk about camels. From an old *National Geographic* or some other magazine, try to find a picture of a camel sitting on the ground as they do when people dismount. Take time to look carefully at the unusual knees, legs, hump, eyes and muzzle. Have your student make a drawing of a camel. He may also want to note the type of region in which the camel lives and works. He may place this information page in the social studies or science section of his notebook.

Social Studies: Family Story- Telling

In the evening, Alice sits on her grandfather's knee and listens to his stories of far-away places. These kind of stories brighten Alice's imagination. They beckon her on to the same kind of adventures. Movies, books and television may all be useful at some time to introduce a new place or activity in an exciting way, but it seems that often stories from your own family can create an even greater excitement. Some of your student's family members may have tales of far-away places. Yet, even tales of living in a different state or region can have meaning and a sense of adventure for your student. A story about a particularly difficult job and how it was accomplished, or an award for some contest and the exciting details of how the contest was won, etc., has the ability to expand your student's mind. This will encourage him in different areas, and challenge him to think about things he might want to do himself someday. These kind of stories bind families together and build intimacy. Encourage your student to seek out family members and let them know of his desire to "hear *their* story." Remind him to wait for a good opportunity, to listen carefully and to thank his story-teller for their time. (A similar theme found in *Grandfather's Journey* by Allen Say included in *FIAR* Volume I. The grandfather tells his grandson of a place called California. Eventually, the grandson travels there from Japan to see for himself.)

Language Arts: Introduction to Library Skills

Miss Rumphius works at a large library. She knows where to find the books that library patrons want to read. She also knows where to find the books in which *she* is interested. There is a system of arranging the books of a library which makes it possible to find the book one wants. It is called the Dewey-Decimal System. You can explore any library using this system, even libraries with which you are not familiar.

Talk with your older student about the Dewey Decimal classification system. You can introduce just one subject number and spend several library trips learning that one number area thoroughly. If your student is interested in history, show him how to find good books for himself in the non-fiction section of the junior library by using the 900 number section of the Dewey Decimal classification system. Maybe the next month could be spent finding science books and learning the general classification number for *that* section of the junior library. The following month, look for a book of poetry, plays or other literature and learn that these books can be found in the 800 section of the junior library, etc. The following is a simplified list of the Dewey Decimal classification system:

000	General, including Bibliographies, books about books, Encyclopedias, etc.
100	Philosophy and Psychology
200	Religion
300	Social Studies
400	Languages
500	Science
600	Applied Science and Useful Arts, Cooking, Automobiles, etc.
700	Fine Arts, including Painting, Theatre, Dance, Music, etc.
800	Literature, Drama, Poetry and Writing
900	History, Geography and Biography

Even your young student may enjoy knowing that different kinds of books come from different areas of the children's library. He may have fun trying, with your help, to match the numbers on the spine of his book to the numbers of each particular section.

Language Arts: Sea Vocabulary

sea	used in this story as a synonym for ocean
wharves	landing places or piers where ships tie up to load or unload
masts	the tall poles that rise vertically from the deck of a boat or ship, used to support the sails and rigging
prow	the forward part of the ship's hull, the bow
figureheads	the decorative human figures on the outer prow of some ships
chandlers	a shop with specific goods or equipment; A ship's chandlery would carry items of rigging, ropes, navigational equipment, etc. (This word appears in the illustrations.)

Art: Medium

The explanation page after the story ends, tells about the medium used by Barbara Cooney for Miss Rumphius. It says she painted with acrylics and accents of Prismacolor pencils on gesso-coated percale fabric which had been mounted on illustration board. Some of the pictures are soft delicate hues of color (pastel shades) and some are full of bright color, like the tropical island. Discuss the concept of multiple medium art. We are not limited to *just* watercolors or *only* pencil. Barbara Cooney combined fabric, illustration board, acrylics, gesso and colored pencils in her drawing. Encourage your student to try combining media. He might paint a watercolor background and draw in his figures using markers, or he might enjoy using colored pencils and pastel chalks together. Some of the most creative art comes from the successful combining of more than one medium.

Art: Detail

Barbara Cooney's paintings are rich in detail and will delight a careful observer. One artist has said of her work, "*...the pictures draw you to keep looking, and the longer you look the more you see and then you want look some more.*"

Look at the title page. The beautiful, stately lupines are painted in natural detail. From this realistic picture, your student would be able to identify the actual plant in a garden, or at a garden center that sells these plants. If possible, take the book along and let him find some lupine.

Notice the picture on the wall of the room where grandfather tells little Alice of far away places. Now look at the same pictures on the wall when Alice is an old woman telling the children her stories. She inherited these paintings. Ask your student if there are pieces of furniture (family heirlooms) or pictures in his home that belonged to his ancestors.

In many of the illustrations, you can look beyond the room of the main subject into side rooms and see people busy at various activities. There is a bedroom dresser which was visible earlier in the story. The dresser is now seen through a doorway, in the picture where she talks to the children at the end of the story. Look through the book for examples. Your older student might try a picture of a room with lots of details. These can include an opening to see into other rooms and areas.

In the picture that shows little Alice and her grandfather at home, there is a calico cat, a shell on the mantle, and books. In the picture where Alice is older, surrounded by children, there is another calico cat, shells on the mantle, lots of books and a fire in the fireplace. We see a full circle of life and common interests and belongings (such as the little brown wicker chair and the paintings), as the generations move along.

Spend some time examining the room, the objects and the people as the elderly Miss Rumphius talks to the children. The carpets, draperies and cushions have textures and design. The children's clothes are completely individual and have personality. You can see sneakers, sandals and dresses, as well as sweaters, tee shirts and jeans. There are also different hair colors and styles. What are the children eating? Where do you think the cockatoo came from? What type of shells and coral are on the mantle? Could the middle shell be the mother-of-pearl shell Alice received from the Bapa Raja?

Ask your student if he thinks it is fun that little Alice paints skies on the pictures when her grandfather is too busy. She obviously shares his love of painting and probably his talent, as well.

Details of a port town are visible in the illustrations on the first two pages. Talk with your student about what happens in each shop. Notice the restaurant under the hotel as there are in many hotels today.

Art: Architecture - Islamic Influence

In the picture where Miss Rumphius rides a camel, the buildings are thick walled, white, and have small windows. If your student does not know, explain the thick walls keep the inside rooms cooler and the white reflects the hot sunlight, for this is a very warm place. The domes and the unusual shaped doorway under the Cafe Djerba sign are examples of Islamic architecture. In previous stories in the *Five In A Row* studies, your student has seen examples of Russian domes and towers, noticed Roman arches and bridges, and learned about French styles of building. These are brief introductions to architectural styles. Such studies help your student become aware of the variety and history of building shapes that are all around him. The Islamic style of doorway in the legendary Land of the Lotus-Eaters (somewhere in Northern Africa) is another architectural type of which to be aware. Help your student make pages for his notebook with brief sketches of these different types of architecture. Then he can quickly compare each style, noting the differences appreciating the variety. (Let a young student trace the shape with his finger on the book or with some tracing paper, just for fun.)

Learning more about the origins of different architectural styles is interesting and will help your student grow in discernment. He will develop an ability to recognize the influences of various geographic areas and cultures on architecture, paintings, etc.

Art: Motion - Evidence of Wind or Breeze

Miss Rumphius says the wind brings the seeds from her garden. You can detect the work of these sea breezes in several of Barbara Cooney's paintings. In the first picture, ask your student how the artist shows the very slight movement of the wind. (The rising smoke from the chimneys has wavy lines. The steamboat smokestack, on the other hand, has smoke going back behind it to show the forward movement of the boat, not necessarily the breeze. However, the fact that there are sail boats in the bay gives another indication of a breeze.) How does the artist show evidence of wind in the picture where Miss Rumphius is in bed? (the movement of the curtains) Can your student find the breeze in the painting where a green-coated Miss Rumphius scatters seed? (The American flag is flying straight out and the flag on the next page is billowing slightly, also.)

In this way, your student will learn that he can draw *evidence* of a breeze or wind if he wants to include it in his picture. He does this by showing blowing leaves, clothes flying up on a line, rain slanting sideways, etc., as well as the ways Barbara Cooney has demonstrated in *Miss Rumphius*. As an exercise, your student may want to look through old magazines and make a small collections of photographs and drawings that show evidence of wind. He can glue them on a page (even collage-style) and place the picture in the art section of his notebook. You may wish to title the work *Ways To Show the Effects of Wind*.

Art: Shadows

FIAR Vol. 1, pp. 40 and 60, has lessons on shadows and finding the light source in pictures. In *Miss Rumphius* there is a good example of the sun at high noon. Look at the picture of Miss Rumphius on the tropical island. Ask your student if he can tell where the sunlight is coming from. Remind him that the shadows will help him figure it out. Because the shadows do not slant in any direction, but rather make a "puddle" under the figures, the sun must be directly overhead. Have him go outside in the noon-time sun and see how the shadows look. Or, use a flashlight in a dark room and hold it directly over an object, noticing how the shadow falls.

In the illustration across from Bapa Raja and Miss Rumphius, the little house on stilts is in the noon sun, also. The palm trees cast a round shade pool about it. Turn the page and see Miss Rumphius on the camel. Now, where is the sunlight coming from? Remember the sun is directly *opposite* the shadow.

Math: Bushels and Pecks

Miss Rumphius sends off to the seed houses to buy five bushels of lupine seed. Ask your student how much seed that is. If you have a bushel basket, show it to him and imagine (if possible!) how many seeds would be in five bushels.

A bushel is a unit of capacity or volume that measures four pecks. A peck is a unit of capacity or volume that measures eight quarts. So a bushel would hold thirty-two quarts. An older student might be interested in this unit of measure and its equivalents. You might also like to do some multiplication work. 5 bushels x 4 pecks = 20 pecks. 20 pecks x 8 quarts = 160 quarts. 160 quarts x 2 pints = 320 pints, etc.

Math: Counting Practice

There are many people in the town where Miss Rumphius lives by the sea, and throughout the book. Have your young student count all the people from the beginning of the story as far as he can count. For additional counting practice, have him try counting only the men, only the women or only the children, etc.

Science: Gardening

If your student has an interest in flowers, find as many examples of good gardens as you can and, if possible, take him to each. Talk about the variety, color of the gardens, and the work that it takes to create and maintain them. Perhaps, if you call ahead, a gardener would be willing to walk around with him and answer any questions he might have or point out unusual flowers. Ideally, this information should be kept to a small amount, while the enjoyment of the garden (the colors and design) shared together provides the main focus of the tour.

Some students take a special interest when there are hands-on activities to bring the story to life. Spring is a good time to look in a nursery or garden center for a lupine plant. Purchase one that is already started from seed and is ready to bloom this season. Let your student plant it (if lupines can be grown in your area), and enjoy the blooms that Miss Rumphius loved so well! If you have room, you might want to scatter seed to begin plants that will bloom next season.

Science: Seeds

Miss Rumphius fills her pockets with lupine seeds and scatters them everywhere. Seeds are a miracle in themselves. There are basic botanical lessons in the structures of seeds (the seed coat, single or double cotyledon, the germ, etc.), the types of seeds (monocotyledon, dicotyledon and gymnosperm), and other classifications that your older student may understand.

However, starting a simple bean seed in a wet paper towel and watching the root and the first leaves is as exciting a way as any to introduce the wonder of seeds to your young student. Growing bean seeds against the sides of a glass jar filled with soil is another good way to introduce the subjects of seeds and germination.In this way, you can watch the arched back of the bean seed as it breaks the ground, witness the first leaves and then the true leaves (the ones that look like the leaves of the mature plant). Your library will have books on seeds and germination. These range from large print simple books for your young student, to more in depth informational books for your older student. Your student will appreciate the colorful illustrations in many of these books.

Take a trip to a garden center and see the hundreds of packets of seeds. Ask your student where the seeds in the packages come from. (Seed companies grow plants and gather the seed to sell in these packets.) Often, if you need a large supply of a certain kind of seed, it is more economical to contact one of these companies than to buy many packages. (Of course, five bushels is a lot!!) Grass seed is a type of seed that people commonly purchase in larger quantities. Spend some time with your student exploring the different kinds of flowers and vegetables that can be grown from seed. An older student who enjoys gardening may be ready to learn about hybrid seeds and plants, or about annuals and perennials.

Think about all the foods at the market. Talk about the fact that someone has to grow them. Depending on the area in which your student lives, have him look for food grown close to his home. (wheat fields, corn fields, soybeans, lettuce, apples, strawberries, potatoes, etc.)

When you scatter seeds you are said to *sow* them. There are stories in the Bible about sowers sowing seed. Also, your student may be acquainted with the story of Johnny Appleseed who planted many apple seeds for trees.

Science: Birds

At the library, where Miss Rumphius works before her travels, there are three stuffed birds on a shelf. Can your student identify them? (an owl, a duck, and a quail) Conservation magazines and *National Geographic Magazine* often have pictures that can be used to make notebook pages. If your student is interested in birds, find pictures to draw, trace or cut out. Let him glue them on a sheet of notebook paper and add a few facts. This approach is a great way to encourage his interest in many topics as he builds his notebook. He will enjoy looking over these pages again and again.

Science: Shells

If your student shows an interest in the shells pictured in Miss Rumphius, find simple books of shells to enjoy for their beauty and variety. Your student may remember one or two names of these shells. However, the appreciation of the shell's color, loveliness, textures and sounds (listen for the "ocean", the roar you hear when you cup something hollow to your ear), is the main reason to explore this subject. If you live near the ocean, a trip to the beach for shell-hunting may be a worthwhile field trip when the tide is out!

Science: Health - Daily Routine

Little Alice *"...got up and washed her face and ate porridge for breakfast. She went to school and came home and did her homework. And pretty soon she was grown up."* These daily habits of routine and discipline promote *health* and the *order* necessary to grow and develop strength, physically and mentally.

Talk about the things that your student does each day to keep physically and mentally fit. (washing his face, brushing his teeth, making the bed, eating good meals, getting exercise, playing outside, having a quiet time, doing homework, helping with chores)

What is the porridge Alice eats for breakfast? (oatmeal probably) Perhaps your student would like to help you make oatmeal and share a bowl of "porridge" together. (Don't forget to use this as an opportunity to explore the mystery of boiling water, cups and measures, etc.!) Oatmeal is generally considered nutritious. Find pictures in newspaper ads or magazines. Cut out a nutritious breakfast, lunch or dinner. Remember to have representative selections from the four basic food groups (grains, meat, dairy, vegetables and fruits). Glue the pictures to a piece of paper and have your student add them to his notebook.

Science: Determining Directions by the Sun

The sun rises in the east and sets in the west. Help your student find the relation of the sun rising and setting to his own home. On which side of his house does the sun rise and set? In this way, he'll learn the directions east and west. Show him that often people use shade trees and awnings on the west side of their homes to keep down the heat and strong afternoon sunlight. (These will also be found on the south side of some buildings.) Speak of the east and west directions over several days. Maybe when you are on an outing, you can talk about the direction you're going. In time, these exercises will help your student develop a good sense of direction. This is a valuable asset.

THE LITTLE RED LIGHT-
HOUSE AND THE GREAT
GRAY BRIDGE

Emma Hinsdale

Title: *The Little Red Lighthouse and the Great Gray Bridge*
Author: Hildegarde H. Swift
Illustrator: Lynd Ward
Copyright: 1942
Award: Parents' Choice Honors, and Reading Rainbow Book
Category: Classic (Children have enjoyed this book for over fifty years.)
Summary: A little red lighthouse looks at circumstances and draws wrong
                conclusions. But, with the help of the great gray bridge, he discovers
                the truth; that he still has useful work to do.

Social Studies: Geography - New York City

The second page says, *"Behind it* [the red lighthouse] *lay New York City where the people lived."* New York City! Where do you begin? New York City is located in the state of New York. It is the most populous city in the United States. With your student, locate the state of New York and the position of New York City. Look at your map or *The World Book Encyclopedia* and notice the water areas surrounding the city, the islands that make up the city. Maybe you can find a simple book at the library about New York City itself. Place your story disk on New York.

If you choose to study New York City, try finding the book *My New York* by Kathy Jacobsen (ISBN 0-316-45653-5). This is an incredibly special book. You can tell the author/artist loves her city and wants the reader to experience the city's wonders, too! Find it at your library or at a bookstore and just open it and gaze! This is a book that your student's father or uncle or grandfather might especially enjoy looking over with him. For a study of New York City, it is splendid!

New York is a fascinating and historic city with myriad opportunities for subject studies. There is much history surrounding New York City. After the Revolutionary War it was the temporary capitol of the United States. George Washington was innaugurated there. Also, New York has been the United States center of manufacturing and trade. It has the garment industry and it is a chief publishing center and world financial center. New York City is a world hub of shipping. And, as well as having famous transit systems and subways, it has world-class museums. It is a major communications center with newspapers, magazines, and the heads of radio and television industries. It is the home of the United Nations, and much more.

(**Teachers Note**: In building a short study of New York City for your young child, you may want to briefly touch on the geography of New York City. Just mention a few famous places or sights. The framework which you lay now will enable you to take up this subject again in years to come and build upon it. You may want to keep track by making a file folder for extensive topics that are likely to be studied in greater depth later. Try keeping a file for New York City, or the human body, or space, etc. Jot down what you teach and the year. When you're ready later to study the subject in more detail, you will know exactly what to review and how to proceed.)

Your older student may want to read an encyclopedia article about the city and explore various areas of study that he finds interesting. A short list of famous topics which your student may begin to recognize in books, magazines, on television and in movies include: Central Park, Fifth Avenue (the name of a street which can even be used today as an adjective meaning "very expensive"), the Bronx Zoo, Shea and Yankee Stadiums, Grand Central Station, Wall Street, the New York and American Stock Exchanges, CBS (Columbia Broadcasting System), NBC and ABC (each are both radio and television networks in New York), Broadway, the Empire State Building, Greenwich Village, Metropolitan Museum of Art, Statue of Liberty, Ellis Island (where immigrants arrived in the U. S.), The New York Times (a paper famous around the world), the New York Post, and the Daily News, the George Washington Bridge and the Brooklyn Bridge, etc!!!

Social Studies: Geography - Travel

If your student lives near New York City or has a chance to travel there, imagine the surprise of actually seeing the Little Red Lighthouse. This has been restored and made part of Fort Washington Park!! Read the back cover of *The Little Red Lighthouse and the Great Gray Bridge* to find out how the little red lighthouse was saved.

Social Studies: Relationships - Pride

After reading *The Little Red Lighthouse and the Great Gray Bridge*, re-read the first page and emphasize VERY, VERY PROUD. Point out the capital letters. Remind your student that the author used them in this way for emphasis. (Add the technique of *capital letter emphasis* to your list of Choices Writers Can Make.) Now, continue reading until you get to the next use of VERY, VERY PROUD. Ask your student why the little red lighthouse is so proud. (Answers may include: because he understands the job he has to do and he knows he does a good job. He feels useful and important. *"What would the boats do without me?"* he says) To understand the importance of one's job and to be proud that it is done well is good. Talk with your student about the jobs (chores) that he is asked to do. Does he feel that they are important? What will his home life be like if he does not do the job or jobs well? Does he feel pride in knowing he has a job to do and in the way he does it?

Skip to the page where the capital letters spell MASTER OF THE RIVER. (See if your young student is recognizing these all capitalized words are different from the rest of the story's print). Discuss the probability that the little red lighthouse has now gone a bit too far in his pride, that it has become the wrong kind of pride. The wrong kind of pride says, *"I am bigger or better or smarter than anyone else!"* This is the kind of pride that often causes a fall or disillusionment. Share any experiences you might have had with your student. Remind him of famous examples such as King Nebuchadnezzar from the book of Daniel in the Bible. By the end of Hildegarde Swift's story the little red lighthouse has learned that though he is little he still has a job to do. Once again, *in the proper way*, he knows that he is doing his very best. And, he is VERY, VERY PROUD.

Social Studies: Thinking Skills - Learning to Make Correct Conclusions and Being Flexible

The little red lighthouse watches the construction of the great gray bridge that spans the Hudson River from shore to shore. He begins to feel very, very small. When the giant light begins to flash on the bridge, the little lighthouse comes to a wrong conclusion: I am needed no longer. In this case, it is not true. The fact that the man does not come to turn the light on deepens this feeling of uselessness and strengthens the belief that the little lighthouse is through. As the story progresses, you find that the bridge serves a different function (job) and the man has been *prevented* from coming to light the lighthouse.

A lot of emotional stress centers around misunderstandings. Discuss with your student the necessity of going slowly in forming conclusions. One must get the facts, communicate. Talk situations out fully, and learn the *true* meanings behind the things that may look obvious.

If you have previously studied *Mike Mulligan and His Steam Shovel, FIAR* Vol. 1, this might be a good time to review the flexibility lesson for that story and apply it to this one. What if the little lighthouse had actually been replaced? (Keep in mind the personification aspect, that the Mike's steam shovel Mary Anne represents people's feelings as does the little red lighthouse.) Rather than despair, a new job is found for Mike Mulligan's steam shovel and a new job could be found for the little red lighthouse, too. Flexibility keeps people open to new possibilities and protects them from depression and despair.

Language Arts: Balance of Title Words

Remind your student that one technique for a good story title is to balance the ideas with the conjunction "and". You can illustrate this by drawing a line with a triangle under the title like a teeter totter. Have your student draw or find a picture of a lighthouse to place on one end of the balance and draw or find a picture of a bridge to place on the other end. Either of you may write the conjunction "*and*" on the fulcrum (middle) of your balance. Have him say the title once or twice, listening for the "*and*" in the center of the title.

For your older student, you could write the title out and have him label the parts of speech under each word of the title. Remind him that the word "*and*" in this title is a balancing word, (it has the same pattern of words before it and after it), as well as a connecting word. There is an article, two adjectives and a noun on the left of the conjunction *and*. There is also an article, two adjectives and a noun after the *and*, making a very balanced title. For example:

The	Little	Red	Lighthouse	*and*	The	Great	Gray	Bridge
art.	adj.	adj.	noun	conj.	art.	adj.	adj.	noun

There are many good ways to write a title. The balanced title is only one of these ways. (**Teacher's Note**: Does your student notice and enjoy the alliterative effect of the words <u>L</u>ittle <u>L</u>ighthouse and <u>G</u>reat <u>G</u>ray Bridge? Alliteration makes a pleasing *sounding* title.)

Language Arts: Compound Words

In this story, by Hildegarde H. Swift, you have an opportunity to mention compound words to your student who is reading. The concept of joining two words and spelling them as one may be a new idea worth introducing. If your student is already aware of compound words, let him find as many as he can in the story of the little red lighthouse. (lighthouse, sometimes, workmen, cannot)

Language Arts: Personification

Personification is giving human characteristics and emotions to non human things. *The Little Red Lighthouse* has several good examples. First, the lighthouse itself is personified in the text by human conversation and emotion, as are the other boats, the great gray bridge, the fog and the wind (which moans). Remind your student that he can give human qualities to things and animals, etc., in the stories he might write. As with Katy, in *Katy and the Big Snow* and Mary Ann in *Mike Mulligan and His Steam Shovel (both in FIAR* Vol. 1), the artist has given human features to the little red lighthouse. Look with your student at each picture starting with the beginning of the story. Notice the changes in expression on the face of the lighthouse. Ask your student if he feels that these expressions coincide (go with) the text of the story.

The other use of personification in this story is in the fog. Lynd Ward has used dark black to represent the fog. (Notice the difference from the other blue sky night pictures, in the illustration opposite the text: *"Sometimes the fog crept up the river."*) This black treatment of fog becomes personification, as the artist actually draws the fog with a human face and hands, and shows the fog trying *"to clutch the boats one by one."*

Language Arts: Reading Comprehension

You can read in the story, *"By day the little red lighthouse did not answer."* But every night the lighthouse speaks to the boats. Ask your student if he remembers that the little red lighthouse has two voices. Ask if he can tell you what they are. One voice is used every night and the other voice is used only if a fog creeps up the river. (The lighthouse's voices are its flashing light *FLASH! FLASH! FLASH!* and its bell *Warn-ing! Warn-ing!*)

Art: Contrast in Size

Enjoy reading *The Little Red Lighthouse and the Great Gray Bridge*. Then, have your student find one of the illustrations that shows the most contrast in *size* between the little red lighthouse and the great gray bridge. (There are several choices, the last picture is good.) Perhaps your student would like to draw his own picture in which there is great contrast in size between two or more figures. It could be a picture of a lion and a mouse, a small tree with a large house, a row of small houses beside a great mansion or a picture with lots of figures in graduated sizes—some small and some large. Whatever subject your student chooses remind him to draw his figures with a great degree of contrast in size as Lynd Ward did in some of this story's illustrations.

Art: Repetition of Line

The artist Lynd Ward showed a repetition of line as he used close parallel lines for the bridge cables and the pickets on the fence around the lighthouse. There is also repetition of line in the X shapes of the bridge bracings. Find some examples, then try a picture with repeating lines. It can be a field of cornstalks or a line of trees, etc. Point out that nearly everywhere your student looks around him, he can find examples of repeating lines. (windowpanes, books in the bookcase, drawers in a dresser, etc.)

Art: Achieving the Effect of Night

Ask your student how the artist portrayed the effect of night. Look near the beginning of the story where the man comes along jingling his keys. (A blue area with just a few stars overhead is a very simple way to suggest night.) Children almost always draw daylight scenes. Suggest that your student try drawing a night scene of his choosing, using Lynd Ward's simple technique.

Art: Details

The printer has used three colors of ink (black, blue and red) to print these classic pictures. In addition, the shading gives variety and roundness to the figures.

Notice the balance in the last illustration with the lights from the little red lighthouse and the great gray bridge shining opposite each other. (Symbolically, the cooperation of the two lights illumines the entire area!)

Math: Counting

Your young student may want to count all the boats or all the people in the story. If he is determined, he could count all the pickets in the fences around the little red lighthouse.

Math: Multiplication and Division

For your older student, create practice problems that center around the subject of the story. For instance, "We probably can't see all the men who work on the bridge. If the cable laying crew consists of twenty men and they go to lunch in shifts of five, how many lunch shifts would they need to feed all the men?" (4) Or, "If there are seven crews of iron workers—each crew made up of six men—how many iron workers work on the great gray bridge?" (42) You can make up as many problems as seem sufficient to cover the math level of your student. Of course, you can design addition and subtraction problems, too.

Science: Rivers

The story of the *Little Red Lighthouse* tells of the Hudson River. It begins high up in the mountains and rolls down looking for the sea. Talk with your students about rivers. This will be an introduction, for your young student, to the ideas that rivers flow from high places to lower ones, where their water is dammed up or eventually reaches the sea. You may want to visit a river, or talk about rivers nearby or in your state. There is a beautifully illustrated picture book on the Amazon called *The River* by Judith Heide Gilliland. You may enjoy finding this book and learning about the Amazon during a study on rivers.

Your older student may be ready for more information on rivers. You could discuss the fact that rivers flow from high to low places, seeking sea level. Remind your student that maps may be deceiving. The Nile River is a good example of this. On a map, the Nile looks like it flows up, from lower (on the page) to higher (on the page.) This, of course, is not true. The Nile flows down from the mountains located the south of Egypt to the lower point of the Mediterranean Sea in the north of Egypt. It is flowing down, always seeking a lower level. If this is a difficult concept for your student (or for your visual learner), use clay, paper mache or plaster to make a relief map with mountains, hills, plains and the lake or sea. (If you made a good depression for the lake or sea, it will catch the water you pour later.) Re-member to make a small channel for the water to flow through. Explain how melting snow or a spring can begin a river. When the model is dry, pour a little water on the highest hill area and let your student see how it must seek a lower level. Set the model so the mountains are directly in front of him, with the plains area further away. He can then see for himself how a river like the Nile flows. This type of hands-on information in early years is valuable for understanding later lessons in geography. And, it is almost always memorable!

Again, your older student may want to study a particular river, whether in the United States or somewhere else in the world. *The Rand McNally Picture Atlas of the World* (ISBN: 0-528-83437-1) has a good illustration on p. 11 which shows the longest rivers of the earth. This picture atlas has many intriguing illustrations and is worth finding.

We study rivers because they are an important source of drinking water, food, energy and a source of transportation and recreation. Your older student may also be interested in conservation measures regarding rivers. Maybe he would enjoy finding out about the process of dam building, or creating man-made lake impoundments with the pro's and con's of such developments. Another study topic is to study the exploration of the United States which took place by river. Your student will discover men named deSoto, de la Salle, Marquette, Jolliet and Lewis and Clark, etc. These men and their explorations provide exciting study adventures.

Remember, if you do a unit study on rivers, the songs, poems and art connected with this topic are rich and varied as well. Be sure to start a notebook on your river study. Add to it whenever you are ready to teach in greater detail, or when you study related topics through the year (or years). It will become a keepsake and an excellent source of review. Many *Five In A Row* stories* have settings with famous rivers mentioned. It will be fun to watch your student take more interest in this subject as he encounters rivers again and again. (*FIAR, Vol. 1: *The Story About Ping*, Yangtze River, China.; *Madeline*, Seine River, Paris, France; FIAR, Vol. 2: *Follow the Drinking Gourd*, Ohio River, United States; FIAR Vol. 3: *Paul Revere's Ride*, Concord, Mystic and Charles Rivers, United States; and many other unnamed rivers in the stories.)

Science: Lighthouses

The little red lighthouse has an important job. Lighthouses are built to warn ships about danger. They are situated on peninsulas, rocky promontories, and sharp points of land. These land formations would endanger ships steering too near them in foggy or stormy weather when visibility is low. There are many famous lighthouses in the United States. Each has its own construction shape and paint scheme. And many lighthouses have amazing circular staircases, because a single flight of steps would be too steep!

Look up lighthouse in *The World Book Encyclopedia*. Examine the pictures with your young student, while your older student may find an interesting topic as he reads the article. He may want to investigate the history of lighthouses, or their methods of operation. The library may have books on lighthouses (search the adult section for books with good photographs). There is a wonderful story called *Keep the Light Burning Abbie*, by Peter Roop. This book tells the exciting story of a young girl who has the responsibility of keeping the light burning in the lighthouse. One of the interesting facts that your student may discover about lighthouses today is that most of them are automated.

If your student lives near a lighthouse or will have an opportunity to travel to an area that has a lighthouse, encourage him to visit and learn more about them. Watch your favorite vendor catalogs for Amanda Bennett's new *Unit Study Adventure: Lighthouses*, soon to be released.

Let your student construct a lighthouse from a piece of paper towel tube and another piece of cardboard in the shape of a semi circle. This can be folded around to form a cone top. Windows may be cut out, too. A tiny flashlight might fit inside and glow out through the windows when your room is darkened. Again, the pictures from actual lighthouses show various paint schemes, bright stripes, etc., for decorating. Your student may want to attempt a model of an actual lighthouse or he may want to create in his own style. Many lighthouses have a small house next to the lighthouse where the lighthouse keeper lived and this could also be modeled easily with a small cardboard box.

Science: Bridges

The great, gray bridge, is actually the George Washington Bridge. It was opened in 1932. By reading and enjoying this story, you have the opportunity to introduce the exciting topic of bridges. From their artistic design, functional strength, and variety of structural styles (including suspension bridges, draw bridges, and covered bridges), to the songs written about them (*London Bridge*, *The Erie Canal*, etc.) bridges are interesting to those who view them, use them, and sing about them.

An excellent children's book explaining the history of bridges from the time man crossed streams on fallen logs to the superstructures of today is called *The Bridge Book* by

Polly Carter! It has delightful, simple drawings with interesting text. *The Bridge Book* is the kind of book that will help you explain different types of bridges to your young student and it's a book that your third grade (and up) student would love to read himself. If you are going to study bridges, this is definitely a book you will enjoy. Soon your student will be pointing out different kinds of bridges to you, whenever you go on an outing.

Also, have your student look for pictures of bridges in books and magazines. Look in the encyclopedia for pictures and help him construct his favorite type of bridge out of cardboard or popsicle-type craft sticks.

Science: Impairment to Sight

The little red lighthouse is important because fog and storms often make visibility difficult. With your student, think of a list of ways that your sight might be impaired: a person could be blind. Also, bright sun or lights, fog and even extreme darkness like in a cave, can all prevent one from seeing clearly. Perhaps your student might be interested in being "sight impaired" briefly by placing a blindfold over his eyes. Help him negotiate a familiar room without sight, feeling his way as he goes. Now he can better understand the importance of a lighthouse with it's bright light and loud bell which warns ships so they do not crash into rocky shorelines during times of fog.

You may also want to use this as an opportunity to discuss vision-related topics including blindness, Braille, seeing eye dogs, glasses, contact lenses, eye exams, eye safety and eye care, etc.

Science: Types of Boats

If your student has an interest, there is a wide range of study topics regarding boat types. Begin with a young student by making a list of all the kinds of boats that he knows. He may have several different types in his bath tub toys! There are canoes, rowboats, kayaks, tugboats, sailboats, barges, submarines, skiffs, inflatable life rafts, trawlers, ferries, aircraft carriers, houseboats, speed boats, battleships, cruisers, destroyers, lobster boats, shrimp boats, whalers, and more!

Boats and boating can lead your older student to studies in navigation, signal flags and lights, astronomy, nautical terminology, ropes and knots, etc., as well as light houses and their keepers. You may even find through this kind of study that your student has an interest in one of the historic boats like the Pilgrims' *Mayflower*, John Paul Jones' the *Bonhomme Richard*, or the famous frigate *Constitution* nicknamed *Old Ironsides*. There is an excellent article about this ship in the *World Book Encyclopedia* under "Constitution." Then, too, there are the boats of the explorers like Columbus (the *Nina*, the *Pinta* and the *Santa Maria*), and Captain Cook's *Endeavor*, etc.

Reading the stories in *Five in a Row*, and allowing your student to investigate topics that interest him (and sometimes those that interest you), is a wonderful way to sample such a variety of things. Your student may find future lifetime interests as well! So, take time to enjoy!!

FOLLOW THE DRINKING GOURD

Title: *Follow the Drinking Gourd*
Author/Illustrator: Jeanette Winter
Copyright: 1988

Summary: A sailor named Peg Leg Joe sees a need and bravely makes a musical plan to help runaway slaves get to the safety of the north.

Social Studies: Pre-Civil War Decades - Cotton Plantation - Slavery

The years *before* the **Civil War** (also called the War Between the States 1861-1865) is the historic time setting for *Follow the Drinking Gourd*. During that time, slavery (you may need to explain this term to your very young student) was practiced throughout the southern states of America. (And, to a much lesser degree, in the northern states.) One of the places slaves worked was on giant southern farms called plantations. Plantation owners often raised large acres of crops such as indigo (used for blue dye), cotton, tobacco, sugar cane, and rice. The slaves planted, tended and harvested these crops, as well as working many other jobs. In the story *Follow the Drinking Gourd*, Peg Leg Joe works for the masters of cotton plantations. (**Teacher's Note:** If you have studied *Mrs. Katz and Tush, FIAR* Vol. 2, you may remember lessons about the Hebrew slavery in Egypt and the references to slavery in the United States as well. In *FIAR* Vol. 1, the story *Who Owns the Sun* also introduces the subject of slavery.)

Social Studies: Underground Railroad

Find the following passage and read it with your student. When Mollie, James, their son Isaiah, old Hattie and her grandson, George, are in the rowboat with Peg Leg Joe, the text reads, *"A path of houses stretched like a train on a secret track leading north to Canada...It carried riders to freedom."* This is a description of the **Underground Railroad.**

The *World Book Encyclopedia* shows a picture map of the networked routes in the Underground Railroad. Your older student might find this map interesting. The states through which most of the "freedom" traffic traveled were Ohio, Indiana and Pennsylvania. In these states the large Quaker population was sympathetic to the plight of the slaves. A few of the runaway slaves settled in the states of the North, but there they could be recaptured and sent back to their owners. Therefore, the most popular destination of the "freedom" travelers was completely out of the United States. Many traveleled into Canada where slavery was illegal and there was safety from being captured and returned.

Social Studies: Geographic Directions

The drinking gourd (the star group known today as the **Big Dipper**), helped the slaves stay on a northward journey. Talk with your student about compass directions and the ways you have to help find them. (the sun, moon, stars, compasses, maps, etc.) Knowing that the sun, moon and stars rise in the east can be helpful knowledge that one might need if he has lost his way. Knowledge of specific pointer stars or the **North Star** can also be helpful as well as interesting.

If possible, obtain a compass and teach your student how to use it. Make up a treasure hunt and give compass directions to find the treasure. Practice saying the directions as you travel, when on an outing. Make and use maps to teach directions and following instructions.

Language Arts: Analogy

An analogy is a comparison of an unfamiliar idea to a simple or more familiar one. The concept of a railroad with tracks and cars that move people and things from one place to another on a schedule is familiar to most people. There came to be a very loosely organized effort to help slaves reach a place of freedom situated a long distance from their beginning point. When many different families and homes were used on the way, and when it was done in secret (mostly at night), the term *underground railroad* was coined. It was based on the analogy of a railroad system. Other railroad words were used as well, including *stations* for the homes used along the way and *conductors* (men who moved people along the underground railroad) such as Peg Leg Joe.

Language Arts: Compound Words

Follow the Drinking Gourd provides opportunities to explore **compound words**. Remind your student that compound words are words created by combining two or more words into a new word. Examples include: trapdoor, underground, steamship, runaways and daylight. It's important to recognize these as compound words, so that they can be spelled accurately.

Language Arts: Theme Study

(**Teacher's Note:** The following lesson suggestion is a departure from the usual *Five In A Row* teaching suggestions because it requires the securing of two more books. Yet, it is an idea that some may find enjoyable and of worth for your older student.)

There are other stories that tell the tale of the underground railroad. R. J. Monjo wrote *The Drinking Gourd,* an I Can Read book, that masterfully tells the story of a family who helps runaway slaves. The story *Sweet Clara and the Freedom Quilt,* by Deborah

Hopkinson tells a similar tale of a quilt, rather than a song as in *Follow the Drinking Gourd*, which secretly reveals a path to freedom.

If you desire, you can find these books and compare them with *Follow the Drinking Gourd*. Notice the differences and similarities in the details of the illustrations. Talk about or list the facts in one story. What additional facts do you learn in the next two stories? For instance, make a list of the specific kinds of danger that the slaves faced as they tried to escape. Or list the types of transportation they used for their getaway. List the different reactions of family members.

Title: <u>Follow the Drinking Gourd</u> by Jeanette Winter	Title: <u>Sweet Clara and the Freedom Quilt</u>	Title: <u>The Drinking Gourd</u> by R.J.Monjo
Danger:_____ _____	Danger:_____ _____	Danger:_____ _____
Transportation:____ _____	Transportation:____ _____	Transportation:____ _____
Reactions:_____ _____	Reactions:_____ _____	Reactions:_____ _____

This type of comparative learning exercise is foundational in helping your student learn to read from many sources to get more facts and to see the different sides of a subject. The ability to pick out details and to be able to compare one thing to another is a quality thinking skill, which can be gently introduced in this way to your student. This entire process is foundational to the research process.

Language Arts:
Uncle Tom's Cabin and Harriet Beecher Stowe

One piece of American literature that greatly influenced the public's opinion toward slavery was *Uncle Tom's Cabin*, written by Harriet Beecher Stowe. A brief mention of her name, the name of the book, and maybe a tiny thumbnail sketch of the story is all you may choose to present to your student at this time. With this introduction, you will build for him a knowledge base for future study. (**Teacher's Note**: You may enjoy reading a biography of Harriet Beecher Stowe for yourself. Her story is an amazing one!)

Art: Details

The illustration on the last page of text shows a vine with white flowers open at night. Moonflowers grow on vines, much like morning glories do, but moonflowers are even larger and they open in the late afternoon or evening and close at morning, while morning glories are the opposite. If your student enjoys gardening, he may enjoy planting some morning glory seeds, along with some moonflower vine seeds near a fence or trellis.

Make sure the ground is quite warm before planting. When the moonflowers bloom, get out *Follow the Drinking Gourd* and let your student compare the artist's pictures with the real blossom!

Art: Texture

Follow The Drinking Gourd provides a rich world of texture in the illustrations by Jeanette Winter. Turn to nearly any page and you'll discover the artist's use of texture, primarily in the backgrounds. You'll find detailed background textures in fields, tree bark, a straw hat, oceans, corn crops, wooden floors, etc. Encourage your student to try a drawing in which he "fills in" large areas of the background with a repetitive texture.

Art: Cut-Away View

After reading the story with your student, open the book to the page where the author describes, "*A trapdoor in the floor that took them under the barn to hide....*" Look at the picture. Talk about what you see. The floor of the stable with straw and horses' hooves is seen *above* the heads of the travelers. This is because under the straw covered barn floor is another cellar-like room where the people are hiding. The picture you see is a cut-away view of the barn. Have your student try drawing a cut-away view of something. It could be as simple as drawingan apple cut in half. You could try drawing what the inside of a car would look like if it were cut in half, or show what you could see in a stack of drawers if the front of the drawers were missing. Building a cut-away view inside a shoe-box, perhaps even a similar scene to the one in this story, could be another project for your older student.

Remind your student that using a cut-away view now and then adds yet more variety to his drawings and paintings. Add *Cut-Away View* to your list of choices an artist can make.

Art: Comparing Artist to Artist

The illustrative style used by Jeanette Winter is reminiscent of the work of Paul Gaugin, both in the stylized figures and especially in the color palette used. Look in the juvenile section of your library for a book on Gaugin that was written for children. (Preview it anyway!) Show your student some of the paintings. See if your student mentions feeling that the pictures have a similarity.

Also, the figures in the paintings of Thomas Hart Benton have a folk-art appearance and a stylized effect (proportions are exaggerated). If you can find any of Benton's work in an art book, compare his paintings, especially the people in them, to those figures of Gaugin and again to Jeanette Winter.

Art: Songs as a Teaching Method

Follow the Drinking Gourd is based on a song that sounded like a folk song, but had the secret plan for escape hidden in the lyrics. The song, with the music, is at the back of the book. It would be fun to teach the song to your student. Read the lyrics with your student and have him find the "hidden directions."

Music is a wonderful way to remember facts and touch the feelings of our past history. Most English-speaking children learn the "ABC Song" as they begin learning their alphabet. The song provides an easy way to help remember the sequence of letters. Many facets of history and past lifestyles are also easily learned and retained by song.

An advanced lesson on "Negro Spirituals" can be taught from this same time period. During the time slaves were brought to North America, they began to learn English and many became Christians. They learned and sang songs, some of which are called "Spirituals," because the lyrics have to do with Christian themes and with going to heaven. Songs like *Swing Low Sweet Chariot, Jacob's Ladder,* and *Go Down Moses,* were sung by the slaves and are still sung today. Your student may already be familiar with some of these songs, yet never have known their historic significance.

Art: Composition and Symbolism

Composition is the placement of figures, background lines and objects in a picture. Find the picture opposite the text, *"Under the starry sky Joe rowed them across the wide Ohio river."* Ask your student what he sees in the picture. Can he see how one side of the illustration (the boat full of people) is balanced by something on the other side (the Big Dipper or Drinking Gourd)? Put your hand over the star group and ask him if he thinks the picture would be just as good without it.

There is up and down, or vertical balance in the picture over the words, *"Walking by night, sleeping by day...."* The tall corn takes the upper two thirds of the picture. The sleeping people, though only in the lower third of the scene, have more mass and therefore balance the illustration. There is diagonal balance in the picture whose text reads, "With danger still near, too close for ease, the farmer sent the five travelers on." The large wagon is in the lower left-hand of this illustration, with the horse moving diagonally across the picture toward the small farm in the upper right. Remind your student that many artists spend much time and thought on the composition of a work before they begin detailed work on it.

There is a touch of symbolism in the picture over the text,*"Then the door opened wide to welcome the freedom travelers."* As the woman opens the door, the artist has drawn her hands spread out wide as if encircling and embracing the travelers. The open-heart welcome of the text is *symbolized* in this illustration.

Math: Measure of Time

Molly, James, Isaiah, Old Hatty and George embark on a dangerous journey to freedom. They hide in trees, cross rivers, rest at the Quaker farmhouse, etc. This is an opportunity to introduce your student to the many ways in which we measure time.

They may have hidden in the trees for several minutes. How long is a minute? How many seconds are in a minute? How many minutes did it take them to cross the river? How many minutes are in an hour? They rested at the farmhouse for several days. How many hours make up a day? How many days in a week? The trip took months to complete.

How many weeks in a month? How many months in a year? Explore these time concepts with your student as they relate to this story, and in ways that relate to their own life.

Math: Counting

As always, there are many opportunities for counting: from corn stalks, to trees, to stars, etc. For your younger student, let him "count" his way through the book several times.

Science: Signals

Throughout history, man has imitated bird calls for hunting and for signaling a companion. The American Indians imitated many different bird calls for signals and Davy Crockett is famous for his backwoods bird-call signaling.

The quail has a very distinctive "Bob White!" call, and owls have various calls. Many people imitate duck, goose and turkey calls when hunting.

If you can, listen to a tape of bird calls. See if your student can make any of the sounds. He may want to teach his friend a bird call, and use it for a secret signal!

Science: Star Groups and Constellations

The sky is full of marvelous things: the sun, the moon, clouds and the stars. Stars have been a source of wonder to man ever since he was created. In an effort to sort and classify the stars, people have learned to recognize pictures that fit the patterns they see in the sky so that they can quickly find the same groups of stars over and over. The Drinking Gourd, or as we know it, the Big Dipper is one of these star groups. It is a pattern of stars which forms part of a larger constellation called Ursa Major, or the Great Bear, according to the 1987 edition of *The World Book Encyclopedia*.

Peg Leg Joe uses a well known sky marker, the Drinking Gourd, to show the escaping slaves how to stay pointed in a northern direction.

If your student seems especially interested in the stars, there is a good book by H. A. Rey called *The Stars,* which you could borrow from your library or find at your bookstore. (ISBN 0-395-24830-2)

The subject of stars is also included in a book called *Adam and His Kin* by Ruth Beechick, chapter 6, page 47. This is an account of creation to "wonder" over and to stimulate your student's thinking.

Science: Cotton

Cotton! Soft, fluffy, white! Cotton was originally grown in Egypt, India and China, but long ago was imported to the New World. Columbus found cotton growing on some of the islands he visited.

Cotton is planted annually, reaches a height of 3-6 feet and is grown in temperate to hot climates from 47 degrees north latitude to 30 degrees south latitude. The cotton plant has a creamy white flower, a three-lobed leaf and, when mature, a cotton boll with fluffy white fiber and cotton seeds. Cotton is planted from March to May and harvested in 16-25 weeks, depending on the variety and the growing conditions.

In 1793, Eli Whitney invented a machine that could comb the cotton seeds from the fiber. This machine was called the cotton gin. Before the cotton gin, the seed was picked out by hand. But, because of this efficient invention, production of cotton in the United States rose rapidly and soon became the top agricultural crop. Encourage your older student to look up the entry **cotton gin** in *The World Book Encyclopedia* to discover the derivation of the word *gin*.

Cotton seed is used for many things (a really interesting topic to study). The oil from the seed is also used for many things, including salad oil. Explore cotton with your student. Touch cotton fabric; feel its softness. Compare it to wool or synthetics. Have fun!

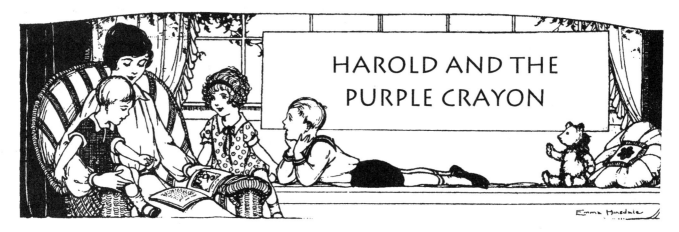

HAROLD AND THE PURPLE CRAYON

Title: *Harold and the Purple Crayon*
Author/Illustrator: Crockett Johnson
Copyright: 1955
Summary: Harold has a crayon and an imagination. The adventures that result are entertaining–filled with drama and humor.

(**Teacher's Note:** This is a short unit to go along with Review Week. *Harold and the Purple Crayon* is strong in art inspiration, and encourages the use of imagination.)

Language Arts: Setting

Harold and the Purple Crayon provides exciting variety in teaching your student about a story's setting. It is unlike some stories that have predetermined settings (real or fictional). The setting of this story is *progressive* and in Harold's imagination. To have the setting unknown at the beginning of the story is unusual. Indeed, Harold is thinking in the initial picture (the lines are just a tangle until he gets an idea). Once he knows that he wants to go for a walk the setting begins. It then changes with each of Harold's new ideas. This *progressive* setting does not stop until Harold drops off to sleep. Crockett Johnson certainly writes and illustrates his story in an unusual way. Your student might want to try writing and drawing a similar type of adventure. In writing this type of story, he could think about what he wants to do, or where he wants to go. Then, in his story, he could design and build (or draw like Harold) the places and things required to make his adventure come to pass!

Language Arts: Humor

The author/illustrator, Crockett Johnson, has used humor in the text of the story through the use of puns. Teach your student about puns and notice them in outside reading, media programs and everyday speech. Some people are very quick to understand and use puns. Perhaps your student is one of them. A pun is humorously using the same word with two different meanings, or two words with different meanings that sound the same. It is basically a play on words for a humorous purpose.

There are examples of the use of puns in this story. *Made land* (which means got to the land, or landed) but Harold is actually drawing or *making* the land! *Made his bed,* usually means to put the sheets and covers on correctly for comfortable sleep. In this case he is drawing *or making* the bed. *Drew up the covers* usually means pulled them up but in this case Harold *drew* them with his crayon.

Another type of humor occurs in the pages describing Harold drawing the forest. A forest, by definition, is a dense area of trees. This means a lot of trees close together, or another name might be woods. Either forest or woods means many trees. So, there is humor as Harold, not wanting to become lost in the woods, decides to make a very small forest, with just one tree in it (which really isn't a forest at all!)

Art: Creativity

What a wonderful book to kick off a discussion about creativity! Creativity is a joyful thing, and some of that joy is captured in the illustration where Harold draws a tree. Harold isn't sure what he is going to draw. He begins and it turns out to be an apple tree. Drawing is fun because one can begin, think and imagine, and often end up with a picture that surprises even the artist! While most finished artists' works are carefully thought out and arranged, the beginning sketches and inspirations are often a process of progressive thoughts.

Harold thinks randomly. Explain that this means Harold's thoughts are going in many directions, not centered on any one specific idea. Have your student trace with his finger the line of thought on the title page and continue onto the copyright page and then to the first page. Talk about how the line represents the random thinking and notice what begins to happen to the line as Harold's thought forms into a single idea (that he should take a walk in the moonlight). In this way Crockett Johnson illustrates the random to specific process of thinking. Give your student a marker and a very large piece of paper. Let him begin in one corner of the paper thinking and drawing randomly. As he forms an idea for a picture have him complete the drawing. It might be fun to do your own picture while your student works on his!

Art: Perspective - Vanishing Point

Perspective is what gives art a three-dimensional look, even though the artist uses a flat surface. Look at a painting or drawing. Ask your student what parts of the picture look far away and what parts look closer. Use the word *perspective*. Explain that artists use various techniques to give the viewer the impression of perspective. The illustrator of this story has used a technique called *vanishing point* on the fifth and sixth page to make the path look like it is going off into the distance. The lines are far apart in the forefront of the picture but join together at the horizon where the path seems to disappear. If your student is interested, he many want to try a drawing that has somewhere in it a path or road that is wider on the lower portion of the picture and converges in the middle or upper part of the drawing. This would be a good technique to point out on occasion as you notice it in illustrations and artist's works. Add *Perspective - Vanishing Point* to your chart of Choices An Artist Can Make.

Art: Perspective - Foreshortening

The picture of Harold laying out a simple picnic lunch is an excellent example of a foreshortened square and a foreshortened circle. Learning the use of these two shapes is invaluable for drawing many things, from boxes and television sets, to buckets and fishbowls, ponds, etc. This technique makes the objects appear to move back into the Foreshortening is another technique for creating perspective.

With your student, notice how Harold's picnic cloth looks like a square that has been pulled out at the side corners, causing the top and bottom corners to become closer together. The tops of the pies are also foreshortened circles. This is a circle that looks as if it has been pulled at the sides. To demonstrate take a fifteen inch piece of heavy string or cord. Knot the two ends together so that you have a loop or circle of string. Lay the string down on a table and shape it into a square. Now pick up two opposing corners and pull outward slightly. Let your student watch what happens to the figure. The top and bottom corner points of the square should be closer together now. You can do the same with a circle. Place the string loop so it approximates a perfect circle. Pinch the string at two opposing points on the circle and pull slightly, creating a foreshortened circle. Then, if he desires, your student may attempt to draw a foreshortened square or circle. Draw attention, now and then, to foreshortened squares and circles that you see in art and illustrations. Add this technique to your chart for Choices An Artist Can Make.

To draw a foreshortened square make two dots like this:

Then add the side, corner dots like this:

Finally, connect the dots with straight lines.

Here are some examples:

A picnic cloth looks square if viewed from above.

A picnic cloth appears to "lay on the ground" if a foreshortened square is used.

A lake might look like a circle if viewed from above.

A lake as it appears if a foreshortened circle is used.

Art: City Scenes

Some young artists are especially fond of drawing buildings—lots of buildings, cities and cities of buildings. Crockett Johnson's illustrations include some of these kind of drawings in the passage describing Harold's attempt to find the right window. If your student would like to make a city, encourage him to try and notice the variety of building shapes and the different kinds of windows.

Math: Counting, and Counting by Twos, etc.

The windows in the city scenes provide ample opportunity for counting. You may also want to try counting by twos threes, fours, fives, and sixes, depending on the window grouping in a single building (in the city illustrations of *Harold and the Purple Crayon*).

Math: Multiplying, Dividing and Using Fractions

Harold makes his favorite picnic lunch–lots of pies! From the picture with five pies, your older student could recite the fives multiplication table. In the same way he could recite the nines multiplication table.

Also, it looks as though Harold ate approximately a third of each pie. Ask your student to count the total number of pies (9). Your student may come to the conclusion that Harold ate nine thirds of a pie. (9/3) This is what is called an improper fraction (when the top number, or the numerator, is larger than the lower number, called the denominator). Make several cardboard rounds divided into thirds. Then, your student can count out nine of the pieces. By putting three pieces together to make a whole pie, he should find that Harold eats three whole pies for dinner. (9/3 = 3)

Science: Transportation - On Land, Sea and Air

Discuss with your student the various methods of travel Harold uses in his adventures. Ask if there are other kinds of travel (possibly under the sea as in a submarine or above the air in outer space). Make a list of ways to travel on land, sea and air. How many modes of travel has your student experienced? Has he flown on a plane? Ridden on a train? In an automobile? On a boat? Motorcycle? Bicycle? Hot Air Balloon? Other?

Science: Survival Skills - Gaining a View from Altitude

Harold knows that if he climbs up a hill, he can see things that are in the distance. Point out to your student, on an outing, that from the top of hills one can see farther. Let him compare this to his view in the lowest part of a road or valley. This is an important thing for your student to know. If he ever becomes lost out doors, gaining altitude by climbing a hill or tree may help him see familiar land marks or the lost path. If this concept seems interesting to your student, go to the library and find pictures taken from space. Show him that, as you continue to gain altitude, you can eventually see the entire planet Earth, the solar system and beyond!

Science: Moon Facts

This is a good chance to review the phases of the moon. See *Owl Moon* in the beginning of *FIAR* Vol. 2, p. 40. Your older, intensely curious science student might be interested in the words **apogee** and **perigee**. These words denote the **elliptical orbit** of the moon about the earth. Perigee is when the moon is closest to the earth in its orbit, while apogee is the most distant point of the moon's orbit.

Title:	*When I Was Young In the Mountains**
Author:	Cynthia Rylant
Illustrator:	Diane Goode
Copyright:	1982
Award:	Caldecott Honor Book (Silver medal given for illustrations)
Summary:	Reminiscing about mountain life brings about a feeling of content ment.

*Alternate Selection for *Down Down the Mountain*

Social Studies: Geography - Appalachia

Writing for the book's dust cover, Cynthia Rylant says, *"The inspiration for this book came from memories of my childhood in Appalachia-Cool Ridge, West Virginia."* In *Five in A Row,* you may have studied two other stories with an Appalachian setting: *Rag Coat* by Lauren Miller Vol. 1, p. 31, and *Down Down the Mountain* by Ellis Credle, Vol. 2, p. 86. Review the information about the Appalachian area in these two units.

Place your story disk on the Appalachian region of your map.

Social Studies: Occupations

When I Was Young In the Mountains, introduces a grandfather who is a coal miner. In this story you also meet a grandmother about whom you could list many accomplishments from housekeeping, cooking, gardening, child care, and livestock tending, to snake killing! In addition, there is a couple who runs a store, a preacher and a traveling photographer. Talk about the type of work and responsibilities for each duty of life and occupation.

The traveling photographer is an interesting occupation. The camera, invented in the mid 1800s, was widely used in America during the late nineteenth century. However, in Appalachia, people were not wealthy or progressive in their possessions and most did not have their own cameras, even well into the 1900s. So, a person could make a living there by taking his equipment from town to town and charging people for photographs. This was similar to the portrait artists. They used to travel from place to place and paint the people and their families for a fee. Then they would move on to another town. The difference between the painters and the photographers was that the earlier portrait artists usually painted the very wealthy families because their art was time-consuming and expensive. The photographers, however, were able to provide a picture more quickly and at far less cost, so working class people began to have their photographic portraits made.

Social Studies: History

Ask your student if he can find examples of a more old-fashioned way of life lived in this coal mining area of Appalachia: candlelight and oil lamps—no flashlights, well water is pumped outside the house and brought in, a johnny house or outhouse—no indoor plumbing, a school-house that doubles as a church, butter churn and wood burning cook stove, and swimming hole—no pools.

If your student has an interest in these kinds of items and this way of living, try to find a museum that has furnished replica rooms of this lifestyle. Or, visit an antique show and look at items used in the past, or a historic house that has been preserved. Allow your student to imagine life in a different era. Compare this way of living to the style in which he lives today. Is there anything he would like to change? Perhaps your student would enjoy writing a short story of his own, set in the early 1900s style of Appalachian mountain life. (Remember before a writing project to have your student review his chart or list of Choices A Writer Can Make.)

A good look at Appalachia today is the book *Appalachia, The Voices of Sleeping Birds* by Cynthia Rylant, ISBN 0-15-201605-8. This book ties the past and present together! It is written by the same author as the book we are currently studying: *When I Was Young In the Mountains*.

Social Studies: Emotions - Crying

Talk about emotions and especially about crying. Remind your student that sometimes people cry because they are so happy. Other times they may cry because they are very sad. It is important for a child to know that crying can be for happiness, as it was for the grandmother at the baptism of her grandson. You might want to use this as an opportunity to discuss the public display of emotions. While men in our culture tend to hide their emotions, increasingly we're told that it is a sign of emotional health to be able to display our emotions when appropriate. Tell your student, particularly boys, that crying is nothing to be ashamed of when circumstances are appropriate, as in cases of great happiness or grief.

Language Arts: Repetition

Ask your student if he can find the repetitious phrase that runs throughout this story. Beginning with the title and repeated seven or eight times is the phrase, *"When I was young in the mountains...."* Talk about the way this phrase ties the story together. See if your student would like to write a story using this technique. He might use, *"When I go to sleep at night..."*, or *"When I go to the store..."*, or *"When I play with my friends, I...."* Remind him by looking back through the story that this repetitious line is not on every

-154-

page. That might be too much. Help your student make a picture book using his repetitious story with pages that turn. Let him illustrate it himself or find an illustrator (parent, sibling, friend, etc.) to do it for him. He could also use pictures from magazines to illustrate his story.

Language Arts: Theme - Contentment

Ask your student what he thinks the author of this story is trying to tell the reader. You may get responses like, "She is trying to portray (show) life in the Appalachian mountains," or "She is showing what the life of a coal miner is like," or "She is showing what the lives of children are like." But underlying these ideas is the theme of the story–the *reason* the story was written. The main idea the author wanted to convey was simply, "I was in the mountains, and that was always *enough*." There is contentment in enjoying the pines, stars, moon, the kiss of the grandfather, the cornbread and the cousins. Even though there isn't a lot of money to do things, the important things are there, and it is enough. This is the main theme of this story.

Talk about the graciousness of contentment. For a person to find happiness and worth in the things around him is a wonderful virtue. Perhaps you and your student could seek to cultivate contentment by pointing out interesting things to each other and enjoying them together. It could be an especially beautiful leaf, a bird call, a pattern of bricks on a building, or having warm toasty muffins on a cold day, etc. The idea is to move a little more slowly, observe and appreciate far more than you might usually do, and begin to let satisfaction with small wonders bring you additional measures of contentment.

The artist takes up this theme of contentment by drawing the children's faces with gentle smiles on nearly every page. Contentment comes from the Grandfather's kiss. It is portrayed in the evening scene on the porch, and the last declaration that *to be in the mountains is enough*. Look through the pictures with your student. Discuss the things in these illustrations that you each find special. Then talk about the things, in your own lives, that bring each of you a special sense of warmth and contentment.

Art: Sky Treatments

Turn with your student to the illustration opposite the page of text about getting the water from the well. Notice the way that illustrator Diane Goode portrays the blue sky. By using a little blue on just part of the white paper page, she has given the *suggestion* of a blue sky. This is different from the more common portrayal of at sky in which the entire sky is a single color. Your student might enjoy composing a picture. Rather than making *all* the area above the horizon a single sky color, instead use color on only part of the paper. Leaving spots of the paper white to show the sun, moon or stars is interesting, too. (Take time to notice in this picture the ferns drooping over the white paper and the splash lines in the pail of water.)

Art: Artistic Effects with Light and Liquid

The second illustration of the Grandparent's table and the cornbread dinner shows an hourglass-shaped stream of light coming from the oil lamp. Some of the light is going upwards and some is cast down onto the table. This effect is made possible on paper by darkening the area around the light rays.

Also, the steam rising from the cornbread is shown by wavy lines while the milk being poured from the pitcher comes out in a curved line. Talk about the way the artist drew the milk. Then pour some for your student from a pitcher into a dark mug. Let him see a side view and witness for himself the curve of the liquid as it pours. Does it look like Goode's illustration? Your student may want to try a picture that has a waterfall (side view) or some kind of liquid being poured, like from a tea kettle, etc. He can try the technique of making the stream of liquid look curved.

Art: Palette

The colors chosen by Diane Goode for *When I Was Young In the Mountains* are subtle (soft) browns, grayed greens and blues, and soft oranges. These are the type of colors used in older paintings. They may have been chosen (rather than modern neon colors) to make the pictures appear old-fashioned. The use of old-fashioned colors accents the old-fashioned subject material.

Again, your older art student may be reminded that an artist may choose a palette which is limited to a few colors (as this story) or one which includes a wide range of colors (sometimes called a full palette). An artist may also choose to work in monochrome (one color). When the artist limits his palette, he chooses a color for the red group, a color for his blue and a color for his yellow. Then he mixes the secondary and tertiary colors from these three colors and stays within these colors for his entire work. The particular color of limited palette in *When I Was Young In the Mountains* causes a unity of theme throughout the work and maintains the subtle, quiet, content mood of the text.

Art: Character Portrayal - Artists' Styles

Look at the faces and bodies in the illustrations of this story. Ask your student if they all seem very different or if they seem similar. (There does not seem to be much variety in the faces, hands and feet of the characters. This does not demean the artist. It only shows that some artists do intense characterizations where every person looks completely different. Remember the faces in *The Story of Ferdinand*? Vol. 2? Each figure was different in size, features, expressions and clothes. At other times, book illustrators focus on the picture as a whole. Their characters are not as highly individualized because they are portraying an overall feeling, or theme, as in this story of contentment.) If your student is interested, look at several books that have many human characters and notice the *style* of the artists. See if you can find a book with highly individualized characters andanother story where the chararcters have a similarity in features, clothes, etc.

Art: Making a List from Illustrations

Make a list of the things you and your student see at the Appalachian general store. This gives your student practice at picking out small details and he will enjoy the search with you. You can help him by answering questions about what certain items might be.

Art: From Cover to Cover

By now, your student is discovering that the illustrations for a story aren't just the pictures connected with the text. They may also be included on the book cover– for a first glimpse of what is to come. Illustrations often appear on the title page, and the dedication page. Sometimes there is a picture at the end of the story after the last page of text. Each of these pictures tells the reader something about the story. These illustrations may add information, symbolism or closure.

On the title page Diane Goode pictured a small house in a woods, amidst a great white background . This picture reminds us of the isolation of the entire Appalachian region. It might also portray the distance between each home in that region.

The table setting on the dedication page depicts the lack of fancy material possessions (shown by the cracked cup). Yet, in the same picture shines the warmth of the lamplight. There is also the love of nature symbolized by the flowers. This warmth and love help, in part, to inspire the contentment portrayed in the story.

The very last picture of the single tree continues and brings closure to the book's theme: The tree might not be overly impressive, but it was good...*and it was enough.*

Math: Weights and Measures

In the general store, there is a scale. This gives you a chance to talk about weighing things. Discuss how pounds and ounces* are used to tell how much something weighs. Take this lesson as far as your student's grade level or interest will allow. Find a scale and let your student measure and record the weight of different items. If possible, show him a scale at the grocery store and measure some items there. Talk about some of the produce in the picture that could be measured on the scale. (coffee beans–or ground coffee, meat, fruit or potatoes, etc.)

There is also a gallon jar pictured, possibly full of pickles. You can use this opportunity to talk about cup, pint, quart and gallon measures* and the type of things that would be measured this way. Also, you may ask how many cups of liquid are in a gallon, etc. (Let your student experiment to find out. He could pour from a measuring cup into a gallon milk jug, using a funnel.)

Although it is not pictured, stores like this one often had yard goods (cloth and ribbons, etc.) for sale. These items had to be measured by inches, feet and yards*. Any of these different types of measurement may be taught from this general store picture, also. Remember to include eggs, muffins and other types of products sold by the dozen.

This is the type of lesson that can turn into an on-going project as you create a small country *store* with your student. Practice measuring, selling and buying common household goods! (***Metric measurements can make another lesson**.)

Math: List and Count

List the animals found in this story and count how many of each appear in the illustrations. Cows-2, Snakes-2 (or 3 if you count what looks like a snake but could be a stick at the swimming hole!), Chickens-8, Dogs-3 (or 4 if you count the cover), Birds-16

This is an excellent opportunity to show your student how to make and read a bar graph.

	1				5				10				15				20
Cows																	
Snakes																	
Dogs																	
Chickens																	
Birds																	

Finally, it might be fun and encourage the use of imagination, to add animals that *could* have been in the pictures but were not: a cat in the store, for instance, an owl and a raccoon in the woods, or a horse in the side yard, a frog near the pump, or insects in the garden, etc. The list goes on!

Math: Adding and Subtracting or Multiplying and Dividing

The children in the story haved three pails at the pump with which to fill two tin tubs for their baths. Using these figures, make up various problems. For example, if they have to have nine pails of water to fill the tubs, how many trips to the pump will they need to make? (3) How much water will go into each tub? (4 1/2 pails). This story scenario can be used to make addition, subtraction, multiplication and division problems at whatever level you need for your student.

Science: Moon

Ask your student if he knows the moon phase the artist has used on the cover of *When I Was Young in the Mountains*. (There is a full moon pictured on the cover and in the next to the last illustration.) In the illustration of the grandmother and young girl on their way to the outhouse, the moon is in a different phase. You may review* what this phase is called–a waning crescent. That means the moon has already been full and is moving toward its new moon phase). Did your student notice the same crescent shape on the outhouse door? (*Review phases of the moon, *Owl Moon*, FIAR Vol. 2, p. 41.)

Science: Snakes

You may be ready to teach your student about snakes. Snakes are **vertebrate** animals (having backbones and craniums). They are also **reptiles** which are animals that are cold-blooded, have lungs and scale-covered skins. There are many different kinds of snakes. Few are harmful to man, but all serve a purpose by helping keep the rodent population in control. Snakes are cold-blooded creatures. That is, their body temperature changes with their surroundings. In order to maintain a proper body temperature snakes move from cooler to warmer locations. Help your student find what this proper body temperature is. Look in *The World Book Encyclopedia* or other reference book. Many students are fascinated with snakes. Consider a trip to the pet store in your area. **Herpetology*** (the study of snakes) has become increasingly popular. Many pet stores carry a wide selection of snakes. For the animal lover teacher and student, keeping a pet snake in a cage or glass aquarium may be a long-term project worth exploring! ***Check the origin and meaning of this word in a good dictionary.**

The grandmother in this story first tries to threaten the snake. Ask your student why it seems she would rather not kill it, unless she feels she has to. (She would rather have scared the snake away because it kills many mice and other rodents.) Snakes are helpful to man because they kill the mice and rodents that cause damage to crops and to food stored in the barn and the house.

Science: Nutrition

The meal that grandmother makes for the family looks good. Ask your student to recall the food groups (studied in *FIAR* Vol. 1 p. 41) and decide if the meal she makes is a nutritious one.

The four basic food groups include:

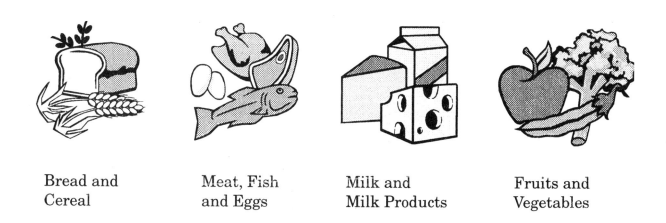

| Bread and | Meat, Fish | Milk and | Fruits and |
| Cereal | and Eggs | Milk Products | Vegetables |

Grandmother's meal consists of hot cornbread (made of corn meal, flour, eggs, milk), pinto beans, okra and milk. Beans and milk combine proteins to make a complete protein base for this meal. The corn meal and flour add carbohydrates and the okra is a green vegetable. Missing might be a fruit of some kind, but the meal is a nutritious one.

Fix some cornbread for a snack, or enjoy some cocoa cocoa together on a rainy morning. Think about what it is like to be in the mountains and practice contentment!

Title: *Gramma's Walk*
Author/Illustrator: Anna Grossnickle Hines
Copyright: 1993
Summary: A loving relationship between a young boy and his gramma provides an opportunity for using imagination to compensate a handicap.

Social Studies: Setting

The setting where Donnie's gramma lives is never revealed. It could be anywhere. Place your story disk wherever you would like, or maybe on the state in which your student's grandparents live.

Gramma's imagined "walk" was set at a seashore. Looking at a map, ask your student where this seashore might have been. Where *are* the seashores? (Anywhere along the east coast or the west coast of the U.S. or Florida or the Gulf states.)

Social Studies: Caring About Others

After reading *Gramma's Walk* with your student, ask him what specific things Donnie does that demonstrates his love, respect, care and concern for his Gramma. (On the very first page, Donnie slips quietly into the sunroom where his Gramma is waiting. He's careful not to bump his hassock into her wheelchair. The reader can tell the close relationship between them by the looks on their faces and the closeness of their bodies. Donnie and his Gramma choose to spend time with each other and enjoy the "walk" they take. Donnie encourages his Gramma with the words, *"Gramma, you're the best walker in the whole world."*) The Gramma, though not able to take an actual walk with Donnie, is still happy and full of imagination and able to provide a special time for her grandson.

Social Studies: Imagination

Few subjects are more controversial in the late twentieth century, but imagination is a wonderful, God-given gift that every child can enjoy. Gramma's use of imagination bridges the gap between her own chair-bound world and the freedom of Donnie's world. Her imagination is basically a memory of days past. She shares it in a way that allows her grandson to experience these adventures "with" her. There is a tremendous difference between imagination and visualization. You want your student to learn to exercise his imagination fully. Perhaps you can "take" your student on a walk with you through the use of imagination. Tell him about a place you went many years ago, perhaps before he was born. Be sure to include plenty of details. Talk about the sights, smells, sounds, tastes and feelings of the place. Then encourage him to take you on a "walk" to a place you've never been with him. Imagination is the seedbed from which storytelling and creative writing grow. Perhaps he'd like to take you on an imaginary "walk" to a place neither of you has ever been before: the moon, China, the bottom of the ocean, etc. Feel free to continue taking imaginative "walks" with your student as opportunities occur.

Social Studies: Handicapped

Gramma has physical disabilities which force her to use a wheelchair. Perhaps your student knows someone who uses a wheelchair. Today, there areas many as 43 million Americans with some form of handicap. This is nearly 17% of our population. You may want to discuss this entire topic with your student, letting him know that there have been several laws passed during the past 20 years to make certain that people with disabilities receive equal opportunities and have access to public buildings.

Your student may have noticed elevator ramps in public buildings. Perhaps he has observed wide, handicapped access doors to public restrooms. Maybe he has observed the Braille labels on public elevators, etc. The important concept for your student to grasp is that handicapped people, though challenged in certain ways, are just like everyone else. They, too, have dreams, hopes, feelings and goals for their lives.There is an internationally accepted sign to to designate reserved parking areas and handicapped access facilities. Maybe your student has already noticed this sign. If not, point it out to him on an outing. This is what the sign looks like:

Language Arts: Structure of Story - Backtracking

The structure of the story *Gramma's Walk* is like a ribbon on a roll. It rolls out to the end and then rolls back up again. Or another way of saying it is that the structure of the story *backtracks*. Donnie and his Gramma take an imaginary walk from a starting point (the lighthouse in the grassy place) to the far point (by the purple jelly-bean rock) and then back again to the starting point. This ribbon-roll structure is fun to try and your student might enjoy writing a story modeled after this work of Anna Grossnickle Hines. (See also *Down Down the Mountain, FIAR* Vol. 2, p. 90)

Your student could also draw a map of "Gramma's walk." Or, he might rather draw a map to illustrate his own story.

Language Arts: Compound Words

Compound words are words made of two or more base words (morphemes). In *Gramma's Walk* there are several good examples of compound words: hoofprints, seashore, sunroom, wheelchair, lighthouse, and seagulls. If your student is spelling on the first or second grade level, you might want to point out these words. Let him know that these words are combined and not spelled as two separate words.

For your young student, you might make two cards. Illustrate the word *sea* (print the word also) on one card. On another illustrate the word *shore* and print the word. Then talk about each word and the meaning and then put the cards together touching, to show these two words are combined into the word *seashore*. Obviously, your young student won't be expected to learn the spellings. However, he will begin to get the idea that some words are combined to make a larger word which utilizes the original meanings of the words.

Art: Illustrations Follow Text

Look carefully at the next to the last picture on the right as Donnie and Gramma wave goodbye. You and your student can see the otter rock, the peeper birds, the barnacle rocks, the smooth rocks, the castle and flag, the seagulls, the rabbit in the grassy place and the lighthouse, as the text traces the homeward path. Each step of the text is visible in the right hand illustration. Let your young student trace the path, stopping at each item, as you re-read the text.

An important skill for an illustrator is to make certain the artwork corresponds directly to the story's text to help the reader understand the story. This does not mean the pictures have to be on the exact same page as the text, but rather that they convey the correct details from the story.

Art: Portraying Quiet Action

There is a time for playing hard and being able to use one's voice and energy to the limit. But this story shows a quiet, yet intensely enjoyable time between a very young person and an older one. Anna Grossnickle Hines has chosen *subtle*, pastel, quiet colors (as opposed to *intense* reds, blues, yellows, or neon bright colors) to convey the gentleness of the time Donnie spent with his grandmother.

The actual action portrayed by the figures of Donnie and Gramma also conveys a gentleness. For instance, there are no fast action lines by Donnie's feet as he pushes the hassock up to the wheelchair. He is moving carefully and slowly. Donnie's head on Gramma's lap (next page) moves slowly to the side as you see him thinking (in the next picture).

Look at the left-hand pictures from the beginning of the book to the end. Watch Donnie and his gramma. Catch the sense of quiet imagining as shown through the movements of their bodies. There is action. Donnie is never in the same position. But it is a calm action, even to the gentle waving goodbye (not an excited flailing of the arms) at the end of the "seashore walk." Don't miss the closing picture of the "walking pair", *after* the last page of text.

You have learned how to show exuberant action in the past *FIAR* art lessons as you have studied action lines, etc. (See *Papa Piccolo, FIAR* Vol. 1, p.80: Creating the Illusion of Speed, as well as *Make Way for Ducklings*, FIAR Vol. 2, p. 98: Speed Lines.) Now invite your student to draw two or more pictures that show slow, gentle action. This could be shown by careful positioning of bodies or objects with subtle changes in their positions.

Art: Double Story Illustrations

Try reading the text of the story while covering all the left hand pictures and only looking at the main scene pictures. Then, try reading it again covering up the right-hand scenes and only looking at the left hand pictures while you read. Consider together what the story would have been like if the illustrator had used only the left hand pictures or only the right hand ones.

This is an interesting method of illustration. The author/illustrator could have used exclusively either the right hand pictures or the left-hand ones and it still would have been a good story. However, by the choice Anna Hines makes to use both sets of illustrations, we get two streams of information and enjoyment. We see both the scenery of "the walk", and we get to watch the close relationship between Donnie and his grandmother. Double good!

Art: Simplicity and Realism

Anna Hines has used simple figures that still look realistic. Some artists create wildly stylized impressions of people and places. Others use a photo-realism style that seeks to capture every texture and wrinkle of the subject. Hines' style is soft, gentle, relaxed and simple, yet it is anatomically accurate and realistic. Examine the illustrations carefully as you discuss the simple use of color and line to define the human form and the ocean shore.

Art: Colors

Look at the fifth major scenic illustration. It shows an aerial view of the beach and the water. Ask your student to count how many colors he can see in the water. The illustrator, with water color and colored pencils, has used pinks, yellows, tans, browns, blues, greens, etc. Some artists use only a deep blue when drawing water. Others use only blue and white. Hines has chosen to use a variety of soft color. Look through the other pages and see if this artist is consistent in her particular portrayal of water. Discuss with your student that there is no *right* way to draw water. Artists use many different styles, techniques and colors to portray water. Perhaps your older artist would like to try using Hines' technique of using several soft, subtle colors to create the appearance of water.

Art: Foreshortened Circles

Foreshortened circles were covered in the art lesson for *Harold and the Purple Crayon, FIAR* Vol. 2, p. 150. Check there for definition and illustration. In *Gramma's Walk* look for examples of foreshortened circles—especially on the sandcastle's turrets. Let your student trace with his finger these elongated circles. See Foreshortening page in Index.

Math: Counting by Twos, Threes and Fours, and Multiplication

To create interest, when teaching your student how to count by twos, talk about Donnie and his gramma being two people. Their pictures appear on the left side of each page. Each time you turn the page you could count higher by twos– two, four, six, etc. The gulls and the peeper birds are seen in groups of three. Begin with the pictures of these birds and count by threes. Continue with scene picture opposite the text where Donnie and his gramma wave good-bye. In this picture you can just see the three gulls and the three peeper birds in the distance. Continue counting by threes as far as you think appropriate. There are four feathers shown on the page opposite the copyright page, four wheels on the wheel chair, and a group of four pebbles on the beach. Practice counting by fours, using these pictures for added interest, according to the level of your student.

With your older student, you might want to do some problems with the twos, threes, and fours multiplication tables. If you have the time, you could make a page of multiplication problems with twos problems and trace a picture of Donnie and his gramma at the top for interest. You could trace the peeper birds or gulls at the top of a page of threes problems, and feathers at the top of a page of fours multiplication tables. This helps create an interesting learning atmosphere. Making these kind of math pages ties math to the enjoyable experience of a reading a story together.

Math: Counting

Open the inside of the book cover. You should see a double page of feathers. These are enough feathers to keep your young student busy counting for a while! Listen to him while he counts and you will notice exactly how high he can count without mistake, and any points at which he makes repeated mistakes. For instance, he may be able to count to fifty each time, but he always leaves out *seventeen*. Careful observation will help you recognize where additional math lessons would be helpful.

Science: Senses

Sight, sound, feeling, taste and smell are the senses that help one experience a situation. The memory of these experiences can recall a situation long after it is over.

Donnie and Gramma are able to take this kind of imaginary walk because one or the other of them has experiences that they can recall. They remember the sights, sounds, touches, tastes and smells. Donnie knows to be quiet around a rabbit. Perhaps this awareness is the result of previous experience with rabbits or other wild animals. Or, he might have learned the information from a book, etc. Gramma has obviously heard the sound of waves and knows the kinds of birds that would be near the water.

With your student, at different times and in different places, pay attention to the sights, smells, feelings, sounds and tastes. When you hear a particular sound, for instance, think of as many descriptive words for it as possible: The town clock bell. Bong! Bong! That sounds like a deep metal striking a note. It reminds me of the bass notes on an organ, the throaty, slow laugh of Uncle Joe, or a lazy old bullfrog.

Try a walk in a garden where you find the herb thyme (or have some fresh thyme on hand). Pick a little and crush it in your fingers. Notice the smell. You could say it is pungent, strong, sharp, or interesting, and that it reminds you of a French soup kitchen or Aunt Mary's closet, etc. These are just ideas to get you started thinking along such lines, but any sights, sounds, smells, etc. will do. With your student, try this exercise from time to time. Make sure you cover the range of all five senses.

As you practice concentrating on the small delights around you, both you and your student will find a wealth of pleasant data being stored in your memories. You can draw from these memories again and again. It will enrich your writing and speech. It may come again to your imagination to encourage you in times that may be not as pleasant, as it certainly did for Donnie's gramma in this story.

Science: Lighthouses

Review the reasons for building lighthouses and the list the areas where you would expect to find one. Using information learned in other stories dealing with lighthouses (*The Little Red Lighthouse and the Great Gray Bridge, FIAR* Vol. 2, etc.), can your student add to this text his own memories to make Gramma's story even longer and more informative? If your student lives near a lighthouse or will have an opportunity to travel to an area that has a lighthouse, encourage him to visit and learn more about them. Watch your favorite vendor catalogs for Amanda Bennett's new *Unit Study Adventure: Lighthouses*, soon to be released.

Science: Beaches

There are ocean* beaches in many areas of the United States. They have some similarities such as tides and waves. But many things surrounding a beach vary from geographic area to area. Beaches can be made of rocks or sand, in differing colors. Some beaches are white, while some are tannish brown and others nearly black due to the differing rocks and sands. The rocks can be different,too. They may be round and smooth from the tumbling in the ocean or they can be sharp and jagged.In *Gramma's Walk,* the rocks are sharp because of barnacles. Barnacles are a marine crustacean (an animal). As adults, these animals form a hard shell and attach themselves to underwater surfaces such as ships, rocks, pilings and piers, etc. When the tide is out, you may find them clinging to rocks and piers.

Each beach area may have different kinds of birds, fish, shells and seaweed-type plants. Even the boats, and houses near the beach may have distinctive cultural differences. Some differences are due to the type of weather that a particular area experiences. If you were to study or visit many different kinds of beaches you could later take an imaginative walk. You would know by the distinctive descriptions whether your "beach walk" took place in Florida, Maine, Southern California or the gulf in Texas!
*Amanda Bennett also has a Unit Study Adventure on Oceans. See vendor catalogs.

If you enjoyed the review week in *FIAR* Volume 1, take a week to review the books in Volume 2, along with the authors, illustrators and illustrations of these stories. Recall titles which were award winners. Figure out which book is the oldest, and which book was written most recently. How many of the titles are more than twenty years old? (If you have returned books to the library, used the information at the beginning of each story in your teacher's manual.)

Discuss the stories you and your student particularly liked. Which characters or ideas were your favorites? Did you have a particular theme that was exciting to you or touched your emotions? What type of story was your favorite: the look back into the past (*Three Names*, or *Down Down the Mountain*), the animal stories (*Ferdinand*, and others that overlap categories), the animal fantasy (*The Tale of Peter Rabbit*), the stories that focus on nature (*Owl Moon, etc.*), the true story (*The Giraffe That Walked to Paris*), or the ribbon roll, back-tracking type of stories (*Down Down the Mountain, Gramma's Walk*), etc.?

Look again at the artwork. Review the elements of art that you have learned. Be sure that you have added the new information in Volume 2 to your art chart or list called "Choices An Artist Can Make". Volume 2 additions might include: foreshortened circles and squares–an element of perspective (*Harold and the Purple Crayon*), knowing your subject (*The Giraffe That Walked to Paris*), vanishing point–an element of perspective (*Three Names*, and *Harold*), interpreting a painting (*Three Names*), surface lines–an element of perspective (*Three Names*), comparing pictures (*Wee Gillis*), cross hatching–an element of shading (*Wee Gillis*), scenes of war time (*A New Coat for Anna* and *They Were Strong and Good*), design and texture (*Mrs. Katz and Tush* and *Follow The Drinking Gourd*), performing artists and promotional posters (*Mirette On The High Wire* and *Babar, to Duet or Not to Duet*), size and distance–elements of perspective (*Ferdinand* and *All Those Secrets of the World*), Islamic architecture (*Miss Rumphius*), additional ways to achieve the effect of night (*Little Red Lighthouse*), rhythm (*Follow the Drinking Gourd*), cut-away view (*Follow the Drinking Gourd*), portraying quiet action (*Gramma's Walk*), and double sets of illustrations for a story (*Gramma's Walk*), etc.

Look now at your student's artwork for the semester. Point out the examples in which you see the most effort, learning or expertise. Let him see how much he has accomplished.

If your student has kept a notebook, leaf through it with him. Recall various projects and review concepts in Social Studies, Geography, Science, and Math. You may find it helpful to use the index (at the end of Volume 2). Use these index topics to guide your review. You may quiz by mentioning the science and geography topics and asking in which story they appear. What were we reading when we talked about cork from trees, or lighthouses, the highlands, bullfights, Niagara Falls, owls, etc? Then, review the information. Ask your student what he remembers about that topic. Then add an additional idea or two that he may have forgotten.

For Language Arts, review the new information in Volume 2, and add it to your literary list or chart called "Choices Writers Can Make," Some of these additions might be Hyperbole (*Three Names*), Writing Description (*Three Names*), Foreshadowing– an element of a story (*Wee Gillis* and *All Those Secrets of the World*), Metaphor–a form of poetic language (*Owl Moon*), Imagery (*Owl Moon*), First Person Point of View and First Person Pronouns (*Owl Moon*), Yiddish (*Mrs. Katz and Tush*), Compound Words (*Mirette* and *Gramma's Walk*), Good Titles (*They Were Strong and Good, Little Red Lighthouse*), Recognizing Latin and Greek Influence (*They Were Strong and Good*), Play on Words (*To Duet or Not to Duet*), Formal Speech (*To Duet or Not to Duet*), Animal Fantasy (*The Tale of Peter Rabbit*), Span of Time Sequence in Stories (*Mr. Gumpy's Motor Car*), Family Storytelling (*Miss Rumphius*), Library Skills (*Miss Rumphius*), Analogy (*Follow the Drinking Gourd*), and Comparative Studies (*Follow the Drinking Gourd*). You may want to do a year-end review of some of the information in Volume 1, as well.

Also, review your student's own writing projects, poetry, etc. Enjoy them again together. Your student will see the variety that he accomplished. He may be encouraged to continue writing and expressing himself in many different forms.

Review the vocabulary lists from the various lessons, If you have made illustrated vocabulary list or illustraed vocabulary cards, use these to review. Recall the stories in which each word appears. Practice using the words in oral sentences.

Again, see how many story disks your student can correctly place on the Literature Map. If you have added your own information, where grandparents live or other geographic places, then be sure to include it in the review. Practice finding directions on a map. Talk about the compass directions while walking in your student's neighborhood, or when traveling,or hiking. Review the Crisis Thinking Skills and Survival Skill Techniques.

For fun, take the story disks from Volume 2 and line them up in front of your student. Then ask, *"In which stories do you remember the characters had to have patience?"* Have him pick up the story disks for the books that he chooses. (*He might answer: Down Down the Mountain, A New Coat for Anna,* and maybe *Owl Moon.*) Whatever the answer, ask where in the story the character had to deal with patience. Even if you do not still have the books, you probably will remember the stories well enough to recap and discuss. This type of comparative discussion,*"How was the character patient in this book, as compared to the other?"* is an important thinking skill, especially for your older student. A great deal of high school and college work is based on this type of comparative discussion.

In the same manner, other review topics and titles might include: Friendship Between Older and Younger People (*Gramma's Walk* and *Mrs. Katz and Tush*), Being Yourself (*Ferdinand* and *Wee Gillis*), Resourcefulness (*Down Down the Mountain, A New Coat for Anna*), Making the Most of Your Situation (*Gramma's Walk, Miss Rumphius*–when she is not well), Disobedience (*Peter Rabbit, All Those Secrets of the World*), and Imagination (*Harold and the Purple Crayon, Gramma's Walk*), etc.

Thank you for spending this year with us in *Five In A Row*, Volumes 1 and 2. We hope that you and your student enjoyed it, had fun together, and found many books to know and love. There is now a Volume 3. If you have enjoyed *Five In A Row*, please tell a friend about it!

Sample Semester Planning Calendar

This is merely a sample semester schedule. It ties *Peter Rabbit* to spring gardening, etc. Feel free to use the titles in any order you wish. *When I was Young in the Mountain* can be used as an alternate title, if you can't find *Down Down the Mountain*. *Gramma's Walk* can be used as an alternate for either *Wee Gillis* or *Babar: To Duet or Not to Duet*. If a certain title is unavailable at your local library this week, simply switch with another title!

January			
The Giraffe that Walked to Paris			

February	**F**ebruary	**F**ebruary	**F**ebruary
Three Names	Wee Gillis	Owl Moon	A New Coat for Anna
March	**M**arch	**M**arch	**M**arch
Mrs. Katz and Tush	Mirette on the High Wire	They Were Strong and Good	Babar: To Duet or Not to Duet
April	**A**pril	**A**pril	**A**pril
Ferdinand	Down Down the Mountain	Make Way for Ducklings	The Tale of Peter Rabbit
May	**M**ay	**M**ay	**M**ay
Mr. Gumpy's Motor Car	All Those Secrets of the World	Miss Rumphius	The Little Red Lighthouse
June	**J**une	**J**une	**J**une
Follow the Drinking Gourd	Harold and the Purple Crayon	When I Was Young in the Mountains	Gramma's Walk

Sample Lesson Planning Sheet

Title:
The Tale of Peter Rabbit

Author:
Beatrix Potter

Illustrator:
Beatrix Potter

Classic-
Written in 1902

	Monday	Tuesday	Wednesday	Thursday	Friday
	Social Studies	Language Arts	Art	Math	Science
	Read story through, then:	Read story through, then:	Read story through, then:	Read story through, then:	Read story through, then:
	Geography-	Exploring Fairy Tales	Drama:	Figuring and grouping using seed packets	Planning a Garden
	English Countryside: trimmed hedges, misty, rainy look English shoes English robin	Vocabulary- sieve for sifting sand or dirt	Act out: FIAR, Vol. 2 p. 106		
	Relationships- Encouragement:	Noticing details: FIAR, Vol. 2. p. 104	Medium: water color- subtle color		Introducing new species:
	sparrows "...implored him to exert himself."	Talk about the illustrations and text and point out details.	If time permits, Art project- Detail:Movement p. 106		native species vs. those brought from afar
	words of encouragement can bring life!				

(Friday, Science column includes a boxed drawing labeled: tomatoes, beans, carrots)

Sample Lesson Planning Page: *The Tale of Peter Rabbit* has 23 suggested lessons in the lesson portion of this manual. The sample planning sheet above shows 12 ideas that *could* be chosen for a one-week study. You are free to choose *any* of the 23 lesson ideas and keep track of your choices by noting them on the reproducible, blank Lesson Planning Sheet (Following page). For more ideas on making the best use of your *Five in a Row* curriculum, be sure to read the *How to Use Five in a Row* section beginning on p. 5.

Blank Lesson Planning Sheet (Reproducible)

Title:

Author:

Illustrator:

Monday	Tuesday	Wednesday	Thursday	Friday
Read story through, then:	Read story through, then:	Read story through, then:	Read story through, then:	Read story through, then:

Human Body - Ear

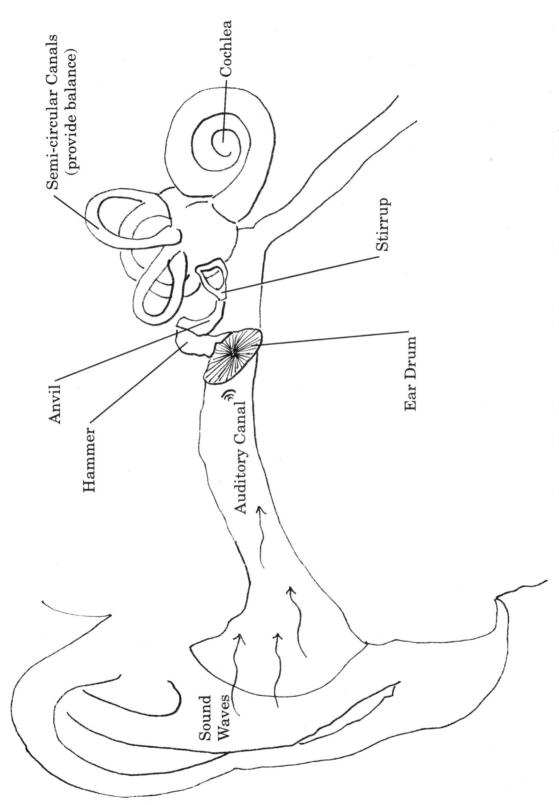

Semi-circular Canals
(provide balance)

Cochlea

Stirrup

Ear Drum

Anvil

Hammer

Auditory Canal

Sound
Waves

For use with *Babar: To Duet or Not to Duet* (p. 79)

Where Is It?
Review Quiz for Volumes 1 and 2

Year-End Review: Where Is It? (Answers)

1. Eiffel (EYE fuhl) Tower

Paris, France. Designed in 1889 for the World's Fair. *Madeline,* Vol. 1, *Apple Pie,* Vol. 1. The Paris setting is used in *The Giraffe,* Vol. 2 and *Mirette,* Vol. 2, but before the building of the tower.

2. Bull Ring

Madrid or Barcelona, Spain. *Ferdinand,* Vol. 2 and *Mirette,* Vol. 2.

3. Pyramids

Egypt. *The Giraffe That Walked to Paris,* Vol. 2

4. The George Washington Bridge

New York, New York *The Little Red Lighthouse, and The Great Gray Bridge,* Vol. 2

5. Ungava Bay

Northern Canada. *The Very Last First Time,* Vol. 1.

6. Boston Public Gardens

Boston, Massachusetts. *Make Way for Ducklings,* Vol. 2.

7. Niagara Falls

On the border between New York, United States and Ontario, Canada. *Mirette,* Vol. 2.

8. Islamic Architecture

Northern Africa. *Miss Rumphius,* Vol. 2.

9. Canals, Venice, Italy

A Gondola on the canals. *Papa Piccolo,* Vol. 1 and *Clown of God,* Vol. 1.

10. Yangtze River, China

Ping, Vol. 1. (Current events 1994: The Yangtze River, almost 4000 miles long, is scheduled to have a dam built at Three Gorges. Research for more details!)

11. Japan

A Pair of Red Clogs, Vol. 1 and *Grandfather's Journey,* Vol. 1.

12. Russian Architecture

(Like St. Basil's in Moscow, Russia) . *Another Celebrated Dancing Bear,* Vol. 1.

---

*Teacher's Note- For a surprise review, find a copy of *Love, Your Bear Pete X,* by Dyan Sheldon. Read it to your student. See how many countries, landmarks and costumes *he* points out to *you.* It's great fun and includes many of the regions, cultures and subjects you've studied together this year in *FIAR,* Volumes 1 and 2.

Student Worksheet: Values and Shading
(Advanced Art Technique)

This lesson is based upon Robert McCloskey's illustrations in *Make Way For Ducklings*. Look with your older student at the drawings. Notice the shading in the picture of the careless boy on the bicycle. (You may also want to look at all the pictures of Michael, the officer.) As you examine the shading, point out the darkest area on the boy (probably his pants). Now point out the lightest areas (his arms, face and shoulder, right leg, and a small patch of his back right elbow). Finally, point out the in-between values—not the darkest or the lightest (front of shirt, left leg and shirt tail).

It is the variety of values of light and dark that create the shading and give a "rounded," or three-dimensional look to the drawings.

Value can be defined as "the lightness or darkness of a color." One #2 pencil can yield several values of gray. Here is a simple chart with five values.

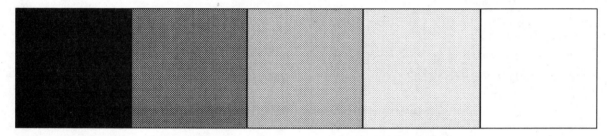

Draw five empty boxes on another sheet of paper. Have your student try to fill in the value scale to match the one above. For the first box he can use his #2 pencil and press as hard as he can, going over the area several times and filling in the box with the darkest value he can obtain from his pencil.

For the second box, he will not press as hard, and will go over the work only once. For the third box, he will use still less pressure. The fourth box will be *very* light, using a delicate sketching stroke for the lightest value his pencil can produce. The fifth box is left white, completely.

In a hands-on way, this exercise demonstrates that while some artists may use many pencils for their sketches, a careful young artist can obtain several values of dark and light from only one pencil, and that shading comes from using color values.

Now, have your older student try sketching a simple object like this ball. He should use at least three different degrees of value. An artist will look at an object he wants to draw and "see" the areas that are darkest and those that are the lightest. Ask you student if he can see the lightest area and the darkest area. He can try to draw what he sees and use an intermediate value for the other areas. Like other artists, he will eventually learn to recognize values!

Light Source

Medium
Value
Shadows

Whitest Area
Lightest Value

Darkest Shadow
Darkest Value

Literary Glossary

Literary Devices

Alliteration

A succession of similar *sounds* (not letters) can occur at the beginning of words or internally. "Susie's galos*hes* made *s*plis*hes* and *s*plos*hes*..."

Apostrophe

A way of addressing an absent person or some inanimate thing not usually spoken to. "*O, Moon!...*"

Hyperbole

An overstatement or exaggeration: "*I've told you a thousand times!*"

Irony

An event or outcome which is opposite what would naturally be expected: "*It was an irony of fate that the girl arrived just as her date left.*"

Mood

The feelings a work of literature brings to the reader: sad, for boding, boyant, etc., derived from the particular descriptive words chosen by the writer.

Onomatopoeia

Representing a thing or action by a word that imitates the sound associated with it: *zoom, ping, ding-dong, buzz.*

Personification

Where a thing, animal or abstract truth is made human, given human characteristics: "*The Man in the moon.*"

Repetition

The repeating of certain words, phrases, or ideas throughout a story or poem: "And I will take you home with me
                Yes, I will take you home with me.

Rhyme

Words where the ending *sounds* (not necessarily the letters) are the same: "Don't blame *me*,
                go and *see*..."

Symbolism

Writing that suggests more than the literal meaning. "*The innocent girl wore a white dress.*" (White being a symbol of purity.)

Elements of a Story

Characters
A person, animal, or thing (wind, for example) that inhabits a story.

Point of view
Who narrates (tells) the story:

> First Person–using I, me, etc.
> Third Person–using he, she, they.

The point of view is usually the same throughout a short story but you will find some stories where it changes. Ask," who is telling this story?" Is the story told through only one character's view? (first person) Or through the overall view of the narrator? (third person)

Mood
The feelings a story stirs in the reader: calm, happy, sad, fearful, etc. The mood of a story can change, e.g., from an ominous beginning to a happy ending, etc. Sometimes there is a pervasive mood throughout a story such as wistfulness, etc.

Plot
The action, the story line. Includes:

Conflict	the problem of the story
Rising Action	the growing excitement
Climax	the high point of excitement
Denouement	the resolution or final outcome

Theme
The general idea or insight revealed in the story. The *heart and soul* of the story.

Setting
Where does the story take place: geography, town, a room, etc.? The time frame for the story: an hour, a day, a certain year or period of years, a season, etc.

Style
Someone once said, "Style is the *clothes* the words wear." In other words, how they are dressed-what *fashion* of words and sentence structure a writer uses to *outfit* his story. Many famous writers have distinctive styles. You can often tell by reading only a few paragraphs who wrote a passage. You would say, "Oh, that story sounds like it was written by ...."

Dictionary of Art Terms

Principles of Design

A picture usually follows certain basic principles of design including:

Center of Interest: the point emphasized in the picture. It should be differentiated by:

    a.) Being larger or smaller than the other things in the picture.
    b.) Being around or near the center of the picture but not usually
        in the exact middle.
    c.) Being a different color, like a slightly darker red apple amid others for instance.
    d.) Being a different shape, like the boat with the sail up on a
        lake full of boats with their sails down.

Unity: Any element of design which holds components of picture together any guides your eye around the picture. Can be line, color, etc.

Rhythm: Repetition of an element in a picture, the line, the color, shape, etc.

Balance: How the elements of a picture are constructed by use of symetry or asymetry.

Elements of Design

The *elements* of design are the tools an artist uses to follow the *principles* of design which include:

Line: The path traced by a moving point. Lines can be straight, curved, zig-zag (as in lightning), broken - - - -, dots................., or wavy. (See *Harold and the Purple Crayon* by Crockett)

Shape: The outward contour or outline; form; figure.

Space: *Positive space:* The house and the tree are positive space. (the objects drawn or painted.)

Negative Space: The space *around* the objects drawn. All the space in this picture that isn't tree or house. An artist makes choices in the amount of positive and negative space in a picture to make a pleasing work. Look at lots of examples of pictures and find positive and negative space and notice how much of each the artist uses.

Texture: Artistically representing an object's surface and how it would *feel*. (bumpy, smooth, etc.) Surface texture is unrelated to color, shape, etc.

Color: There are many components which make up the element of color including:

Color Hue: The name of the color: red, blue, etc.

Shade of Color: Black added to a particular color hue produces a *shade*.

Tint: of Color: White added to a particular color hue produces a *tint*.

Tone of Color: Gray (black and white together) added to a particular color hue produces a *tone*.

Primary colors: Red, yellow, blue. These colors cannot be obtained from mix. All other colors are produced by mixing these three *primary colors*.

Secondary colors: Orange (made by mixing red and yellow), green (made by mixing yellow and blue) and violet (made by mixing blue and red).

Tertiary colors: Made by mixing a secondary and a primary color. Yellow orange, red orange, yellow green, blue green, red violet and blue violet made by mixing the colors that the names suggest. (Brown *not* considered a ter tiary color) can be made mixing orange with a little blue and in other ways.)

Complementary Colors: Sometimes called opposites because of their place on the color wheel. In other words, if you look on your color wheel at red, the opposite color is green. Green and red are complementary colors. As red is added in small amounts to green and visa versa, the effect is a greying or neutralizing of the original color.

Warm colors: Colors that give a feeling of warmth, including the yellows, oranges and reds. These colors are chosen by the artist when he wants to show the warmth of the sun or a light or fire, etc. and when he desires to show symbolically the warmth of a scene, as a homey scene. (This is an *enormous* subject with many subtleties, but this is a simple, working definition for young students.)

Warm Palette: Limiting colors used for a picture to the warm color hues (list ed above), without using cool colors too (which is called *using a full palette*).

Cool Colors: Colors that give a feeling of coolness including the blues, greens and purples. (Again, this is a *simple* definition for primary students.)

Cool Palette: Limiting the colors used for a picture to only the cool colors (list ed above) without using warmer colors (which would be considered a *full palette*).

Full Palette: Using both warm and cool colors in the same picture.

Principles of Drawing for Depth (Perspective)

Surface: Making objects seem closer by drawing them closer to the botton of the picture that the other components of the composition.

Size: Drawing some objects larger than others will make them appear closer to the viewer.

Foreshortening: A method of shortening the lines of <u>any</u> object, distorting the image to give the impression of depth. Let's look at circles and squares as examples.

Foreshortened Circles

Foreshortened Squares

Overlapping: Drawing objects behind and partly obscured by the front objects in order to make the front objects appear closer.

Surface Lines: Lines used on an objects to give a 3-dimensional look, like the "wrapping around" of short lines to make a pencil seem round.

Intensity: Another method of producing depth by drawing or painting close objects with more color and detail than objects that are in the background. The background objects are drawn with less detail and often have *greyed color,* made by adding to the color used on the main objects mixed with a little of their complement (opposite on the color wheel). This *greyed color* is used to paint objects in the background.

Shadows: Shadows give depth to a drawing and are often used to cause the subject to stand out more clearly. Shadows cause the object to *come forward* in the drawing or painting. Shadows indicate the direction of the picture's light source.

With shadows, it is important to remember the light source in your drawing and keep consistant, having the shadows *all* flowing in from the same direction. The shadows will be on the *opposite* side of the light source.

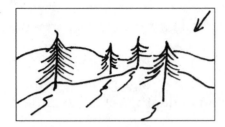

Shading: Helps make things appear rounded or three-dimensional by the use of shadows.

Additonal Terms

Medium: The type of art material you use to create a picture. For drawing, you might choose: pencil, pen and ink, charcoal, chalk or oil pastel, crayon, colored pencils or markers. For painting, the choices include: oil paints, water colors, acrylic (a water based pigment that works like oil but dries more quickly), tempra (pigment is mixed with egg or other substances instead of oil), gouache (*opaque* water colors made by mixing pigments with water and gum) or finger paint (probably a type of tempera). We might say an artist chose oil paints *as his medium.*

View point: The point from which an artist views his subject. In some drawings and paintings, we find ourselves looking down on the subject as if we were perched in a tree. (*The Glorious Flight* is an example) In other pictures we might feel as if we were seeing everything from the view point of sitting or lying on the ground looking up. (*Night of the Moonjellies, Stopping by the Woods on a Snowy Evening*)

Bibliography

The Giraffe That Walked to Paris by Nancy Milton, Crown Publishing. ISBN 0517581329

Three Names by Patricia MacLachlan, Harper Collins Publishers. ISBN 0060240350 also available in paperback ISBN 0064433609

Wee Gillis by Munro Leaf, Viking Press. ISBN Unknown

Owl Moon by Jane Yolen, Philomel Books. ISBN 0399214577

A New Coat for Anna by Harriet Ziefert, Alfred A. Knopf. ISBN 0394874269 also available in paperback ISBN 0394898613

Mrs. Katz and Tush by Patricia Polacco, Dell Publishing. ISBN 0440409365

Mirette on the High Wire by Emily Arnold McCully, G. Putnam's Sons . ISBN 0399221301

They Were Strong and Good by Alice and Robert Lawson, Viking Press. ISBN 0670699497

Babar, To Duet or Not to Duet by De Brunhoff, Binky Books. ISBN 1856270947

Ferdinand by Munro Leaf, Viking Press. ISBN 0670674249

Down, Down the Mountain by Ellis Credle, Thomas Nelson. ISBN 0840760205

Make Way for Ducklings by Robert McCloskey, Viking Press. ISBN 0670451495

The Tale of Peter Rabbit by Beatrix Potter, Viking Penguin. ISBN 0723234604

Mr. Gumpy's Motor Car by John Burningham, Puffin Books. ISBN 0140502467

All Those Secrets of the World by Jane Yolen, Little Brown & Co. ISBN 0316968919 also available in paperback ISBN 0316968951

Miss Rumphius by Barbara Cooney, Puffin Books. ISBN 0140505393 (paperback)

The Little Red Lighthouse and the Great Gray Bridge by Hildegarde H. Swift, Harcourt Brace Jovanovitch Publishers. ISBN 0152470409 also available in paperback ISBN 0156528401

Follow the Drinking Gourd by Jeanette Winter, Alfred A. Knopf. ISBN 0679819975

Harold and the Purple Crayon by Crocket Johnson, Harper Collins. ISBN 0060229357

When I Was Young in the Mountains by Cynthia Rylan, E.P. Dutton. ISBN 052542525X

Gramma's Walk by Anna Grossnickle Hines, Greenwillow Books. ISBN 0688114806

Finding the Books

In our experience, a "typical" library may actually have 20-25 of the 55 *Five in a Row* titles within their own system. The rest they will have to obtain through Inter-library loan (ILL). We've also observed that juvenile fiction is frequently mis-shelved because children examine books at random while mother makes her selections, replacing the books on the shelves *wherever is convenient*! The result is that even though the computer may indicate a given volume is "available," you may have a very difficult time locating it on the shelf.

We've found the most time-effective way to utilize the library system is to get a stack of library request cards from your librarian. If you own all 3 volumes of *Five in a Row*, you'll need 55 cards. Then, take the hour needed to fill them *all* out and put a rubber band around them, placing them in your purse or organizer. Keep them with you. Whenever you go to the library, simply turn in two or three cards for any titles that are not on the shelf and let *them* do the searching. *They* will locate the mis-shelved book when the computer indicates it's available. *They* will flag the computer to automatically "hold" the title for you when another library patron returns the book. *They* will request books via ILL and hold them for you when they arrive.

(Note- Some library systems and some librarians are still resistant to doing ILL, but that is changing. A recent article by one of the foremost authorities on library science in the world suggested that while ILL was practically unknown a few years ago, it is common practice today in most libraries. She went on to say that ILL will continue to grow as libraries inter-connect their computerized catalogs. She concluded by saying that a good librarian today should *never* tell a patron, *"I'm sorry but we don't have that book,"* without quickly adding, *"but I'll be happy to locate a copy for you!"*)

As your local library collects your requested titles they will call you every week or two to let you know another book or two is being held for you. Then, when you go to check out your new acquisitions, turn in two or three more cards and let them begin the search/request/hold cycle all over again. You will discover a comfortable rhythm of swinging by the library every two weeks or so and picking up your next title or two. It can be very painless!

Another note on the subject. One of the benefits of requesting a title is that often a library will eventually purchase the book if it's requested often enough. If the library comes up empty handed on a particular title, keep requesting it every few weeks. Encourage your friends to request it too! You'd be surprised how many wonderful books end up in the system that way.

A personal anecdote: A dear friend who began reviewing *Five in a Row* several years ago obtained *Who Owns the Sun?* via ILL. When she returned it suggested the librarian consider purchasing a copy for the local library. The busy librarian quickly brushed her aside saying, *"I'm sorry, but we've already spent our budget for this year; it's out of the question."* Our friend simply opened the book and began reading it aloud to the librarian right at the check-out desk! Before she was halfway through, the librarian was wiping away tears as she listened to the poignant story, and by the time our friend finished reading, the librarian grabbed the book from her saying, "*I'm going to take $15 from our office supply budget and order this book immediately!*"

Sadly, many of the most wonderful books being written today, as well as the marvelous classics like *The Story About Ping* are being supplanted on limited library shelf space by books of far less merit. The library system is designed to respond to patron usage and requests. They buy and maintain what the most people are reading. One of our more subtle opportunities is to bless our communities with wholesome, solid books by requesting them, sharing them with local librarians, or even donating a copy of a special title from time to time. Our libraries are what we make them!

One final note on the titles of *Five in a Row*. We're well aware that several of the books are difficult to locate and several others are currently out of print for those who wish to *purchase* them. While we struggled with this issue, in the final analysis we concluded that we wanted to offer the very *best* of the more than 5000 children's books we've explored and examined. In the three volumes, we've supplied 55 lesson plans; 55 weeks of unit study to keep you going through a calendar year. (The joy of reading wonderful books and discussing what you've read can be a year-round activity.)

We know that even if you keep going year-round, you're only likely to actually use 43-45 titles because of vacation breaks, Christmas breaks, etc. The "extra" titles are provided so that if there are several books you cannot locate or which are unavailable through your local library, you'll still have more than enough material to keep your young ones learning for a full year. *But,* for those who are willing to leave no stone unturned in their search for all 55 titles, we're sure you'll be blessed and rewarded for your trouble. Some of the most difficult titles to find are some of the richest!

The cost of *Five in a Row* is just slightly more than $1 per unit study. Even if you only locate two thirds of the titles successfully, you'll still be getting wonderful, inspired unit studies for less than $1.50 each. And in the meantime, keep on the lookout for other titles, by trading with friends, having relatives check their libraries, requesting again and again locally, exploring used bookstores and flea markets, etc.

In the final analysis, we've tried to give you the very "best of the best" from the more than 5,000 children's books Jane has explored in the hopes that each one will be a present tense joy and a lifetime friend for both you and your children. God bless you and your children as you set out on the wonderful adventure of learning with *Five in a Row*.

Integrating *Five in a Row* with Additional Curriculum

For teaching three, four and some five-year-olds, you will find *Five in a Row* to be an exciting and complete curriculum. Once you make the decision that your student is ready to begin phonics, reading and mathematics you will want to supplement your *Five in a Row* curriculum with additional materials.

Thereare many wonderful products available to help you teach phonics/reading and mathematics. You will find helpful descriptions of available products in homeschool curriculum catalogs. You may also want to make plans to see and review these materials first hand by planning to attend a homeschool convention or curriculum fair in your area. Most of these events occur between March and July each year.

Once you integrate your new reading/phonics and mathematics curricula with *Five in a Row* your teaching day may look something like this:

Morning
Math instruction
Five in a Row (read the story aloud and discuss one of the five subject areas)
Lunch (Nap?)

Afternoon
Phonics/Reading instruction

Or perhaps you'll want to do phonics and mathematics in the morning and save your *Five in a Row* until after lunch as a sort of *reward* for the morning's work. Other mothers prefer to do *all* their work in the morning when their student is *fresh*. Arrange your teaching day in whatever way works best for you and your student. Don't be afraid to change or rearrange your schedule to provide variety, flexibility or to try new schedules until you find what works best for you. There is *no* right or wrong way to do it! Some mothers like to create a chart for their schedule. Perhaps your schedule might look like this:

Monday	Tuesday	Wednesday	Thursday	Friday
Math	Math	Math	Math*	Math
Phonics	Phonics	Phonics	Phonics	Phonics
FIAR Social Studies	FIAR Language Arts	FIAR Art	FIAR Applied Math	FIAR Science

*You may or may not want to omit your math curriculum lesson on Thursday and concentrate on the *Five in a Row* math lesson instead. We believe it's important *not* to skip the *Five in a Row* math lesson however, because *it* teaches your student how mathematics is applied in life all around him including measuring, telling time, counting money, sewing, building, etc. This lesson time will stimulate math curiosity and motivate your student to learn math!

Finally, if you are using *Five in a Row* with older students, third grade and older, consider adding brief grammar and punctuation lessons. Workbooks containing these lessons are available through curriculum catalogs, teacher's stores, bookstores and even at your local Wal-Mart! Some of these books are quite good and cost less than $3.00. One series that we've found useful (and there are many) is the *Brighter Child Series*. One book is entitled *English Grammar and Writing for Grade 3*. ISBN 1 56189-083-9 published by American Education Publishing, 150 E.Wilson Bridge Rd., Suite 145, Columbus, OH 43085. Of course there are other books available for grade four, five, etc. These simple, affordable booklets can supplement *Five in a Row* for your older students, supplying the needed sequential learning that's appropriate for language arts.

For Science and Social Studies, you might consider having your older student do additional, self-directed research and reporting on several of the hundreds of topics you will encounter while doing *Five in a Row*.

By enriching *Five in a Row* using advanced, student-directed research and reporting and by supplementing the curriculum with additional work in mathematics, grammar and punctuation, you'll find *Five in a Row* can serve as the educational base from which you build for children from pre-school through elementary school.

Supplemental Books & Poetry
Included in Lessons of Volume 2

Stokes Nature Guides: A Guide to Nature in Winter by Donald Stokes,
(*Owl Moon,* p. 41)

Sweet Clara and the Freedom Quilt, by Deborah Hopkinson,
(*Drinking Gourd,* p. 144)

Tale of Mrs. Tiggywinkle, The, by Beatrix Potter, (*Peter Rabbit,* p. 105)

The River, by Judith Heide Gilliland, (*Red Lighthouse,* p. 139)

The Stars, by H.A. Ray, (*Drinking Gourd,* p. 147) *Keep the Lights Burning Abbie,* by

Tortoise and the Hare, The, by Aesop, (*Babar,* p. 73)

Uncle Tom's Cabin, by Harriet Beecher Stowe, (*Drinking Gourd,* p. 144)

Winnie the Pooh, "In Which Pooh and Piglet Go Hunting..." by A.A. Milne, (*Owl Moon,* p. 41)

Supplemental Songs & Music Included in Lessons of Volume 2

ABC Song, The, (*Drinking Gourd,* p. 145)

Ba Ba Black Sheep, (*Babar,* p. 77)

God Down Moses, (*Drinking Gourd,* p. 146)

Home on the Range, (*Three Names,* p. 23)

Jacob's Ladder, (*Drinking Gourd,* p. 146)

London Bridge is Falling Down, (*Lighthouse,* p. 140)

Over There, by George M. Cohen, (*Secrets,* p. 122)

Surprise Symphony or Symphony No. 94 in G Major, by Franz Joseph Haydn,
(*Babar,* p. 77)

Swing Low Sweet Chariot, (*Drinking Gourd,* p. 146)

The Erie Canal, (*Lighthouse,* p. 140)

Westward Ho, Hear and Learn Tape, (*Three Names,* p. 23)

Supplemental Videos Included in Lessons of Volume 2

My Side of the Mountain, (*Owl Moon,* p. 39)

Wee Gillis, (*Wee Gillis,* p. 30)

MASTER INDEX

Social Studies Index

Social Studies History

Social Studies Culture

Language Arts Index

Language Arts

Choices Writers Make

Elements of a Story

Literary Devices

Spelling

Making a List

Title Index

Math Index

Geometry

Science Index

Products from Five in a Row Publishing

Before Five in a Row by Jane Claire Lambert- This wonderful new treasury of creative ideas helps inspire learning readiness in children ages 2 thru 4. Mothers who want to devote special time to these littlest ones will delight in this sweet and ever-so-gentle beginning to the lifelong adventure of learning. Through *Before Five in a Row* you will share times of joy, laughter, wonder and insight with your youngest pre-schoolers. These ideas and activites, built around 23 outstanding children's books, provide the perfect introduction to the joys of parent-directed learning in just a few very special minutes each day.   ISBN 1-888659-04-1 $24.95

Five in a Row *Volume 1* by Jane Claire Lambert- First published in 1994, the new, revised, second edition is now available. Volume 1 contains 19 unit studies built around 19 of the very best children's books ever printed. Each unit takes five days to complete. Created primarily for children ages 4-8 but don't be afraid to include other ages too!   ISBN 1-888659-00-9 $19.95

Five in a Row *Volume 2* by Jane Claire Lambert- An all new, revised, second edition is now available. Volume 2 explores 21 more outstanding children's books. Each unit takes five days to complete. Created for ages 4-8.   ISBN 1-888659-01-7 $24.95

Five in a Row *Volume 3* by Jane Claire Lambert- An all new, revised, second edition is now available. Volume 3 explores 15 additional outstanding children's books. Each unit takes five days to complete. Created for ages 4-8.   ISBN 1-888659-02-5 $19.95

Five in a Row Christian Character and Bible Study Supplement by Jane Claire Lambert- This wonderful resource teaches hundreds of non-denominational Bible lessons and concepts using the first *three* volumes of *Five in a Row*. Teach your children about obeying parents, kindness, generosity, good stewardship, forgiveness and more. Ages 4-8.   ISBN 1-888659-03-3 $17.95

Laminated Full Color Story Disks by Jane Claire Lambert- Each volume of *Five in a Row* contains black and white *story disks*. Use these little half-dollar sized drawings to teach children geography by attaching them to your own large, world map as you explore each new *Five in a Row* story. Just cut out the disks, color and laminate them. *However*, we offer this *optional* set of already colored, laminated disks for those who prefer to save the time needed to prepare their own. These disks are printed in full color and heat laminated- ready to use. One set of these disks covers all *three* volumes of *Five in a Row*. Beautiful and ready to enjoy! $15.00

Beyond Five in a Row *Volume 1* by Becky Jane Lambert- This exciting new curriculum is the answer for all those moms who have asked, "What do I do <u>after</u> *Five in a Row?*" You'll find the same creative, thought-provoking activities and lesson ideas you've come to expect from *Five in a Row* using outstanding chapter books for older children. Volume 1 will keep your students busy for a full semester with history, geography, science, language arts, fine arts and issues of human relationship. Each unit also includes numerous essay questions, career path investigations, optional internet sites to explore and much more. Volume 1 requires *The Boxcar Children, Homer Price,* and the *Childhood of Famous American Series* biographies of *Thomas A. Edison- Young Inventor* and *Betsy Ross- Designer of Our Flag*. Created for ages 8-12.   ISBN 1-888659-05-X $24.95

Beyond Five in a Row Bible Christian Character and Bible Supplement *Volume 1* by Becky Jane Lambert- This companion volume to *Beyond Five in a Row Volume 1* provides a rich selection of the wonderful Bible links and strong character lessons you've come to expect from *Five in a Row*. This valuable supplement teaches traditional Christian values such as honoring parents, forgiveness, generosity, etc. Easy to use!   ISBN 1-888659-06-8 $ 9.95

Feel free to photocopy this page

PLEASE SHARE *FIVE IN A ROW* WITH A FRIEND

Name _____

Address _____

Phone _____

City/State/Zip _____

Item	Qty.	Price Ea.	Total
Five in a Row-Volume 1		$19.95	
Five in a Row-Volume 2		$24.95	
Five in a Row-Volume 3		$19.95	
All 3 Volumes (Save 10%)		$58.50	
Five in a Row Bible Supplement		$17.95	
Laminated Full Color Story Disks		$15.00	
Before Five in a Row (Ages 2-4)		$24.95	
Beyond Five in a Row Vol. 1 (Ages 8-12)		$24.95	
Beyond Five in a Row Bible Supplement		$ 9.95	
	Merchandise Total		
	*Shipping Charges		
	MO Residents Add 6.475% Tax		
	Order Total		

Make Check Payable To:
Jane Claire Lambert
14901 Pineview Dr.
Grandview, MO 64030

*For each order be sure to add:
$5.00 for UPS (5-7 days) or $3.50 for 4th Class Mail, (3 weeks)

Thank you for ordering *FIVE IN A ROW!*

PLEASE SHARE *FIVE IN A ROW* WITH A FRIEND

Name _____

Address _____

Phone _____

City/State/Zip _____

Item	Qty.	Price Ea.	Total
Five in a Row-Volume 1		$19.95	
Five in a Row-Volume 2		$24.95	
Five in a Row-Volume 3		$19.95	
All 3 Volumes (Save 10%)		$58.50	
Five in a Row Bible Supplement		$17.95	
Laminated Full Color Story Disks		$15.00	
Before Five in a Row (Ages 2-4)		$24.95	
Beyond Five in a Row Vol. 1 (Ages 8-12)		$24.95	
Beyond Five in a Row Bible Supplement		$ 9.95	
	Merchandise Total		
	*Shipping Charges		
	MO Residents Add 6.475% Tax		
	Order Total		

Make Check Payable To:
Jane Claire Lambert
14901 Pineview Dr.
Grandview, MO 64030

*For each order be sure to add:
$5.00 for UPS (5-7 days) or $3.50 for 4th Class Mail, (3 weeks)

Thank you for ordering *FIVE IN A ROW!*